THE DIALECTICS OF SCHIZOPHRENIA

THE DIALECTICS OF SCHIZOPHRENIA

PHILIP THOMAS

FREE ASSOCIATION BOOKS / LONDON / NEW YORK

Published in 1997 by
Free Association Books Ltd
57 Warren Street, London W1P 5PA
and 70 Washington Square South,
New York, NY 10012-1091

ISBN 1 85343 362 4 hardback

    1 85343 361 6 paperback

A CIP catalogue record for this book is available from
the British Library.

Produced for Free Association Books Ltd by
Chase Production Services, Chadlington, OX7 3LN
Printed in the EC by J.W. Arrowsmith Ltd, Bristol

'You must always be puzzled by mental illness.
The thing I would dread most, if I became mentally ill,
would be your adopting a common sense attitude;
that you could take it for granted that I was deluded.'

Ludwig Wittgenstein
Recollections of Wittgenstein

For Stella

Contents

Acknowledgements

Many people have contributed ideas that have helped to shape this book, and I apologise for any omissions. I am indebted to those people who have shared their first-hand experiences of psychiatry with me. Without their willingness to try to help me understand this, I simply could not have written this book. In one way or another every patient that I have ever seen has contributed to this understanding, but there are some to whom I am particularly grateful. My first teachers were the many clients of the Manchester African-Caribbean Mental Health Project. They were followed by members of the Hearing Voices Network, in Britain and Holland. Peg Davies is a voice hearer with whom I have worked closely over the last three years, and I am particularly grateful to her for allowing me to provide a detailed account of our work. Ron Coleman deserves special mention. His strength of character and courage in getting out of the psychiatric system, and his willingness to share this with others, has forged a special bond between us. Ron's is a remarkable story which he will no doubt write about soon. The same applies to Sharon Lefevre whose play, *On the Edge of a Dilemma*, is discussed in the final chapter. There are many professional colleagues whose ideas and comments have been invaluable. These include Gilroy Ferguson, who, in 1989, was appointed as the development worker with the Manchester African-Caribbean Mental Health Project, Ivan Leudar, Terry McLaughlin, Tom Butler, David Healy and Pat Bracken. Over the last four years my work with two nursing colleagues, Ian Murray and Mike Greenwood, has played an important part in helping to turn some of the ideas developed in this book into practice. In addition to this, there are two particularly gratifying sources of inspiration. My discussions with a group of young trainee psychiatrists in North Wales, including Jaap Hamelinjk, Marie Savage and Tom McMonagle, have played an important part in helping to shape these ideas. Then there is Europe. Britain has always retained a distance from European philosophical thought, but it is time that this changed, especially as far as British psychiatry is concerned. Marius Romme and Sandra Escher in Maastricht have become good friends, in their willingness to teach me about social psychiatry and working with service users. I am particularly grateful to Michael Langenbach, a psychiatrist working in Dusseldorf, who has made detailed comments about Chapters 7 and 8. I despaired of ever getting this book published, until I spoke to Gill Davies at Free Association Books. She provided the sort of advice that all putative authors need and, in addition, has been helpful and supportive at all stages. I am particularly grateful to her for this. But there is one person whose help and support was essential in writing this book. My wife, Stella, has had the unenviable task of acting as midwife, helping to deliver these ideas into the light of day. She has listened, supported, disagreed, read, criticised, encouraged and believed in what I have tried to say. Without her, the task would have been impossible.

Introduction

There was a great deal on my mind as I drove to Manchester from Edinburgh, that night in early September 1983. It was a wild night, as an early autumn gale tore through the Scottish borders, but I drove on barely noticing the twisting, waving shapes of the trees picked out by the car's headlights. I was miles away. The peaceful conclusion of a Bruckner Mass (No. 3, in F) kept repeating itself, going round and round in my head. This always happened after a performance, but on this occasion it was particularly significant because it was the last time that I would sing with the Edinburgh Festival Chorus. I was amused because I could not put the end of the piece out of my head. The end? I was leaving the Chorus. I was also leaving Edinburgh to start my first job as a consultant psychiatrist. After five years of higher professional training I had achieved my ambition. I was particularly excited because I was returning to Manchester, to the hospital where I had trained in medicine. I was apprehensive, but confident that the years spent training and learning my speciality had prepared me well to undertake the task that lay before me.

At least that is what I thought at the time. What I was not prepared for were the differences between Edinburgh and Manchester. Of course there was urban decay and poverty in Edinburgh, especially in Pilton and Muirhouse, areas which I got to know well in my five years in the city. Nor had my training sheltered me within the comfortable confines of the asylum. My first consultant, the late Jim Affleck, had given me every encouragement to spend as much time working in the community as possible, not that I needed any. As a result, I had an excellent grounding in community psychiatry. In Manchester my catchment area included some of the poorest inner-city areas in Britain, areas such as Hulme, Moss Side, Brunswick and Ardwick. The difference between the two cities became apparent from the moment I walked onto the ward where my in-patient beds were located. I looked at the names on the board, and the black faces, old and young, in the corridor outside. Most of my in-patients were Afro-Caribbean, many of them admitted on Sections of the Mental Health Act. This puzzled me. I had encountered nothing like this in Edinburgh. What was going on here? What did this indicate?

Then, gradually, I became aware of more subtle differences. In Edinburgh we lived near the city centre in Tollcross, a stone's throw from the King's Theatre. To get to work I walked *out* of the city centre, to the Royal Edinburgh Hospital, two miles to the South. Edinburgh is a living city. Its centre has shops, businesses, offices, banks, pubs, theatres and concert halls, but people live there. In Manchester we moved to a leafy, middle-class suburb ten miles south of the city centre. As I made my daily journey to and from work, it struck me that I was travelling through a living museum of urban planning since Victorian times. The first part of my journey home took me through parts of Hulme, where the old back-to-back slums had been replaced long ago by those icons of 1960's concrete modernism, the crescents. Whose idea was it to name these dehumanising monstrosities after Robert Adams and John Nash? Was this deliberate, intended as an ironic gesture? Or were they being sincere? In any case, the crescents have now gone, flattened by the bulldozers of brave new partnerships, residents, architects and city council working together. Then, driving south down Cambridge Street, I would cross Great Western Street to enter a maze of 1970s estates. Here was a different set of problems. If the Hulme crescents were dehumanising, their monolithic blankness making residents feel insignificant, then the estates had a different effect. Superficially, they appeared more user-friendly. Neat rows of terraces, soft red bricks broken up with patches of green and trees. At least that is how it seemed during the day. It was a different matter at night, when the maze of poorly lit, poorly sign-posted paths became heavy with threat. Then continuing south across Claremont Road, took you back a hundred years in time. Here it seems that the planners and municipal developers had finally recognised the error of their ways. Instead of demolishing the old back-to-back slums they were busy refurbishing and redecorating them, turning them back into homes. Houses and streets that had stood for a hundred years would be left to stand for another hundred. Corner shops were starting to flourish again, as were the old small local pubs. Communities were starting to grow again.

What really struck me after a few months' commuting was that I was not a part of any of these communities. Like most of my professional colleagues, we were strangers to them, people who travelled in from another world to work for the people who lived in this part of the city, in their homes, in places where they spent all their lives.

Each day I sneaked in by car, did my bit, and sneaked home again. No wonder that they regarded me with suspicion. One day, shortly after I started, I went to visit the mother of a young Afro-Caribbean man whom I had admitted to hospital on Section. The social worker had phoned to tell her that I wanted to discuss her son's problems with her, but when I arrived at the door of her small terraced house in Moss Side she was terrified. It emerged that she believed that I had come to arrest her, because she thought that psychiatrists were like the police. I simply wanted to speak with her to try to understand her son's problems. This was because the great majority of the Afro-Caribbean men (most of them were men) under my care puzzled me greatly. It was indisputable that a small number were suffering from the psychiatric disorders that I had been trained to diagnose and treat, but for the majority this was not so. Many of them behaved in ways that were difficult to understand, but very few of them appeared to have the experiences that indicated the presence of mental illness. Most of them came into hospital at night, brought in by the police off the streets. Some were referred by social workers and probation officers, who were equally as puzzled by their behaviour. It soon became clear that my main function was not to treat the person, but to dispose of them by providing a convenient and 'humane' way out for the other agencies who had become involved. This, and similar experiences, made me realise how little I really understood the people I was supposed to be helping. It was difficult to escape the conclusion that my role was not that of psychiatrist, but that of a gaoler with a social conscience.

There was only one way to deal with this. I decided that I had to establish much closer links with the community. In any case, the Afro-Caribbean community was already well aware of the problems that British society posed its members. Fifteen years or so earlier, parents, Church leaders and other prominent members of the community in Moss Side had started to take action to deal with the increasing problem of homelessness amongst its young men, which led to the opening of George Jackson House, a hostel for homeless young black people. The mental health of many of these young people had suffered as a result of the stresses they had experienced, a combination of racism, unemployment, poverty and homelessness. The community was already deeply concerned about the way that some of its finest young people disappeared off the streets, only to reappear weeks later in one of Manchester's psychiatric hospitals. The time for dialogue had come, and thus started the slow and difficult process which gave birth to the Manchester African-Caribbean Mental Health Project. It was this work more than anything else which set in motion the train of ideas which led to this book. I became more aware of the way the community perceived my role as a psychiatrist, and it became clear that there was a great discrepancy between the way I saw my role, and their experience of it. Then I began to understand that this problem not only affected my relationship with the black community, but the majority of people whom I thought I was helping. Like most doctors, I had been brought up to believe that psychiatry, like medicine, was an area of knowledge unsullied by the complications of society and politics. But as I struggled to understand the world as experienced by my patients, it became impossible for me to remain in this state of detachment. I began to understand why many service users are so dissatisfied with psychiatry.

This dissatisfaction started to gain expression as a small group of users started to write about their experiences of psychiatric services. Survivor accounts describe mental health services as 'dehumanising' (Pembroke, 1993). Others articulate the view that, despite their shortcomings, community-based mental health services are far superior to the asylum system they replaced (Campbell, 1993). In 1990, MIND undertook a survey of local mental health associations, advocacy groups and workers in statutory services (Rogers et al., 1993), the purpose of which was to obtain some idea of the views of people who have received mental health services. Every one of the 516 people who participated had had at least one period of in-patient care for psychiatric illness. Over 32% of respondents said that they had found psychiatric nurses to be the most helpful group, whereas only 12% found psychiatrists helpful. Psychiatrists were reported to be the least helpful group by more than 21% of respondents. These figures are not based on equal amounts of contact with each of the groups listed; for example, only 3.5% of respondents said that they had found psychotherapists helpful. But only a very small proportion of in-patients are likely to be under the care of a psychotherapist, whereas all in-patients will be under the care of a psychiatrist. Over 38% found their psychiatrists' attitudes unhelpful or very unhelpful, and comments about bad medical practice make interesting reading:

'I felt that there has been little understanding of my problems and more of an emphasis on drugs and prescriptions.'

'(Psychiatrists) appear unconcerned about the problem. They come across as being more interested in what they have to say about the problem than what the patient has to say.'

(Rogers et al., 1993, pp. 49–50)

Others used adjectives such as 'reserved, detached, godly' or 'condescending, complacent benevolence' to describe the attitudes adopted by some psychiatrists towards their patients. In fairness, there were some users who found their psychiatrists helpful, and this is useful because it helps to establish how users see good practice:

'... Explained things right from the beginning when asked.'

'They understand my problems and they have always given an appointment when I've asked for one.'

'... now they have [discussed properly with me my illness, diagnosis and medication] it has been very helpful. They are always there if I need them.'

(Rogers *et al.*, 1993, p. 48)

According to Anne Rogers and her colleagues there are three components to good medical practice from a service users' perspective. Psychiatrists should be empathic. This means that they should be sympathetic and understanding of their patients' problems. Psychiatrists should be open. They should demonstrate a willingness to share information with patients, and to provide full explanations about the nature of the problem and the help on offer. Finally, psychiatrists should be available and accessible. In my view there is something else which emerges from some of the comments. Consider the following:

'I feel that I was treated too much as an object rather than a person.'

'They have a set diagnosis which they work to and treat with ECT [electro-convulsive therapy] and drugs. They do not search out the reasons for your illness with you so the illness just repeats itself again and again.'

(Rogers *et al.*, 1993, p. 50)

These statements reveal some important problems with the nature of psychiatry as far as service users are concerned. Many patients do not feel that psychiatrists are really interested in them as people. Instead, they are regarded as objects, things rather than people. This suggests that psychiatrists are not really concerned with their patients' experiences as human beings; that their feelings and their understanding of why they are the way they are, are of no consequence. The second quotation suggests that this may have something to do with the fact that psychiatrists regard the processes of diagnosis and treatment as more important than helping patients to understand the reasons for their illness. Professional concerns are placed in front of patients' concerns.

This may come as a surprise. Most doctors passionately believe that they have their patients' interests at heart. Most psychiatrists would add that they are indeed concerned to understand their patients' problems. What has gone wrong here? Why is it that a profession which regards caring as a core value, is seen as uncaring by many of the people it is supposed to help? These problems take us to the core of this book. I want to try to understand why psychiatry evokes such negative responses. To do this, I believe that we must examine the knowledge upon which psychiatry is based, and the best way of doing this is to examine the nature of psychiatric discourse. An analysis of the languages which underpin the practice of psychiatry can take place in different ways. We can examine the nature of the scientific, psychological and social languages used by psychiatrists in their attempts to deal with their patients' problems. We can compare and contrast them. We can examine their advantages and disadvantages. Most important of all is the fact that we can step outside these languages and examine their social significance, such as their effect on the relationships that exist between all professionals and service users. The argument developed in this book has a dialectical structure, which juxtaposes conflicting perspectives. Part I consists of four chapters which examine the psychiatric view of schizophrenia. This condition is chosen because it demonstrates so well the conflicts between different explanatory languages. We establish what psychiatrists think schizophrenia is, what they think its causes are, and how they treat it. The central part of my argument is developed in Part II, consisting of four chapters which challenge the evidence presented in Part I. Chapter 5 challenges a number of assumptions that psychiatrists have about the disease nature of schizophrenia. Chapter 6 questions the emphasis on the role of medication that follows from an uncritical acceptance of the medical model of schizophrenia. Chapter 7 contextualises this model by examining its significance in relation to recent political changes in Western societies, and Chapter 8 deals critically with a number of assumptions inherent in the philosophy of neuroscience. Part III consists of two chapters which try to find a way forward. It examines new ways of thinking about and working with people who hear voices. It also looks in detail at psychiatrists as members of the medical profession, and considers the nature of the barriers which many users feel exist between them and their psychiatrists, before drawing conclusions about the training of psychiatrists.

In the past, critical debate about the nature of psychiatry has been characterised by polarised arguments between the profession and anti-psychiatrists. This is unhelpful. It makes it difficult to move the profession on. Indeed, it is arguable that the ascendancy of neuroscience in the 1980s and 1990s is a legacy of the attacks on psychiatry in the 1960s and 1970s. It is easy for psychiatrists to dismiss the protests of the anti-psychiatrists because of the latter's insistence that psychiatry has nothing to offer people experiencing mental health problems. I believe that psychiatry, neuroscience included, has much to offer, but this is hampered by psychiatrists' uncritical, thoughtless application of theory (whether neuroscience, cognitive, psychoanalytic, social or political) without considering the individual who is subject to this theory. In one sense, an important purpose of this book is to stimulate a debate between mental health professionals and service users. I want to encourage a critical approach to understanding the nature and origins of mental health problems. Most of all, I want to try to revive the notion of critical psychiatry. In this sense the book tries to set out a context against which the value of critical psychiatry can be seen, and, hopefully, will pave the way for future texts dealing more specifically with the nature of critical psychiatry.

Part I   THESIS

1 Medicine and Madness

Unless we are explicit about the nature of the languages we use to talk about ourselves, and the world we live in, we will misunderstand each other. We shall remain divided by impenetrable barriers of discourse. Nowhere is this more true than in psychiatry and the disputed nature of mental illness, especially serious mental illness such as schizophrenia. What is the best way of conceptualising the problems that are lumped together under the rubric of 'mental illness'? Are they illnesses caused by disturbances in brain function, or are they labels given by society to deviant individuals? Are they cultural artefacts, nothing more than social constructions bound and constrained by the temporal and cultural contexts in which they are used? Or are they ordinary people's responses to poverty and social adversity, the inevitable outcome of the growth of inequality in our society over the last quarter of a century? All these views have been popular at one time or another over the course of the twentieth century, depending upon fashion. The real problem is that the proponents of these views usually believe that theirs is the only truth, so if we believe that 'mental illness' is in fact a social construction, then this precludes the possibility that the medical model might have anything to offer. We may form a clearer view of these conflicts if we consider the following vignettes.

An old man is rushed into a medical ward two days after his wife dies. When he gets there he believes that he is in prison and the nurses are warders. He has no idea of the date, or time. He mumbles incoherently to himself and keeps brushing at the bedclothes, trying to remove the insects he sees crawling up the duvet. He is extremely restless, particularly at night, when he shouts out in terror at the voices which, in their broken fragmented way, threaten him. The bedclothes are damp with his sweat, and his heart is racing. His lips are a dusky red colour, he has a high temperature and a cough. His restlessness is extremely difficult for the doctors and nurses to manage on a medical ward, so they give him a small dose of a major tranquilliser. The nursing staff find out from his son that the old man's memory has been failing for two years. His wife cared for him.

The doctors discover that he has acute pneumonia which responds well to treatment with antibiotics. His acute confusional state settles as his temperature falls, but the psychiatrist who assesses him several days later finds that his memory is extremely poor, and he still has no idea of the date or where he is. Eventually he has to go and live in an old people's home.

A middle-aged woman is admitted to a psychiatric unit three months after the sudden death of her husband from a stroke. She has stopped going to work and had been housebound for two months prior to admission. Her weight has fallen by two stones because she has been taking fluids only. Normally she takes great care in her appearance, but on admission her hair has not been touched for four weeks and she smells. She believes that she is to blame for her husband's death because twenty years before she had an affair with another man which she never disclosed to him. In her view she is wicked, a sinner. She believes that she is going to be punished. Because she is so profoundly depressed and agitated, the psychiatrist suggests that she starts on a small dose of a major tranquilliser, and has a course of ECT, which she agrees to. Six weeks later she is back at work, and is having a course of bereavement counselling from her community psychiatric nurse. Over the course of the next three months she comes to terms not only with her husband's death, but also with her guilt.

A young Asian man in his first year at university studying computer science, is arrested by the police outside the house of the parents of the girl to whom he is engaged. He smashes a window and threatens to kill her father, who, with his own father, arranged the marriage. The young man has a white girlfriend at university with whom he is in love. He has told his father that he doesn't wish to marry the girl they have chosen for him. In the police cells he shouts and screams, and appears to be talking to himself. He is assessed by a psychiatrist who arranges his admission on Section 2 of the Mental Health Act to the local psychiatric hospital, where he is seen to be overactive and overtalkative. In the first forty-eight hours of his admission he sleeps only for one. He is given large doses of major tranquillisers and develops unpleasant side-effects, which result in peculiar writhing movements of his right arm. Some of the doctors say that he is catatonic, others that he is hysterical. Despite the disagreements the young man is still in hospital four months later, hearing distressing voices that are not controlled by high doses of neuroleptic medication, which cause him many distressing side-effects. His family are utterly perplexed by what has happened. No one seems able or willing to explain to them what is going on.

An eighteen-year-old girl, the daughter of an army sergeant, is admitted to a psychiatric unit when her weight falls to five and a half stones. She started dieting three years before when she was sent to a boarding school when her father and mother were posted abroad. Now she runs four miles a day, consumes large amounts of laxatives, and can cause herself to vomit at will. Her parents are at their wits' end to know how best to encourage her to eat. In hospital she is given a small dose of a major tranquilliser, and is placed on a strict contract which means that she can gain privileges, such as getting out of bed, watching television or going horse-riding, by gradually increasing her food intake and gaining weight. Three weeks after admission she tells a nurse of a recurrent nightmare in which she thinks she might be attacked by a strange and terrifying figure. She describes Priapus, the Greek god of eroticism, son of Aphrodite and Dionysus. Later, she goes on to disclose systematic sexual abuse at the hands of a close relative. In doing so she gains weight rapidly. She is given the opportunity to discuss these horrifying experiences in detail with a nurse, and also has a course of Art Therapy. She gains weight rapidly and shortly after leaving hospital finds a job.

These vignettes give some idea of the wide range of problems that psychiatrists have to deal with. They share certain features that we shall examine in some detail later on. All the patients received neuroleptic drugs,[1] an important group of drugs widely used to treat people suffering from schizophrenia. Yet none of the patients was actually suffering from schizophrenia. This has always struck me as odd. In all four cases the disturbance that ultimately resulted in hospitalisation occurred after a major change in the individual's life circumstances. These changes, or life events, include bereavement (in the first two cases) or role conflict (third case), or an overwhelming trauma such as sexual abuse (the last case). In the first case the patient's physical state of health was also an important factor that resulted in hospitalisation.

---

1   These drugs are also known as major tranquillisers or anti-psychotic drugs.

Perhaps most important of all, with the possible exception of the first case, is the presence of uncertainty as to what is the most appropriate way of understanding the presenting problem. What exactly has happened to these people? Why did they come under psychiatric care? Is the lady in the second vignette suffering from affective disorder, or has she become overwhelmed by grief and guilt? Is her disturbance a physical one brought about by complex changes in her brain chemistry, or is she experiencing a deep spiritual malaise understandable in terms of the problems of her existence? Is the young man in the third vignette suffering from an acute hypomanic illness (a severe form of mood disorder, with a biological basis), or is he experiencing an understandable adjustment to a severe life crisis, in which his notion of himself and his cultural identity are shaken to their foundations because of his life circumstances? Or is he a victim, caught in the clash of two oppressive cultures, Western materialism and Islam? Is the young girl in the last vignette suffering from anorexia nervosa, an eating disorder which some consider to have a physical basis which involves the regulation of appetite in the brain, or is she using her food intake as the only means of control she has over her life, in the face of a sexually abusive relationship in which she is forced to believe that she has no control? Each of these stories may be analysed in different ways, depending upon your theoretical perspective, medical, psychological or social. Each perspective leads to different conclusions. A detailed examination of this conflict, between different interpretations of people's distress, illness, call it what you will, lies at the heart of this book. We shall examine the features of the *languages* that underpin these different models, in an attempt to establish how they may relate, or may lie in conflict. In particular I shall try to show that the most profound problem associated with the use of these languages is their exclusivity. To speak one of these languages brings with it the risk of excluding others, especially the voice of the subject whose problems are being described. At issue here is the interaction between professionals and the subject's account, especially the particular significance of individual experience and the reinterpretation of this by professional languages.

These vignettes share another important feature; that is a breakdown in the individual's habitual coping mechanisms. It is very easy for mental health professionals to forget that the people whom they are trying to help have been put in that position not so much because of the existence of the problem that resulted in referral, but because they are no longer able to cope with the problem. The coping mechanisms that people use to help deal with emotional distress or psychiatric symptoms vary enormously, and until recently professionals knew very little about them. This is why self-help groups for conditions like benzodiazepine dependence, or eating disorders for example, have become a very important component of help. Until recently, self-help, or self-management, has not played an important part in the care of those suffering with the most severe types of mental health problems such as psychotic illnesses like schizophrenia. This, as we shall see, is beginning to change.

Before we can develop these themes further, we need to understand more about the most severe forms of psychiatric disorders, so I shall present the traditional medical view of psychiatric disorders. The purpose of this is to lay open, for detailed examination and criticism, the way that psychiatrists have been trained to think about mental illness for almost a hundred years. This will become clear if we consider the condition that psychiatrists call schizophrenia as an example. Schizophrenia has become an ideological battleground. In no other condition have the adversaries drawn up such clearly demarcated lines and formations. No other condition, with the possible exception of acquired immune deficiency syndrome (AIDS), invokes such fear and misunderstanding in the minds of ordinary people. For these reasons it is important that we examine the origins of the concept, the latest theories about its nature, and how psychiatrists try to treat and manage the condition. I want to present this view of the condition first, without deconstructing it. The criticism will come later. My reason for wanting to do it this way is simple: it is not often that a psychiatrist is given the opportunity to present modern theories of schizophrenia to a general audience. The main purpose here is to present the medical 'language' that is used to think about and describe the condition. Once this has been achieved we will be in a better position to examine the conflicts between these languages. My purpose in presenting these theories is not necessarily to attack the theories themselves, but, in later chapters, to attack the uncritical application of these theories without thought for the individual whose experience becomes buried beneath a welter of specialist terms and jargon.

SCHIZOPHRENIA

The Centre for Health Economics in the University of York has estimated that the total cost to the National Health Service (NHS) of treating schizophrenia is £397 million a year at 1992 costs. This is equivalent to 1.6% of the total spent on health care in Britain. The same group has estimated that the total economic cost to the country in terms of lost production through schizophrenia is around £1.7 billion (Davies and Drummond, 1994). In the popular mind the term evokes the epitome of madness. Every day we hear people use the word out of context. I once heard a music critic on the radio talking about a 'schizophrenic' performance of Mahler's Ninth Symphony. I presume that he used the term to refer to the fact that the performance reflected the intense extremes of emotion that this great work undoubtedly displays. Whenever we are confronted by expressions of emotional intensity or behaviour that swings from one extreme to another, we reach for the word 'schizophrenic' to reflect the duality, the two extremes, the contradictions bound up in the whole. But what exactly do psychiatrists mean when they use the word? The best way to answer this question is to describe it in terms of epidemiology, genetics, biochemistry, neurodevelopment and cognition. These theories provide much of the scientific basis underlying modern approaches to treatment and therapy, which I shall also describe in some detail. But first, what are the symptoms of the condition?

Peter was nineteen years old and in his first year at a northern university reading mathematics when his parents became concerned about him. His girlfriend phoned them up to say that she had not seen him for four weeks because he had locked himself in his room, spending hours by himself. At night the sound of loud music could be heard coming from his room in the Hall of Residence, and sometimes he could be heard carrying on long conversations with himself. He had also stopped attending lectures. His tutor had written to him several times, but there had been no reply. His parents visited him and were shocked to see the state that he was in. He was filthy and hadn't washed or combed his hair for several weeks. He had also lost over a stone in weight. His room was in a mess, the carpet covered with cigarette ends and ash, and old newspapers were scattered over the floor. His desk was covered with hundreds of pieces of note-paper on which were scribbled repeated phrases and disjointed ramblings, none of which appeared to make sense. They brought him home and took him to see his General Practitioner (GP) who immediately referred him to the local psychiatric service. Peter appeared to accept this passively, without questioning what was happening to him. In the hospital he was seen by a young psychiatrist who asked him a series of questions. At first Peter appeared reluctant to answer them, but as he became more settled during the course of the interview he opened up. In response to the questions he admitted that he had been hearing voices talking about him, saying that he was a 'plank', and that he would be sawn up into little pieces. This terrified him. He also believed that a metal bar had been implanted in his body, because he had a strange sensation in the pit of his stomach. He didn't know how the bar had got there, but he believed that it enabled the people whose voices he heard to control his thoughts, and, on occasions, his actions. For example, he thought they were able to use the bar to put their thoughts into his mind. On one occasion he had the idea that he should cut off his right hand, a thought that was not his own, and that he thought must have come from the voices. He agreed to admission to hospital and was started on a course of trifluoperazine (stelazine), a neuroleptic. His physical and neurological state were investigated in detail, although no abnormalities were detected. A social worker interviewed his parents in detail. Peter had had a perfectly ordinary and happy childhood. He was a loved child who had had no traumatic experiences. Following admission and treatment with stelazine there was a slight improvement in his condition. He appeared less troubled by his experiences, although they did not go altogether, and he continued to experience distressing voices. At this stage, in the opinion of his consultant, Peter also showed evidence of a restriction in the range of his emotional expressiveness, as well as a reduction in the amount of spontaneous conversation. She told his parents that these signs indicated that their son was unlikely to make a full recovery. Two years later he had not returned to university and was living in a hostel for the mentally ill. Although his medication had stopped the voices, he remained flat and disinterested in anything around him. He spent most of the day by himself, watching the television and chain-smoking.

Symptoms and signs

Peter's story is typical of the thousands of young people who are diagnosed with schizophrenia ('schizophrenic') each year. At this point it is worth noting this change in title, from 'person' to 'schizophrenic'. It relates to a number of issues that I want to deal with later in this book. The psychiatrist makes the diagnosis on the basis of the experiences described by the patient (or symptoms), using additional information (signs) based on observation of the patient's behaviour at interview. It is also customary for the psychiatrist to gain additional information from a third party who knows the patient well, to corroborate the history and also to obtain an independent view of the historical development of the problem. This is particularly important in situations where it is helpful to know something about the early life and development of the individual. Once this information has been obtained, the psychiatrist then tries to draw it together by making a diagnostic formulation, which is a statement of all the factors that the psychiatrist considers to be important in explaining the disturbance. There is a strong tradition that regards two groups of symptoms as being of particular importance in diagnosing schizophrenia, or, to be precise, one group of symptoms (abnormal experiences) and one group of signs (features noticed by the doctor at interview, and not necessarily of concern to the patient). These are referred to as 'positive' and 'negative' symptoms.

Positive and negative symptoms

For many years these have constituted the *sine qua non* for schizophrenia. Without one or more of these symptoms you are unlikely to be diagnosed with the condition. They have also come to form an important component of modern systems of classification of the disorder which are widely used in scientific research. There is nothing new in the distinction between positive and negative symptoms. In the nineteenth century the neurologist Hughlings Jackson (1889) compared the symptoms of mental illness with those found in neurological disorders such as epilepsy. He concluded that negative symptoms arose directly from the effects of pathology on the brain, whereas positive symptoms arose through the release of healthy activity in the lower levels of the central nervous system by the pathological process. This model was in turn based on Jackson's hierarchical model of the way the central nervous system was organised. Berrios has argued (1985) that the distinction between positive and negative symptoms should more correctly be attributed to the physician J.R. Reynolds, who had a simpler view of the relationship between the two sets of symptoms, claiming that there was no functional relationship between them. Despite the controversies of academic discussion, the distinction has been an influential and useful one over the last twenty years. To put it simply, positive symptoms are experiences that should not be there, but which are, whereas negative symptoms are features that should be present but which are not. This will become clearer if I describe each group in turn.

Positive symptoms correspond closely to a group of symptoms described by the German psychiatrist Schneider (1957) and which have since come to be known as Schneider's First Rank Symptoms

(FRSs). Schneider maintained that the presence of one or more of these symptoms, in the absence of evidence to suggest that the patient was suffering from organic brain disease, indicated a diagnosis of schizophrenia. These symptoms have become enormously influential and have formed the basis for most modern systems of diagnosing schizophrenia. The First Rank Symptoms are as follows:

1. *Three types of auditory hallucinations*. Hallucinations are said to occur if we have a perception (we see, hear, smell, feel or taste something) in the absence of a physical event in the external world to bring about the perception. In schizophrenia the most characteristic type of hallucinations are auditory verbal ones, or the experience of hearing voices when there is no one else about and nothing else to explain it. Schneider described three types of verbal hallucinations which he considered to be pathognomonic[2] of schizophrenia: hearing voices that speak your thoughts aloud; hearing two or more voices talking about you, perhaps arguing or having a discussion, in which they talk about you in the third person (that is referring to you as 'he' or 'she'); hearing one or more voice carrying on a running commentary in which your actions, or sometimes your thoughts, are commented on. It is worth noting at this stage that in order to diagnose schizophrenia on the basis of hearing voices, psychiatrists are only interested in certain very restricted features of the voices. They are only interested to establish whether the voices fall into one of the three categories above, so that they can make the diagnosis of schizophrenia. Most other features of the voices are disregarded.

2. *Interference in thinking processes*. In some ways this is the most difficult set of experiences to relate to. In Western culture (and this is an important qualification) there is a shared notion that people's minds, and what goes on in them, is a private inner world, inaccessible to other people. There is, if you like, a very clear boundary between what is me and what is not me, outside and 'other'. The hallmark of this second set of symptoms is that this boundary breaks down, so that I lose the sense that my thought processes are personal and private. Other people gain access to them. Schneider described three main symptoms in this group: the experience that other people are able to insert their thoughts into my mind (thought insertion), or that they are able to take thoughts out of my mind (thought

---

2   A pathognomonic symptom is one which is considered to be essential in diagnosing a particular disease.

withdrawal), and thought broadcasting in which I have the experience that other people know what I am thinking at the same time that my thoughts pass through my mind.

3. *Passivity experiences*. This group of symptoms closely resembles thought insertion and withdrawal, in that the experience involves a breakdown in the sense of control and autonomy that I possess over my body. This can manifest itself in a variety of ways. Sometimes it takes the form of bodily hallucinations, strange physical sensations located within my body, or, alternatively, it may take the form of urges to do things, or simple motor acts like raising an arm or picking up a packet of cigarettes, which I experience as not intended by myself. It is as if I am no longer the author of my own actions, merely an amanuensis obeying the dictates of another's will.

4. *The primary delusional experience*. Although Schneider claimed that this experience was at the core of the 'schizophrenic' experience, it is in fact extremely rare. I have only encountered a very small number of people who have described it clearly. In his description there appear to be three components. The first consists of delusional mood.[3] In this state I might have a sense of unease, a feeling that something is about to happen, that in some way is personal and involves me in a profound way. This feeling may last for weeks, and is followed by the second stage, the delusional perception, in which I have a normal perception to which I attach a strange new meaning, usually of personal significance. For example I might go for a walk and see a real crow settle on a real telegraph pole, but in my mind this otherwise insignificant event becomes imbued with great personal significance, because I take it to mean that the Masons are convinced that I am a homosexual, and that they are going to persecute me. In the final stage this delusional idea[4] becomes elaborated into a complex delusional system, forming a network of beliefs about the world that only I hold,

---

3   This is an extremely difficult experience to describe. One of the best recent accounts is to be found in Chapter 2 of Louis Sass' book *Madness and Modernism* (1992). In it, he draws parallels between delusional mood and the work of the Italian painter de Chirico, and the literary works of Kafka, Hugo von Hofmannsthal and André Breton.

4   A delusion is a false unshakeable belief held despite evidence to the contrary, and out of keeping with the individual's social, educational, cultural and religious background.

and which places me in the centre of a (usually) persecutory universe.

There are two other groups of symptoms that I want to mention at this point, although neither are First Rank Symptoms. For many years psychiatrists regarded thought disorder as an important symptom of schizophrenia, so much so that the phenomenon is often called 'schizophrenic' thought disorder. Anyone who showed evidence of this would, in the past, almost certainly be diagnosed schizophrenic. The reason for this is that over eighty years ago the Swiss psychiatrist Eugen Bleuler considered disorders of thinking to be a central feature of the psychological breakdown in schizophrenia (Bleuler, 1911). Psychiatrists generally consider a speaker to be thought disordered when they find it difficult to follow what is being said. I shall have more to say about this in Chapter 5, but there can be no doubt that thought disorder has played an important part in the diagnosis of schizophrenia in the past. The other group are the catatonic symptoms, in which behaviour becomes very disorganised. These include disturbances of posture in which the subject may hold a bizarre and uncomfortable position for hours at a time, and negativism, in which the subject does the opposite of what was expected. These symptoms are now extremely rare, and are seen much less frequently than was the case a hundred years ago. Many catatonic symptoms probably have an organic basis (i.e. arising from a major disturbance in brain function brought about by physical illness), and for this reason less weight is attached to their importance in diagnosing schizophrenia these days.

The young man, Peter, whose problems I described above, experienced most of Schneider's First Rank Symptoms. He heard voices talking about him, he had strange bodily experiences, and he also had the strange idea that there was a metal bar in his body. He also told the psychiatrist that he believed that people could interfere with his thoughts. It was because he described this range of experiences that the psychiatrist decided that he was suffering from schizophrenia. But the psychiatrist also noticed certain features of his behaviour which she considered to be abnormal. These are the negative symptoms of schizophrenia. Strictly speaking a more appropriate (medical) term would be negative signs, because they are things that doctors notice on examination and the people who evince them generally do not complain about them. It is only relatively recently that psychiatrists have become interested in them, and a good account of negative symptoms has been provided by Andreasen (1982a, 1982b) in America. She describes five groups of symptoms under this heading.

Blunting of affect. Affect is the expression used by psychiatrists to describe our emotional reactivity. It is an indication of the extent to which we are emotionally engaged with our environments, especially with the people we encounter in it. If you watch two friends having a conversation you will notice a rich variety of complex behaviours that demonstrate their emotional warmth towards each other. Their eyes are involved in a complex dance, establishing, breaking and then re-establishing gaze. Their faces change in expression reflecting their emotional states. Subtle shifts in body posture may indicate the degree of interest they have in the topic under discussion. Hands and arms are used in an endless variety of expressive gestures to add weight or emphasis to particular aspects of their conversation. Voice pitch and volume change in complex patterns indicating distinct changes in mood: sadness, happiness, anger, love, sexual arousal and so on. We are all experts in other people's behaviour. Clinicians decide that blunting of affect is present if, during the course of an interview, the individual shows evidence of a reduction of these behaviours. According to clinical descriptions, people who show blunt affect have fixed and expressionless faces. They establish little or no eye contact, or sometimes they are said to have a peculiar quality of eye contact, in which the interviewer feels that she is being stared through. There is little reciprocal change in posture, and a reduction in the amount of expressive gestural movements. The voice is said to be dull and monotonous. Anyone with these features will be said by a psychiatrist to show evidence of blunting of affect.

Poverty of speech. Poverty of speech is a reduction in the amount of spontaneous speech observed during the course of a psychiatric interview. When this occurs the interviewer finds that she has to make most of the running in trying to get the subject to open up. Many of the subject's replies may be monosyllabic ('Yes' or 'No'), or the interviewer's questions may remain unanswered. The experience for the interviewer is a little like trying to get blood from a stone. The sentences out of which such speech is constructed tend to be very short and contain fewer complex clause structures (Thomas *et al.*, 1987; Thomas, Kearney *et al.*, 1996). Poverty of content of speech is a slightly different phenomenon. Here, although the subject produces an adequate amount of speech, it does not contain a great deal of information. The amount of speech could be considerably reduced in order to convey the same amount of information. This is because it is repetitive, and contains vague ideas that are poorly knitted together. The difficulty here is that such speech is commonly encountered in people who have never been diagnosed with schizophrenia.

Lack of drive, lack of pleasure and poor attention. I have grouped the last three negative symptoms together because some authorities do not consider them to be true negative symptoms. Lack of drive, or avolition, refers to an apparent reduction in the subject's will to get up and do things, or face new challenges. Such individuals may remain inert or idle for long periods of time, with a general disinclination to become involved in any form of activity. Similarly, lack of pleasure (or anhedonia) is revealed by a reduction in the individual's drive to engage in pleasurable activities such as friendships, sex and so on. Poor attention can manifest itself in a number of ways, but is traditionally regarded as an important cognitive deficit that has, for many years, been regarded as a major psychological feature of schizophrenia. In its simplest form it may be regarded as an inability on the part of the subject to direct his or her psychological processes to the task in hand.

At this point it is worth contrasting positive and negative symptoms, for they differ in a number of important respects. Most psychiatrists would agree that positive symptoms appear suddenly and respond well to neuroleptic medication. On the other hand, negative symptoms appear gradually and do not respond to neuroleptics. There is also evidence (see, for example, Andreasen, 1985) that some people who have negative symptoms may have subtle forms of brain damage, demonstrated by brain scans and psychological tests, whereas this is not the case in people who have positive symptoms. In Peter's case, the psychiatrist noticed the presence of negative symptoms two years after he first presented, because he showed evidence both of blunting of affect and of poverty of speech. The concept of negative symptoms is central to the classical form of schizophrenia, but, as we shall see in Chapter 5, their relationship to positive symptoms is far from clear.

The main purpose of this chapter has been to introduce the main symptoms by which psychiatrists diagnose schizophrenia. But there is something in addition that I want to bring out. The phenomena which we have considered here have a unique status. They represent varieties of human experience which have become identified as symptoms of disease, and in order to legitimise this, psychiatry has evolved a special language to talk about these experiences as symptoms. The language is psychopathology, a name which implies that these experiences arise out of disease processes located in the mind. According to Berrios (1991), the word psychopathology first appeared in a translation of a German textbook of 1847 by the Austrian physician Feuchtersleben, who set out the principles of medical psychology. The word was slow to catch on in Britain, where medical explanations of mental diseases were subsumed under a number of headings, such as mental science, mental pathology, psychological medicine or mental physiology. Some authorities (Lanteri-Laura, quoted in Berrios, 1991) have outlined two approaches to psychopathology at the end of the nineteenth century. Some used the term 'pathological psychology' to refer to that branch of psychology concerned with phenomena which arose from disturbances of normal mental processes in mental diseases. In contrast, psychological pathology, favoured by psychiatrists, regarded psychopathology as the study of abnormal mental phenomena which only occurred in mental disease. In an earlier paper, Berrios (1984) has used the terms 'continuity' and 'discontinuity' to describe these conflicting models.

Berrios' description is useful because it highlights the extent to which psychiatrists examine the symptoms of people suffering from mental illness in a way which sets these experiences apart from normal experience. In pathological psychology the 'symptoms' of mental illness arise from disturbances of normal psychological functioning. Implicit in this approach is the idea that there is no qualitative difference between 'normal' and 'pathological' experience. The latter are inherent in the former. There is no barrier between normal and abnormal experience. Psychological pathology, on the other hand, presupposes that hallucinations, for example, are inherently abnormal, a manifestation of a morbid psychological process. This effectively sets these experiences outside the range of what is considered to be normal. This resulted in a setting apart of psychotic experiences. Here we face a paradox. The mind (psyche) is immaterial. It has no substance. Pathology is the study of physical disease processes as they affect the (material) body. How, then, is it possible for physical processes to act in an immaterial domain? I shall return to this question later in this book, but there is a further point to be made about psychopathology. In psychiatry the term is widely used to refer to the study of psychiatric symptoms, and is often taken to be synonymous with phenomenology. Psychiatrist freely talk about the 'phenomenology' of schizophrenia, or depression, when in fact they are referring to the symptoms of what they regard to be mental diseases. In the second part of this book I want to examine a serious misunderstanding of the word, by referring to its true meaning in reference to a major body of nineteenth- and twentieth-century philosophy. But before I can develop these ideas we have to consider contemporary psychiatric theories concerning the nature of schizophrenia. This we shall do in the next two chapters, in which we shall examine the evidence that is used to justify not only drug treatment, but also social and psychological interventions for the condition.

2 The Tricks of the Trade?

Medicine follows a well-trodden path in its approach to understanding disease. The roots of this approach extend back 2500 years to the island of Cos in the Aegean, where Hippocrates taught his students the secrets of diseases, using the earliest version of what is now called the medical model. Over the last 150 years, developments in science have honed the medical model into a cutting edge that has realised some remarkable successes in conquering disease. We start with epidemiology, to understand the frequency and distribution of a disease in different populations. This may provide important clues about the cause of the disease. Then we examine the genetic and biological basis of the disease. In all areas of medicine, social and psychological factors have an important part to play. This is especially so in psychiatry where there are conspicuous tensions between these models. Biological theories (genetics and biochemistry) provide explanations which are rooted firmly in the physical characteristics of our brains. The argument here is that disturbances in brain function, however caused, result in symptoms in the mind, the abnormal experiences we examined in Chapter 1. This is an important assumption that will be subject to close scrutiny in Chapter 8. Psychological and social theories are very different. Psychological theories offer explanations in terms of mind, and seek to explain the symptoms of psychiatric disorders through disturbances in such mechanisms as perception, memory and language, which are important components of mind. Mind and brain are closely related, but they are not the same thing. This constitutes a central conflict in psychiatry, which we shall also consider in Chapter 8. Social theories examine how factors such as employment, social class, family structures and culture influence psychiatric disorders. They also pose difficult questions for the cultural assumptions that lie beneath psychiatric talk about categories like schizophrenia.

THE EPIDEMIOLOGY OF SCHIZOPHRENIA

The science of epidemiology examines the distribution of an illness in a given population at a particular time. Most of us are familiar with some of the more striking successes of epidemiology. A good example is the discovery of a link between cigarette smoking and lung cancer. In studies of large numbers of people, it became clear that there was an increased risk of developing lung cancer the more you smoked. By examining the distribution of illnesses in populations, epidemiology reveals clues about the causes of disease. In Chapter 1 we saw that Peter was given a diagnosis of schizophrenia on the basis of his responses to questions in a clinical interview. In this respect psychiatry is unlike any other branch of medicine, where diagnoses are usually made on the basis not only of history, but also through the use of diagnostic tests. A physician may be able to establish the diagnosis of lung cancer unequivocally through the use of chest X-rays. If doubt remains, then an endoscopy makes it possible to examine the tumour directly through a fibre-optic tube passed down into the air passages. If there is still doubt at this stage, then a minute amount of the tumour tissue may be removed through the endoscope and sent off for histological examination. If this happens a pathologist will examine the tissue under a microscope and will then be able to say without any doubt whatsoever whether the patient is suffering from lung cancer. There can be no doubt about the recognition of the illness. This means that when we come to count its frequency in the population as a whole we can be reasonably certain that our figures are accurate. This simply is not the case with schizophrenia. There is no diagnostic or laboratory test for the condition, a fact which has hampered epidemiological studies of schizophrenia for years. The diagnosis is based largely upon clinical convention. Because there are differences of opinion about the criteria that should be used to diagnose the condition, psychiatrists have placed great emphasis on the importance of standardised diagnostic criteria. These are lists of symptoms, such as Schneider's FRSs which we met in the last chapter, whose purpose is to ensure that no matter in which part of the world they work, psychiatrists can be reasonably certain that the same criteria are being used.

Over the last thirty years, the World Health Organisation (WHO) has invested enormous resources into epidemiological surveys of the frequency of schizophrenia in different countries. The methods used have been described in detail by Sartorius (1993).

The first of these studies, the International Pilot Study of Schizophrenia (IPSS) was undertaken in nine countries (Taiwan, Colombia, Czechoslovakia, Denmark, India, Nigeria, UK, USA, USSR). Its objectives included the development of research assessment instruments, such as the Present State Examination (PSE), a standardised psychiatric diagnostic interview. Investigators from the study centres were trained in the use of the PSE and their reliability checked, to ensure that the investigators were using the same criteria to judge the presence of a particular symptom. Jablensky (1988) has summarised the main findings of these studies. Schizophrenia appears to be a universal syndrome affecting 5 adults out of every 1000 in all cultures, there being only a modest variation in the incidence rates[1] in different cultures. Depending on the way schizophrenia is defined, the incidence varies from 1.5 cases per 10,000 population per annum in Denmark, to 4.2 per 10,000 in Chandigarh, rural India. Gender appears to influence the incidence rate by age. Although the total risk of developing the condition by the age of fifty-four is the same for men and women, women tend to be older than men when they develop the condition. According to Jablensky, the WHO studies provide evidence in support of a significant genetic component in the cause of schizophrenia. In addition, they also provide support for the idea, outlined in Chapter 1, of the existence of two distinct types of symptoms, one characterised by acute (or positive) symptoms, and another characterised by gradual onset (negative symptoms). Perhaps the most striking finding was the fact that people diagnosed with the disorder in different cultures had quite different outcomes, with those living in non-industrial societies generally having a more favourable outcome. This suggests that culture and social factors play an important role in the condition.

Over the last ten years some researchers have raised the possibility that the incidence of schizophrenia may be falling. Is the condition becoming less common? Using figures of admissions of patients to hospitals in Scotland, Eagles and Whalley (1985) found a marked decline in the apparent incidence of schizophrenia. Der et al. (1990) in London have made similar observations. A related claim, by Zubin et al. (1983), is that the nature of schizophrenia has changed over the last fifty years. They have suggested that it is becoming a less severe illness with a more

---

1　Incidence rates are the total number of new cases presenting to services over the period of one year.

favourable outcome. This echoes the WHO's finding that the condition has a more favourable outcome in non-industrial cultures. Harrison and Mason (1993) have reviewed the evidence here, pointing out that the most obvious explanation is that the shift to community care over the last twenty years means that people suffering from schizophrenia are more likely to be treated at home, rather than being admitted to hospital. This means that any comparison based on hospital admissions over time will show an apparent fall. Another possibility is that psychiatrists' diagnostic habits have changed, as they have adopted narrower definitions of schizophrenia under the influence of more rigorous diagnostic criteria. Harrison and Mason conclude that, with the exception of some subtypes of the condition, there is nothing to suggest that there has been a real change in the course and outcome of schizophrenia, although the possibility of such trends cannot be discounted.

There remains one final, but important, thread of evidence to be gleaned from epidemiological studies. A consistent finding over the years has been the association between schizophrenia, lower social class and urban life. The condition appears to be more common in inner-city areas. Cooper and Sartorius (1977) suggested that schizophrenia may have emerged as a consequence of the profound upheavals in social organisation that occurred with the industrialisation of Western societies in the nineteenth century. When they were widely dispersed in rural communities, people suffering from schizophrenia presented no threat to society. This changed dramatically with urbanisation and the concentration of large numbers of people in towns and cities. The problem of schizophrenia simply became more conspicuous. The relationship between urban life and schizophrenia was most clearly demonstrated in a well-known study by Faris and Dunham (1939). They found that the frequency of first admissions to hospitals in Chicago for schizophrenia gradually decreased as people moved away from the poor inner-city areas to the more prosperous suburbs. Two opposing explanations were proposed for this observation. The 'social drift' theory maintains that people suffering from chronic and disabling mental illnesses such as schizophrenia drift into inner-city areas because they face fewer social demands there. Support for this idea comes from a study by Goldberg and Morrison (1963), who found that although the social class distribution of people admitted to an urban hospital was skewed in favour of those from social classes IV and V, the distribution of the social class of their families of origin was no different from that of the general population. People with schizophrenia, it was argued, 'drift' down the social ladder, *as part of the disease process*. Such people, it is argued, are unable to meet the complex demands made upon those who live in more prosperous areas, so they drift into inner-city areas where social demands are reduced. A variant of this explanation is that the upwardly mobile migrate out of inner-city areas. These are people whose mental health is good, and who are successfully at work, raising families. This selective migration of the mentally healthy out of the inner-city areas further increases the prevalence[2] of schizophrenia in the city. An important factor here is the great change in the composition of the population in the inner city. In Britain, Hugh Freeman (1984) has made an extensive study of these factors in the town of Salford. He found that the dramatic fall in the population of Salford from 1928 on was largely accounted for by the migration out of families containing employed adults. This left behind the mentally ill, the chronically sick, single-parent families and the elderly.

The alternative explanation has been called the 'breeder' hypothesis. This holds that schizophrenia is caused by the social adversity facing those who live in urban areas. Factors such as social disorganisation characterised by excessive mobility, poor housing, poverty and ethnic conflict constitute important stressors that are capable of causing schizophrenia. Freeman (1994) has reviewed the evidence for and against these opposing models. One difficulty is that the term 'urban' has a number of different meanings. In addition there are social and non-social environmental factors associated with urban life. He concludes that the 'urban' effect may be largely explained through migration and social class. I shall return to the complex relationship between schizophrenia, urban life and poverty in Chapter 7. Although Jablensky (1988) concludes that there is compelling evidence for a biological basis for schizophrenia, and that social and cultural factors play what he calls a 'non-specific' role in shaping the development and course of the disorder, much of the evidence suggests that social factors, especially the nature of urban life, have an important influence on the diagnosis and outcome of schizophrenia.

---

2   Prevalence is the term used by epidemiologists to describe the total proportion of a given population said to be suffering from the condition in question, at a particular time.

GENETICS AND SCHIZOPHRENIA

The amalgamation of genetics and the science of molecular biology has profound implications for psychiatry. The link between the two is quite straightforward. Genes are the sequences of chemicals found along the length of each of the forty-six chromosomes located in the nuclei of the cells of our bodies. Each chromosome consists of a tightly coiled double spiral of deoxyribonucleic acid (DNA) formed by a constantly changing sequence of chemicals called base pairs. There are four of these base pairs, so called because they pair off together like the rungs of a ladder, joining the two spirals of DNA. Each gene consists of a sequence of base pairs which forms a special code responsible for controlling the production of a particular protein molecule, usually an enzyme. These molecules play a central role in the control of the complex chemical reactions to be found in our cells, and so ultimately control our physical characteristics. These include simple features such as hair or eye colour, as well as more complex aspects such as the growth, development and ageing of our bodies, from the moment of fertilisation to death. The physical aspects of the development of our brains are also under genetic control. This has the potential for being an extremely deterministic view of the nature of man, one in which there is little room for environmental, let alone psychological or spiritual, considerations. To show that genetic factors are important in causing disease, we have to show that the risk of developing it increases the closer your relationship to someone who has the disorder. This is because the closer your blood relationship to someone, the more genetic information you share in common. We inherit half our genes from each parent, so that children of the same parents share 50% of their genes in common. For this reason the most informative genetic studies have involved the two types of twins, identical and non-identical. The latter come from the fertilisation of two eggs by two sperms, and so are no more similar in genetic terms than ordinary brothers or sisters, having 50% of their genetic material in common. Identical twins are formed when a single egg, fertilised by a single sperm, divides shortly after fertilisation to form two genetically identical embryos.

In addition to twin studies, family and adoption studies have also been widely used to investigate genetic factors in disease. Family studies examine the incidence of disease in the members of families where one person is already affected. If genetic factors are important, then we would expect the risk of developing the condition to increase with the closeness of the relationship to the affected person. Twin studies are similar. Here, the concordance rate (CR) is compared in identical and non-identical twins. The CR is the proportion of affected twin-pairs. A twin pair is concordant if both develop the condition. They are discordant if only one twin is affected. If heredity is important then we would expect to see higher concordance rates in identical twins than non-identical twins, because the former are genetically identical. One of the main criticisms of the use of family and twin studies is that they are unable to separate the environmental effects of parenting and early family life from heredity. In this view, the debate becomes focused on the relative contributions of heredity and environment, sometimes referred to as 'nature versus nurture'. This distinction plays an important part in theories of most psychiatric disorders, and hinges upon the fact that our biological closeness to our parents or siblings brings with it shared family, social and environmental experiences. Geneticists have attempted to tackle this problem by using adoptive studies. These rely on identifying children born to mothers diagnosed with schizophrenia, and adopted away from their biological families to be brought up by psychiatrically 'normal' mothers.[3] The risk of schizophrenia in this group is then compared with a control group of children born to psychiatrically healthy mothers and adopted by psychiatrically 'normal' mothers. The argument runs that if genetic factors are more important than environmental ones, then the children of the schizophrenic mothers will still be at a higher risk of developing the disorder as adults, compared with the children of non-schizophrenic mothers. What can we learn from such approaches?

Family and twin studies

Gottesman *et al.* (1987) have summarised the results of all published European family and twin studies of schizophrenia, over a sixty-year period. If you have a relative who suffers from

---

3   Throughout the text I shall enclose the term normal in quote marks. This is to indicate that the adjective is one which, whilst in wide and general use, is incapable of satisfactory definition. A number of authorities have attempted definitions of normality in relation to psychiatric disorder, ranging from the statistical to the idea of biological disadvantage (see Kendell, 1975, and Kraupl Taylor, 1976, for discussions). Shortage of space precludes a full discussion of these issues here.

schizophrenia, then the chances that you will be affected appear to increase as your relationship to the sufferer becomes closer. If the general population risk is just under 1%, then the risk for the family members of those affected is presented in Table 2.1. The risk gradually increases from about 1.5% for first cousins, to 12% for non-identical twins and 44% for identical twins.

Table 2.1:
Risk of schizophrenia in relatives of people diagnosed with schizophrenia

Relationship to patient	Average lifetime risk (%)
First cousins	1.56
Nieces or nephews	2.65
Brothers or sisters	7.30
Children	9.35
Non-identical twins	12.08
Identical twins	44.30

Source: McGue et al., 1985.

There have been many studies of concordance rates for schizophrenia in identical and non-identical twins. Gottesman and Shields (1982) summarised the results of five studies, yielding risks of 47% in identical twins and 12% for non-identical twins. These figures are similar to those of McGue et al. in Table 2.1. They suggest that genetic factors make a significant contribution to the risk of developing schizophrenia. But if schizophrenia was entirely genetically determined, then we would expect a much higher CR in identical twins. This is not the case. In over 50% of identical twins, only one of the pair is affected. This suggests that environmental factors must play an important role. One way of disentangling the contribution of heredity and environment is through the use of adoption studies.

Adoption studies

The Finnish psychiatrist Tienari has recently summarised the important findings to emerge from adoption studies (Tienari, 1992). Although there are different types of adoptive studies, they all rely on estimations of the prevalence of schizophrenia in the children of affected parents, and who are adopted by non-schizophrenic families. If these children carry a genetic risk it is argued that they will subsequently develop schizophrenia, even though they have been brought up in 'normal' families. It is worth noting here that the original purpose of these studies had as much to do with disproving theories that families caused schizophrenia as they had to do with investigating the genetic basis of the condition. One of the earliest adoptive studies was performed by Heston (1966), who found a very high rate of schizophrenia in the children of schizophrenic mothers reared in foster homes. However, he also found a wide variety of other conditions in these children, including personality disorders, neurotic disorders and learning disabilities. Another study by Rosenthal et al. (1971) failed to find a significant excess of children who subsequently developed schizophrenia, if strict criteria were used to diagnose schizophrenia in the biological parents. The most comprehensive study was undertaken by Tienari et al. (1987), who identified over 164 Finnish women suffering from schizophrenia, and who had adopted away 179 children. The importance of this study is that both the biological and the adoptive parents were examined for psychiatric illness. They found that 10% of the children of affected mothers subsequently developed psychotic illnesses, but only half of these suffered from schizophrenia. The remainder had a mixture of problems, including paranoid psychoses, atypical psychoses and affective psychoses. This suggests that the mechanisms of genetic transmission in schizophrenia are far from clear, and, if anything, favour some sort of interaction between genetic and environmental factors. Tienari (1992) has described how this might occur. In the gene–environment interaction, the effect of genes only becomes apparent in the presence of certain environmental conditions. There is a well-established model for this in medicine. The condition known as phenylketonuria (PKU) is a genetically transmitted disorder of metabolism in which affected individuals are unable to break down the amino acid phenylalanine, an essential amino acid present in many foodstuffs. The clinical symptoms of PKU, which include brain damage and epilepsy, only appear if the individual takes phenylalanine in the diet. Avoiding foods that contain it prevents the clinical manifestations of the disease. Such a model demonstrates that interactions between genes and environment do occur, and may possibly be important in schizophrenia, as we shall see later in this chapter.

The results of twin studies show that genes may play an important part in determining the risk of developing schizophrenia, but the way the condition is transmitted from one generation to the next is far from clear. Classical genetic theory originated in the work of the Austrian monk, Gregor Mendel, who observed how certain characteristics, such as flower colour or leaf shape in plants, pass from one generation to the next. He was able to predict accurately the proportion of plants having a particular feature using the presence of these features in the parents. Some always appeared in the next generation if present in one parent only. Mendel described this as dominant transmission. Recessive transmission required the feature to be present in both parents if it was to appear in the next generation. Since then more complex modes of transmission have been described. The problem in psychiatry is that it is very difficult to fit the data from twin and family studies into any clear pattern of transmission. Peter McGuffin (McGuffin *et al.*, 1984) in Cardiff has commented that schizophrenia and manic depressive illness almost never show typical Mendelian segregation ratios (patterns of transmission from one generation to the next) within pedigrees. This means that there is no single gene responsible for schizophrenia, so more complex models have been proposed. The single major locus model claims that transmission is by a single gene, but the extent to which this shows itself in the next generation (its penetrance) varies for reasons that are not clear. In the polygenic model, schizophrenia is seen as the end result of an interaction between a number of different genes as well as environmental effects. Because it is not clear which, if any, of these models is best, psychiatrists have adopted two strategies in an attempt to clarify the situation. One involves examining the heterogeneity[4] of schizophrenia and the other depends on the search for biological markers.

The recent revolution in genetics has resulted in rapid progress in mapping the function of our genes, with the hope that it may be possible to link biological markers of disease to relatives in affected families. If a marker is associated with the presence of the disorder in affected members, then it is likely that the genes responsible for the marker and the illness are closely situated on the same chromosome. There has been particular interest in the possibility that there may be a marker for schizophrenia on chromosome 5 (Sherrington *et al.*, 1988), although two groups (Kennedy *et al.*, 1988; St Clair *et al.*, 1989) have failed to confirm this. In part the problem here goes back

---

4   Heterogeneity refers to the idea that there are different types of schizophrenia, in which the role of genetic factors varies.

to the absence of an unequivocal diagnostic test for schizophrenia. One way around this is to look for enduring physical or psychological characteristics of affected individuals, features that are not just associated with the presence of First Rank Symptoms, and to see if the same features occur in unaffected family members. If so, then this feature may be regarded as an important marker possibly associated with the genetic risk for developing schizophrenia. The important distinction here is between states and traits. Let us say, for example, that I think that there may be a deficit of attention in schizophrenia. How should I go about investigating this? If I measured performance on tasks of attention in people suffering from the acute illness, I might find that they performed poorly compared with non-schizophrenic subjects. The problem is that I cannot conclude that poor performance in schizophrenia is an intrinsic feature of the illness. It could have arisen because the subjects were so preoccupied with their abnormal experiences (hearing voices and so on), that they were unable or unwilling to perform the test. Medication, too, could also affect performance. In other words they performed badly because of the state they were in at the time of testing. To be able to show that attentional impairment is an integral feature of schizophrenia, I must re-test subjects when they no longer have acute symptoms such as hallucinations or delusions. Only if they perform badly at that stage can I be reasonably certain that attentional impairment is a stable and enduring trait of schizophrenia.

For most of the twentieth century psychologists believed that the symptoms of schizophrenia could be explained through disturbances in attention. The problem is that attention is a complex phenomenon that can be measured in different ways. The most widely used technique to measure attention, at least as a vulnerability marker in family studies, is the Continuous Performance Test (CPT). This involves presenting the subject rapidly with a large number of stimuli. The subject is told to make a response whenever a specified target stimulus appears. Cornblatt and Keilp (1994) reviewed over forty studies in which the CPT was used as a marker, and concluded that poor performance on the test appeared to be a stable and enduring trait in people suffering from schizophrenia, which was independent of their clinical state at the time of testing. Furthermore, people carrying a genetic risk of developing schizophrenia also tended to perform badly at these tasks. This supports the idea that impaired attention is a trait feature associated with a susceptibility to schizophrenia.

BIOCHEMICAL THEORIES OF SCHIZOPHRENIA

If we accept that genes are important in causing schizophrenia, then this implies that the disorder has a biochemical basis. This idea has a long pedigree. The physicians of Classical Greece thought hysteria was caused by an obstruction of the circulation of the four humours (blood, phlegm, yellow bile and black bile) by the wandering uterus. Likewise, the biochemical theories of today are humoral theories. Brain tissue consists of two main parts. Under the microscope the grey matter consists of millions of nerve cells. Each cell has a number of lengthy fibres branching out to establish contact with other nerve cells. These fibres have a fatty layer of myelin as insulation so they appear white to the naked eye, hence the term white matter. If we were to magnify the point of contact between the fibre of one cell with the cell body of another, we would see that there was no physical contact, and that the two were separated by a minute gap, called a synapse. When a nerve impulse reaches the gap, chemical transmitters are released which diffuse rapidly across to the next cell body. Here, they engage with special sites on the cell membrane called receptors, triggering off a nerve impulse in the cell. There are many different types of chemical, or neurotransmitters, each acting on different receptors. The one that has received the greatest attention in schizophrenia is dopamine.

The biochemistry of the brain is complex, and there have been many biochemical theories of schizophrenia over the years, most of which have been rejected because of a lack of supporting evidence. The dopamine theory, proposed by Snyder (1976), maintains that the symptoms of schizophrenia occur because of overactivity in the nerve fibres that use dopamine in nerve impulse transmission. These fibres extend from deep within the base of the brain (midbrain) to the temporal and frontal lobes. Dopamine is an important neurotransmitter in a number of pathways in the brain, but there are two that are particularly important here, the striatum and meso-limbic system. The latter is thought to be important in relation to the acute symptoms of schizophrenia, whereas the former is important in the regulation of voluntary movements. There are two strands of evidence in support of the dopamine theory; amphetamine psychosis and the action of the neuroleptics. People who abuse amphetamines occasionally develop an acute psychosis indistinguishable from acute schizophrenia, with delusions and hallucinations. Laboratory experiments have shown that amphetamines increase the turnover of dopamine in the brain, thus increasing the activity of nerve fibres using this transmitter. Although this model helps to explain positive symptoms, it fails to account for negative symptoms. In fact there is much evidence to suggest that negative symptoms are associated with reduced dopamine activity. For this reason, the amphetamine model has recently been replaced by the phencyclidine model (Javitt and Zukin, 1991). Phencyclidine is a hallucinogenic drug, sometimes called 'Angel Dust', which can induce both negative and positive symptoms. This is because it has effects on a number of neurotransmitter systems including dopamine.

The clearest evidence in support of the dopamine theory concerns the mode of action of the neuroleptics, the drugs used to treat positive symptoms. Seeman et al. (1976) demonstrated that the clinical potency of neuroleptics was directly related to their efficacy in blocking dopamine transmission. This stimulated much research into dopamine systems in the brain. Some scientists examined the effects of dopamine-blocking drugs in animal brains. Others performed post-mortem examinations on the brains of people who had suffered from schizophrenia in life, searching for evidence of increased dopamine receptor activity. Others searched for biochemical evidence of increased dopamine activity, either in the cerebrospinal fluid (CSF) which bathes the brain and spinal cord, or in other body tissues. Wyatt (1986), who reviewed the results of these studies, concluded that the results were conflicting. In general there do not appear to be differences between psychiatrically healthy control subjects and those suffering from schizophrenia. Owen et al. (1978) performed a post-mortem study and found that the density of dopamine receptors was increased in the brains of people diagnosed with schizophrenia, but in this study the patients had been on neuroleptics for many years. There is evidence that after a year on neuroleptics the same changes occur in animal brains (Clow et al., 1980). In addition, these changes were not found in the brains of patients who were free of neuroleptics before death (Reynolds et al., 1981). This suggests that the increase in number and sensitivity of dopamine receptors is secondary to the effects of drug treatment, and is not an intrinsic feature of the illness. As we shall see, this has important clinical implications.

The introduction of new brain imaging techniques has not helped to clarify the situation. Positron emission tomography (PET) scanning allows us to examine brain activity directly by giving subjects small amounts of chemicals labelled with a harmless radioactive marker, which are selectively taken up by brain dopamine systems. By using special detectors it is possible to measure and picture the activity in dopamine systems. The evidence from these studies is equivocal. Wong *et al.* (1986) found an increase in dopamine receptors in people suffering from schizophrenia who were medication-free, but another group (Farde *et al.*, 1987) failed to confirm this. The jury is still out on the dopamine theory, although Carlsson (1990) regards it as no longer tenable. This is because it takes between two and four weeks before neuroleptics have any effect on symptoms, yet these drugs block dopamine receptors in a matter of hours following ingestion. This discrepancy has long puzzled psychopharmacologists, who have had to resort to a series of ingenious twists and turns in juggling their theories to match the clinical facts. Another serious problem for the dopamine theory is that the neuroleptics have effects on a number of neurotransmitter systems in the brain. Indeed the name 'largactil', the trade-name for chlorpromazine, was coined because it had a large number of actions on the brain. In this case why has the antipsychotic effect been linked specifically to dopamine? Finally, recent developments in neuropharmacology have identified different types of dopamine receptors. They all respond to dopamine, but have distinct biochemical characteristics, and are found in different areas of the brain. These have been labelled D_2, D_3 and D_4 (Reynolds, 1994).

NEURODEVELOPMENTAL MODEL OF SCHIZOPHRENIA

This model views schizophrenia as a disease caused by an abnormality of brain development. Although this abnormality may have a genetic basis, environmental events are necessary for the disease to become apparent. In this respect the model is one version of the genetic–environment interaction proposed by Tienari (1992). The outcome of this interaction is a delay in certain aspects of development, long before the appearance of positive symptoms. There are three sources of evidence to support this model: epidemiological; the presence of structural abnormalities in the brains of some people suffering from schizophrenia; and evidence of developmental abnormalities in childhood in some people who later develop the condition. Let us consider each in turn.

Over the last twenty years there have been more than 200 studies suggesting that structural abnormalities are common in the brains of some people suffering from schizophrenia (Cannon and Marco, 1994). Most of the early studies were post-mortem examinations, but more recently these have been supplemented by the new generation of brain imaging techniques, especially computerised axial tomography (CT) scanning, and nuclear magnetic resonance (NMR) scanning. CT scans rely on computer enhancements of specially taken X-rays to produce high-definition images of the brain. NMR scans are different. If hydrogen atoms are exposed to intense magnetic fields, they behave like tiny magnets, and organise themselves in line with the magnetic field. If they are then exposed to a pulse of high-frequency radio waves, they are deflected, and emit a brief pulse of electromagnetic radiation. The detection of this radiation makes it possible to obtain accurate measures of hydrogen atom distribution in tissue which, in effect, is a measure of its water distribution. These measures may be used directly, or they may be converted into high-definition pictures of the brain. The particular advantage of this technique is that it is possible to visualise white matter (the nerve fibres in the brain) and grey matter (the nerve cells themselves). Both techniques allow accurate measurements of the width of the folds and convolutions of the brain's surface (the sulci), as well as the central fluid-filled chambers (the lateral and third ventricles).

A number of post-mortem studies have found a reduction in weight and volume of the brains of people who suffered from schizophrenia (for example, Brown et al., 1986; Pakkenberg, 1987; Bruton et al., 1990), compared with people suffering from other psychiatric disorders and non-psychiatric groups. Microscopic examination of brain tissue removed at post-mortem has also revealed abnormalities in the complex organisation of cells in the grey matter, or cortex, of the brain. For example, Jakob and Beckman (1986) found some cells to be in the wrong place. They had failed to migrate to their usual position in the temporal lobes in schizophrenia. Murray (1994) has argued that these findings could arise from a failure of cerebral development, either in the foetus or shortly after birth. One of the earliest CT studies was performed by Johnstone et al. (1976) who found that some schizophrenic people had enlarged ventricles, a finding that has been repeated on numerous occasions. Recent studies have found that this abnormality is present in the earliest stages of the illness (Weinberger et al., 1980; Lewis, 1993) and appears to be related to the presence of abnormalities of personality prior to the onset of symptoms. Similar findings have emerged from NMR scan studies. For example, Harvey et al. (1993) found a small but significant reduction in total cerebral volume in people suffering from schizophrenia, and these reductions were not apparent in the brains of people diagnosed with serious depression (Harvey *et al.*, 1994). Others have found that these changes are prominent in certain areas, especially the temporal lobes and related structures (Suddath *et al.*, 1989; Bogerts *et al.*, 1990). Other studies have found differences in the brains of identical twins who are discordant for schizophrenia (that is, where one twin only has developed the condition). Reveley *et al.* (1982) found that in discordant identical twins, the twin who developed schizophrenia had larger ventricles (on CT scans) than the unaffected twin. Suddath *et al.* (1990) obtained similar results using NMR scans. They also found that affected twins had smaller left temporal lobes. These last two studies are important because they are difficult to reconcile with the view that schizophrenia is largely genetically determined. If this was the case, then we would expect no differences in the brains of identical twins. This implies that environmental factors have an important influence on brain development. What might they be?

Jones and Murray (1994) point out that there is a lot of evidence that people suffering from schizophrenia are more likely to have experienced birth injuries, and that these complications are associated with enlarged ventricles (Lewis and Murray, 1987; Lewis *et al.*, 1989). This suggests that the processes that cause schizophrenia may start many years before the illness develops. If so, then we might expect to find evidence of abnormal development in childhood before schizophrenia appears. Is this the case? Lane and Albee (1965) found evidence that people admitted to hospital with schizophrenia had lower intelligence quotients (IQs) than either their classmates or their brothers and sisters in childhood. Fish *et al.* (1992) reviewed twelve studies of infants at risk of developing schizophrenia, and found evidence of delayed development in the infants of schizophrenic parents. Ideally, the best way of investigating this is to identify a large sample of children, study their development through childhood, then find out who develops schizophrenia in adulthood, and then go back to compare their development with those who do not. The Perinatal Mortality Survey made it possible to perform such a study. In the week of 3–9 March, 1958, nearly all births registered in England, Scotland and Wales were included in the survey, which sought to establish the main causes of infant deaths. Subsequently, four attempts were made to trace the children of this original group, at ages seven, eleven, sixteen and twenty-three. Even at the age of twenty-three, 74% of the original group could still be traced. The four follow-up points, known as the National Child Development Study (NCDS), made it possible to measure socialisation and behaviour. Using the Mental

Health Enquiry, a national register of admissions to psychiatric hospital, most of the 12,000 subjects followed up to age twenty-three who subsequently developed schizophrenia were identified. Done *et al.* (1994) compared the development of forty of these NCDS subjects suffering from schizophrenia, with those suffering from a variety of other psychiatric disorders and a large number of NCDS subjects who had no psychiatric disorders. At the age of seven years, the children who later developed schizophrenia were considered by their teachers to show more evidence of social mal-adaptation. This particularly applied to boys. The same group (Crow *et al.*, 1994) found that academic impairments were more common in the pre-schizophrenic children at ages seven, eleven and sixteen. These children were slow in reading and had speech difficulties. Jones *et al.* (1994) reported similar findings in a group of nearly 5000 children followed up into adulthood.

The evidence we have considered so far suggests that there is a subgroup of people suffering from schizophrenia who may have an abnormality of brain development, which places them at a developmental disadvantage in childhood, as well as predisposing them to the disorder as adults. The abnormality may arise from an interaction between the genes controlling the development of the brain, and environmental factors. We have already seen that birth trauma may constitute one such factor, but are there others? There is evidence to suggest that people who develop schizophrenia tend to be born in late winter and early spring (Hare, 1988). Viral illnesses, such as influenza, are particularly common at this time of year, so is it possible that maternal infection with influenza predisposes the developing infant to schizophrenia in later life. This has been investigated by Mednick, who examined the outcome of the 1957 influenza epidemic in Helsinki (Mednick *et al.*, 1988). He found that several months after the epidemic, the number of births of people who subsequently developed schizophrenia doubled. In a further study (Mednick *et al.*, 1994) the risk of the child developing schizophrenia as an adult was greater if the mother had contracted influenza during the second trimester of pregnancy. O'Callaghan *et al.* (1991) reported similar findings in England and Wales. It appears, therefore, that infants whose mothers developed influenza in pregnancy are at higher risk of schizophrenia later on. It is possible that either the virus, or the mother's immune response to it, may have an adverse effect upon the growth and development of the foetus' brain. This may be exaggerated by the occurrence of minor brain damage associated with birth injuries, leaving the infant at a developmental disadvantage.

So, where does this lead? The neurodevelopmental model of schizophrenia takes us in two directions. Murray (1994) argues that the genetic contribution to schizophrenia has been overestimated. Whilst these factors are important, he believes that some people suffering from schizophrenia have a disorder of brain development. This is caused either by abnormal genes responsible for regulating brain growth, or environmental events, such as birth injury or maternal viral infections, which also adversely affect brain development in the foetus or infant. These abnormalities produce negative symptoms in the child, poor social adjustment, delayed intellectual development and delayed language acquisition. As the brain matures in adolescence positive symptoms appear. Men appear to be more vulnerable to neurodevelopmental schizophrenia than women, possibly because oestrogens (female hormones) may have a protective influence on the brain, or because the male brain is a more fragile organ. It is worth noting that other developmental disorders, such as autism, dyslexia and hyperactivity, are more common in males.

Another neurodevelopmental route has been followed by Tim Crow in Oxford. In a number of recent papers (Crow 1993a, 1993b, 1995) he adopts an evolutionary perspective, arguing that the most characteristic feature of *Homo sapiens* is the complexity of our social organisation. This is reflected by our capacity for language and social communication. To make this possible there has been an enormous increase in the complexity of our brains in comparison with the apes. Most of this complexity is accounted for by the need for increasingly complex social interactions, particularly our use of language and the need to predict the intentions and dispositions of our neighbours. This has resulted in the evolution of the 'social brain', which includes the mechanisms for identifying emotional cues, such as facial expression, gesture and so on, as well as the development of language. The complexity of these mechanisms means that there is much that can go wrong, and, when this happens, we see the emergence of psychosis. There is some evidence in support of this model from my own research into the language of people suffering from schizophrenia (Thomas, Kearney et al., 1996). The speech of people in their first episode of schizophrenia is structurally less complex than that of other psychiatric and non-psychiatric patients. These features were particularly associated with the presence of negative symptoms (Thomas, Leudar et al., 1996). This suggests that linguistic development in schizophrenia lags behind that of other groups, implying that there may well be problems in those areas of the brain concerned with language. Language is so important here. It unites the three areas of human experience that are central to an understanding of the nature of schizophrenia: biological, psychological and social. It provides a natural bridge to the psychological and social theories which we shall consider in the next chapter.

3 Mind or Society?

The single most important feature of biological explanations is that they are rooted in the physical substrate of our bodies. All aspects of our experience, our thoughts, memories, desires, intentions, feelings, language, imagination, everything about us that is subjective, that is to do with the fact that we are sentient and reflexive beings, is viewed as secondary to physical events in our brain. There should be little surprise, therefore, to hear 'mind' referred to as 'the ghost in the machine'. But explanations based on the machine throw little if any light on the peculiar nature of the subjective experiences of schizophrenia. After all, it is these features that allow psychiatrists to make a diagnosis of schizophrenia, and not a disturbance in the way the machine functions. As we move to psychological explanations we are crossing a linguistic divide. The language of psychology makes it possible for us to ask the question: why and how do people hear voices? At present we are largely concerned with the explanatory value of different languages. In Part II we shall return to another question concerning the values that are attached to these different explanations. Theories of schizophrenia are either psychological or social, yet another gulf separates psychology and sociology, although it is perhaps smaller than that between biology and psychology. There can be no doubt that at the end of the twentieth century biological explanations are in the ascendancy. This has not always been so. The name 'schizophrenia' was coined because at that time psychology was considered to be the best way of understanding the condition. Psychology still provides powerful tools with which we can examine the nature of the condition.

PSYCHOLOGICAL THEORIES OF SCHIZOPHRENIA

Historically, these theories have played an important role in our thinking about schizophrenia. Bleuler (1911) invented the word, which literally means 'split mind', to highlight the splitting of the psychological processes which he thought was at the root of the illness. Since then there has been no shortage of psychological theories purporting to explain the disorder. The problem with most of these was that they reduced all the symptoms to an underlying deficit in attention or information processing. Both may be disturbed in schizophrenia, but this can also happen in other serious psychiatric conditions, such as dementia or affective disorders. This makes it difficult to see how such disturbances can produce the symptoms of schizophrenia, positive or negative. The situation has changed considerably over the last fifteen years with the emergence of cognitive science as a conspicuous feature of modern psychology. This arose largely as a revolt against the simple reductionist approach of behaviourism which until then had dominated psychology. In its simplest form, behaviourism states that all human actions can be understood in terms of learning and theories of association. In contrast, cognitive science emphasises the role that thinking processes play in our behaviour. It places 'mind' firmly in the domain of psychology. The most fruitful developments in this field have been inspired by linguistic theory, computer science and philosophy, all of which have offered us new models of mind and consciousness. Those who work in this area have followed one of two routes. The first, exemplified by the work of Ralph Hoffman in Yale, attempts to integrate cognitive models developed from analogies with computer science, with biochemical models. The other, associated with the work of Chris Frith in London, introduces ideas from neurology, cognitive psychology and philosophy in order to explain the symptoms of schizophrenia. We shall examine each of these in turn.

In the last chapter we examined biochemical theories of schizophrenia. The problem here is, what difference does it make if dopamine activity is increased in schizophrenia? How does this explain the particular features of the symptoms? After all, these are *subjective* experiences located in our minds. Surely abnormalities of brain chemistry are incapable of explaining this. Cohen and Servan-Schreiber have developed a model which attempts to integrate our knowledge of brain chemistry, with theories drawn from computer science, to explain how disturbances in dopamine systems can produce the symptoms of schizophrenia. Central to this theory are parallel distributed processing (PDP) systems which have been developed to provide models of information processing in the latest generation of super-computers. Cohen and Servan-Schreiber (1993) have described how this can be adapted to provide a model of the way the brain processes information. PDP systems, whether in computer or brain, share a number of features. They consist of a group of interconnected processing units, each of which is responsible for a particular computation. Each unit is widely connected to other units, receiving both excitatory and inhibitory influences. The level of activity in a particular unit is governed by the balance of excitatory and inhibitory influences. The more excitatory inputs it receives, the more likely it is that the level of activity in that unit will increase. The more inhibitory inputs it receives, the more likely that its level of activity will fall. As far as the brain is concerned, these units may correspond to single nerve cells and fibres, or larger groups of these. Cohen and Servan-Schreiber argue that in the brain, information is represented by the pattern of activity between units, and information processing is represented by the spread of activity (or change of pattern in activity) amongst units. In this model, knowledge is indicated by the ability to generate an appropriate response for a given input, and is represented as a set of weights which determine the probability that the spread of activity (information processing) will follow one path rather than another. Learning occurs whenever these weights, or probabilities, are altered. This means that one pattern of activity will occur in preference to another. An important feature of learning, however, is that when these weights are changed and new behaviour learnt, the old weights (knowledge) should not be lost.

Similar models have been used successfully to explain how the brain deals with a number of complex psychological or linguistic information-processing problems. It can, for example, show how the brain can compute shapes from simple information about light and shade. It has also been used to model the difficulties that the brain has in accessing word-meaning in dyslexia. But how does dopamine and schizophrenia fit into such a model? Cohen and Servan-Schreiber (1992) have suggested that dopamine systems play a key role in modulating or controlling the level of activity in many brain systems whose function is the processing of information. In this model, dopamine systems may improve the quality of information processed by these other systems, making them less likely to be distorted by extraneous information. To put it another way, dopamine systems influence the signal–noise ratio in other systems. In healthy subjects, increasing the level of dopamine activity improves signal detection, making it less likely that noise (extraneous or irrelevant information) will detract from signal quality. As we saw in the last chapter, there is evidence from continuous performance tasks that people with schizophrenia perform badly in detecting signals. Cohen and Servan-Schreiber suggest that this occurs because of a failure of dopamine systems situated in the frontal lobes, whose function it is to represent environmental context. This means that the subjects are less well able to modify appropriately their responses to environmental signals. These dopamine systems are therefore important in maintaining our attention.

Ralph Hoffman has taken the computer analogy further than anyone else (Hoffman and McGlashan, 1993a, 1993b). He uses the term 'neurodynamics' to refer to the interaction of large numbers of neurones in processing information, and also to explain how these patterns of connections develop and are reinforced. He argues that schizophrenia occurs as a result of abnormalities in the complex neuronal circuits responsible for our experience of the world, our beliefs and the production of language. These networks consist of millions of nerve cells and fibres. Like Cohen and Servan-Schreiber, he believes that dopamine plays an important role in modulating the level of activity in the connections in the network, but there is an important departure in his model. He regards the traditional neuropsychological approach, in which specific psychological functions are thought to be located in particular brain areas, as being inadequate and inappropriate for schizophrenia. Hoffman regards the brain as an integrated organ in which changes in one circuit produce changes in others. In this model the symptoms of schizophrenia arise from what he calls 'dysmodularity', in which information spreads inappropriately from one module to another, in the cortex of the brain. Although there are serious difficulties with both these models, they are important for two reasons. First, they are genuine attempts to relate what we know about the biochemical basis of schizophrenia to the psychological features of the condition. This is long overdue. Second, they have the potential for generating new hypotheses about schizophrenia, and thus opening up our understanding of the condition through new research. Hoffman in particular tries to get closer to understanding how the symptoms of schizophrenia arise, but we are still left feeling that his explanation fails to account for the peculiarly alien nature of these experiences. If we are to succeed in this we must use a different approach. This is exactly what Chris Frith has done.

Frith (1992) has proposed a comprehensive theory to account both for positive and negative symptoms. In doing so he makes two important assumptions. First, he suggests that schizophrenia can best be understood as disorder of self-awareness. Second, he argues that a failure in Theory of Mind (ToM) may help us to understand the nature of symptoms. Theory of Mind refers to our ability to form an accurate impression of other people's intentions and dispositions towards us. In neurology the importance of self-awareness has been recognised for many years. In order to initiate and complete a simple motor act, like picking up a cup, I must be able to monitor what is going on. The first step involves the formation of an intention to pick up the cup. The idea must form in my mind if I am to carry it out. Next, I must establish a plan of action to complete the task. In this case the plan involves the accurate co-ordination of the activity of many different groups of muscles. This activity is regulated automatically, without my being conscious of it. This is managed by special receptors found in muscles and tendons, which send information back to my brain, letting it know exactly where my arm is in relation to the plan of action. In this way I know when to stop moving my arm. These feedback mechanisms are fully integrated into all aspects of the nervous system's activity, and function completely automatically. Self-monitoring has long been established as an essential component of the neurophysiology of motor acts and perception. In the nineteenth century, the German physiologist Helmholtz (1866) observed that when we move our eyes the image of the world moves across our retinas, yet the world remains still. To achieve this there must be some mechanism which enables us to distinguish between movements on the retina due to eye movements, and those due to movements in the outside world. When we move our eyes, receptors situated in our eye muscles send information (corollary discharge) to a central monitoring system which tells us to compensate for eye movements so we perceive a stationary image of the world. Movement of the image on the retina brought about by movement in the real world is perceived as movement because there is no corollary discharge. This mechanism depends on comparison between intentions to move and actual movements, and can be upset by moving one's eye passively by gently poking it, in which case the image of the world appears to jerk unsteadily. Frith extends this principle to higher cognitive processes, arguing that a problem in self-monitoring is one of a triad of problems in schizophrenia which he calls disorders of self-awareness.

It is parsimonious to suppose that the brain developed such control mechanisms to control motor activity only. Frith argues that similar mechanisms exist for psychological faculties such as thinking. If these break down, then we may have an explanation of positive and negative symptoms. In the first stage I must form an intention to act in some way, for example to communicate with someone. If this does not happen, then I do not communicate. In other words I show evidence of the negative symptom, poverty of speech. Now let us consider what might happen if I do form the intention to communicate. To do so successfully, Frith argues that I must be able to use a Theory of Mind. For example, let us assume that I am worried because I think my friend John believes that I drink too much. Such a state of affairs may be represented in my mind by the following statement:

(John thinks that [Phil drinks too much])

This sentence consists of two parts, a statement (Phil drinks too much) with a prefix (John thinks that) which indicates that the statement is an attribution made by me to another person. Such a sentence indicates that I am operating a Theory of Mind. The important point here is that the sentence in the curved brackets is formulated in my mind, as part of my intention to talk with John. Now let us assume that there is a mechanism in our minds responsible for monitoring our thinking processes, just as there are feedback mechanisms for monitoring our motor actions. If this mechanism fails, then the first part of the sentence (John thinks that) may become separated from the second (Phil drinks too much). In this case one of two things may happen. I might experience the second part of the sentence (the part in square brackets) as a thought inserted into my head by John. Alternatively, I may hear a voice speaking out the words 'Phil drinks too much', possibly attributed by me to John. Either way the failure of this monitoring system means that a part of my own conscious experience becomes detached from my sense of intentionality. It is this that results in its being experienced as alien and not belonging to me. Frith has extended this basic mechanism to explain how most First Rank Symptoms of schizophrenia, as well as negative symptoms, may be explained.

Frith's ideas have much in common with earlier work by Hoffman (1987) in which he proposed a mechanism to explain the occurrence of verbal hallucinations. Underlying Hoffman's model is the idea that in order to communicate effectively, we must have a clear plan of what we intend to say, and we must also monitor the plan as we speak. If this does not happen we may flit from unrelated topic to unrelated topic leaving our conversational partner confused. Such problems in communication are occasionally seen in people suffering from schizophrenia, although they can also occur in non-schizophrenic speakers. When it happens, psychiatrists usually decide that the speaker shows evidence of thought disorder. Thought disorder is a complex disturbance of communica-

tion involving different linguistic levels, and is not simply a disturbance in the subject's thinking processes (Thomas, 1995). The
most significant linguistic disturbance in thought disorder occurs at
the level of discourse. Hoffman proposes that in thought disorder,
communication problems arise as a result of a failure in planning
and monitoring discourse. The discourse plan becomes disjointed
and broken up so that fragments of the plan are experienced as
non-intended and therefore 'alien'. When this happens, these 'parasitic' fragments are experienced as verbal hallucinations.

Both Frith's and Hoffman's theories are brave attempts to place
cognition, thinking and the individual's will firmly back in the
frame. They are important because they are capable of generating
many hypotheses for researchers to investigate. My colleague Ivan
Leudar and I (Leudar et al., 1992, 1994) have investigated both
models by examining features of the speech of different groups of
subjects. If we are to be successful conversationalists it is important that we monitor and self-regulate our own contributions, as
well as those of our conversational partner. The extent to which
we monitor successfully should be apparent in how well we detect
errors, both our own and our partner's, as well as how we repair
these errors. In one study (Leudar et al., 1992) we found that
people who suffer from schizophrenia and who have auditory hallucinations tend to correct their own speech errors less often than
they correct the errors of their conversational partners. This suggests that they do have problems in self-monitoring their communication, a finding consistent with Frith's and Hoffman's theories.

SOCIAL THEORIES OF SCHIZOPHRENIA

The one thing shared by biological and psychological models is that
they both regard the origins of schizophrenia as being located
firmly in the brain or mind of the individual. However, the words
of John Donne ('No man is an Island, entire of itself') suggest that
we should never overlook the relationship between the individual
and his or her social world. We must consider our relationships to
others and society, in order to understand schizophrenia properly.
Of course, as we shall see, society as a concept is neither fashion-
able nor politically correct. Despite this there is considerable evidence that society, including family, social, economic and political
factors, is inextricably linked to the nature of schizophrenia. We
are concerned with two particular aspects here: the first is the
relationship between social environment and the course of schizo-

phrenia, particularly the quality of our relationships, and life events; the second involves the perspective adopted by Richard Warner, who has examined the relationship between culture, economic factors and outcome of schizophrenia.

The most important early evidence of a link between social circumstances and the clinical features of schizophrenia came from work by a sociologist, Erving Goffman (1968). He explored the features of closed institutions, such as the old mental hospitals, and the effect that these had upon the lives of their inmates. He considered that the 'symptoms' of chronic mental illness, especially the negative symptoms of apathy and social withdrawal, were not due to the illness at all but were understandable in terms of the inmates' response to institutional life. Goffman was not the only person to claim this. A psychiatrist, Russell Barton (1959), described 'institutional neurosis' as the response of chronically hospitalised patients, the majority of them suffering from schizophrenia, to long-term institutional care. The descriptive work of Goffman and Barton created much interest in the relationship between social environment and illness, and influenced the early studies by George Brown and his colleagues in the Social Psychiatry Research Unit at the Institute of Psychiatry. Brown & Wing (1962) investigated the relationship between the institutional characteristics of three mental hospitals in the south-east of England, and the clinical features of their inmates. Two of the hospitals represented two extremes of practice. One was characterised by the progressive and enlightened attitudes of its senior nursing staff, who took great interest in the well-being of the residents, and engaged them in active rehabilitation programmes. In the other, staff were disinterested and apathetic, taking little interest in the residents. They found important differences in the clinical features of the patients in the different settings. In the first hospital, patients appeared livelier and less apathetic, whereas in the second hospital, most of the patients appeared more withdrawn and were more disturbed. Of course it could be argued that these clinical features determined the differences in staff attitudes in the two hospitals. We have no way of knowing this, but this study was important because it showed that there was a relationship between the social environment and clinical symptoms.

An important consequence of the Second World War was the growth of military psychiatry, and research in this area suggested that stressful situations played an important role in triggering off episodes of schizophrenia in young men who were predisposed to the condition. This was investigated by Wallis (1965) in the Royal

Navy, and Steinberg and Durell (1968) in the US army. Both found an unexpected increase in the rate of schizophrenia in young men shortly after enlistment. This increase was not accounted for by the detection of schizophrenia in those who had already developed the condition. In other words this appeared to be a genuine increase, possibly related in some way to adaptation to military life. People became interested in the possibility that life events, major stressful changes in our life circumstances, might play an important part in precipitating schizophrenia. This was investigated by Brown and Birley (1968) who interviewed fifty patients admitted to hospital with acute schizophrenia, and in whom the onset of the illness had occurred within three months of admission. Patients and relatives were asked about the occurrence of life events prior to admission, including bereavement, births, marriage, moving house, divorce and changes of employment. These events were classified as 'independent', such as being burgled, where the occurrence of the event was unlikely to have been brought about by the early stages of schizophrenia, or 'possibly independent', such as being made unemployed, where, you could argue, the event was brought about by the illness. They found that in the three weeks before the onset of symptoms, 46% of the patients had experienced at least one independent life event, compared with 12% of such events occurring in earlier three-week periods. This suggests that life events are common just before admission to hospital.

Since then there have been many studies of life events and schizophrenia in three main areas. Some studies have examined whether the onset of schizophrenia was associated with a higher incidence of life events than was the case with other psychiatric conditions. Some considered whether the onset of schizophrenia is associated with more life events than occur in the general population. Others have examined the relationship between life events in schizophrenia and the severity of symptoms. This evidence has been reviewed in detail by Norman and Malla (1993), who concluded that there was good evidence in support of a relationship between stressful life events and schizophrenia *within* groups of patients suffering from the condition. Such studies overcome some methodological problems because patients were used as their own controls, in other words the presence of symptoms was examined over time in each patient, in relation to life events. However, the evidence also suggests that life events are just as important in triggering other psychiatric disorders. This suggests that life events are non-specific and are unrelated to particular psychiatric illnesses. Hirsch *et al.* (1992) came to similar conclusions, finding inconsistent evidence to support the role of life events in triggering schizo-phrenia. It seems probable therefore that these events play a part in precipitating not just schizophrenia, but a variety of psychiatric problems, including depression. The same is probably also true of family environment.

The early work on family environment was undertaken by Brown *et al.* (1972), who were interested in the family environment and the quality of the relationships between family members, where one member was suffering from schizophrenia. Earlier work suggested that expressed emotion (EE) had an important influence on the out-come of the illness in the affected family member. They refined the definition of EE, making it possible for them to measure it with a high degree of reliability. According to Brown, expressed emotion is indicated by the number of critical comments made about the patient, and the amount of emotional over-involvement and hostility demonstrated by family members. Using these measures, the level of EE expressed by key relatives at the time of admission was a powerful predictor of the relapse of illness in the nine months following dis-charge. The risk of relapse could be reduced by medication. Relapse occurred in 66% of patients from high EE homes in the nine-month follow-up period if they were not taking medication, and this number fell to 46% if they took medication. In addition, the amount of time the patients spent in face-to-face contact with their families also appeared to influence the risk of relapse. Relapse occurred in 79% of those in high EE homes if they spent more than thirty-five hours a week in direct contact with other family members. This number fell to 29% if this contact was reduced to less than thirty-five hours a week. These figures indicate that family atmosphere has an impor-tant effect on the course of schizophrenia, and that medication and social interventions aimed at reducing contact between families and patients may be valuable in reducing the risk of relapse.

Since then, there have been many studies confirming these ini-tial findings, although one study by a team working at Northwick Park in London found that EE had little or no effect on the risk of relapse. McMillan *et al.* (1986) found that when chronicity of ill-ness and compliance with medication were accounted for, neither EE (in the form of critical comments) nor social contact related to relapse. But there were several problems with this study. Many patients lived alone and were not in regular contact with their families. This may have weakened the effect of EE on relapse. Kavanagh (1992) examined the results of twenty-six studies of EE in schizophrenia. Overall he found that the risk of relapse over a twelve-month period in high EE homes is nearly 50%, compared with just over 20% in low EE homes. Many studies have since failed to confirm the effect of the amount of contact with relatives. Other studies, however, have confirmed the value of medication, often in combination with social interventions, in preventing relapse in high EE homes. There is disagreement as to which aspect of EE is important in determining relapse. Some studies have found that critical comments are more important, others have found hostility to be more important. The greatest difficulty lies in trying to establish the relationship between EE and symptoms in relapse. There are two possible models for this. One views EE as the determinant, in which family attitudes cause a recurrence of symptoms in the affected member. The other regards EE as an understandable response by the family, to the difficulties of having to live with someone who suffers from schizophrenia. The problem with the first model is that it means that families may be blamed for causing schizophrenia. The problem with the second is that the patient is blamed for causing high EE. Kavanagh suggests one way around this is by adopting an interactional model, in which a series of factors, including individual vulnerability to schizophrenia, life events and family atmosphere, all contribute to relapse. We shall see in the next chapter that the most important outcome of these studies has been the development of social and psychological interventions aimed at reducing EE.

Earlier, we saw that the results of the WHO's international study suggested that social factors have an important effect on the course of schizophrenia. In his book *Recovery from Schizophrenia: Psychiatry and Political Economy*, Richard Warner (1985) develops the idea that there is an important relationship between the prevalence and outcome of schizophrenia and social factors such as unemployment and standard of living. He looked at the results of dozens of studies which examined outcome and recovery in people diagnosed from schizophrenia, over five different periods in the last 100 years, each of which had different socio-economic characteristics. Some studies were performed in times of relative economic prosperity with high levels of employment (for example, 1941–55; unemployment rates US = 4.1%, UK = 1.5%). Others were performed in recessions with high levels of unemployment (for example, 1921–40; US = 11.9%, UK = 14%). Warner found a very high correlation between unemployment rates and the extent to which people suffering from schizophrenia were able to make a full recovery. In other words more people recovered when employment levels were high and their chances of getting back to work were good.

We have already seen that an important result to emerge from the WHO studies is that schizophrenia appears to have a better outcome in traditional cultures. Warner examined this in some detail. He suggests that it is easier for patients recovering from the condition to be reintegrated back to some form of useful occupation in traditional cultures, although this very much depends upon the nature of the culture. One of the tragic consequences of the 'Westernisation' of indigenous cultures is the loss of traditional roles within the society and the disintegration of traditional family, social and economic structures. Warner compared the prevalence of schizophrenia of two groups, the Canadian Indians of Saskatchewan and Australian Aborigines, with the Amish and Hutterite communities of North America. Both the Indian and Aboriginal societies have experienced 'Westernisation' with high levels of unemployment. Both have high rates of schizophrenia. In comparison, the Hutterite and Amish communities, who have successfully preserved the integrity of their traditional eighteenth-century social structures and subsistence agricultural economy, have a much lower prevalence of schizophrenia. It is difficult to resist the conclusion that the economic and cultural circumstances of a society have a profound influence on the outlook for those suffering from schizophrenia. These influences occur both on a large scale, affecting thousands of individuals, as well as smaller groups such as families. In Chapter 7 I will examine more critically the relationship between schizophrenia, unemployment and society.

4 Panaceas, Nostrums or Cures?

So far we have examined the symptoms of schizophrenia and the theories which attempt to explain it. These theories provide the rationale of a number of therapeutic interventions aimed at controlling symptoms or enabling the individual to cope with them. This is important, for there is no cure for schizophrenia. In part this is because we still do not understand how the condition is caused. At this point it may be useful to examine how an understanding of the causation of disease can lead to treatment and cure. Diphtheria was a common cause of death in the overcrowded slum conditions of Victorian Britain.[1] The bacteria which cause the disease spread from person to person by minute droplets of water present in the air we breathe out. Whilst the local effects of the infection are hazardous and can lead to death through obstruction of the air passages, the invading bacteria produce a toxin which is distributed throughout the body via the bloodstream. This toxin is particularly noxious for the heart and central nervous system, causing irregularities of the heartbeat and nerve paralysis, both of which may be fatal. The discovery of the responsible organism in the nineteenth century made possible the manufacture of an antitoxin which neutralises the effects of the toxin in the body. This, together with developments in pharmacology in the early twentieth century which resulted in the introduction of the antibiotic drugs such as penicillin to kill the bacteria, means that diphtheria is no longer the life-threatening condition it used to be. Here we can see a clear link between our understanding of the cause of the disease and its cure. Now let us consider a quite different condition, arthritis. Recent developments in molecular biology, immunology and rheumatology have considerably extended our understanding of the complex changes that account for the chronic, disfiguring and disabling symptoms of this range of diseases. Despite this, there

---

1   It is, of course, worth noting at this point the importance of what are ultimately political factors (poverty) even in such 'medical' conditions as diphtheria.

remain few satisfactory 'cures' for the majority. In this situation our understanding of the cause of disease does not necessarily lead to the development of a cure. To some extent this is because many of the features of arthritis arise because of the destruction of tissue, which, given the current state of technology, is irreversible. Under these circumstances the psychological and social aspects of management play an important role. Coping with chronic illness, pain and disability, becomes the keystone of long-term management in arthritis. Sufferers may be unable to continue work or follow leisure activities and so experience psychological adjustments relating to the loss of social roles. Because of this they may require psychological support to adjust to the restrictions imposed on their lives through disability. Their environments may require modification to enable them to maintain independence for as long as possible. Social interventions aimed at helping families to help and support the sufferer are important.

In this respect, in so far as we can consider schizophrenia to be an 'illness', it has much more in common with arthritis than diphtheria. There is no cure and so a large number of different drugs and physical treatments have been used to treat it. Although it is true that medication may help to control some symptoms, many people are left with distressing experiences such as hallucinations and delusions, which interfere with their quality of life. Over and above the psychological and social adjustments that people suffering from chronic physical disease are forced to make, people who have mental illness also have to cope with stigmatisation. Psychological and social interventions are particularly important in the management of schizophrenia. We must now examine the effectiveness of three approaches to the management of schizophrenia: drug management, psychological interventions and social interventions.

DRUG MANAGEMENT OF SCHIZOPHRENIA

The evolution of a body of research evidence in support of the value of drugs in the treatment of schizophrenia is a conspicuous feature of the psychiatric literature in the second half of the twentieth century. This has been a major growth area. Until the early 1950s there were no drugs to treat the condition. The introduction of chlorpromazine by Delay and Deniker (1952) in France represented not only the first drug treatment for schizophrenia, but also the birth of a new industry – psychopharmacology, the scientific study of the effects of drugs acting on the central nervous system. The competition became fierce as the pharmaceutical industry realised that huge profits were to be made in developing new and more effective drugs to 'treat' hitherto untreatable psychotic illnesses, and invested huge sums of money in research and development. But what is the evidence that these drugs are effective? Do they help to prevent relapse? What are the drawbacks associated with their use? Before we examine the evidence, it may be useful if we consider a couple of points. First, we need to outline the main category of drugs used in psychiatry. Second, we must understand how the effectiveness of drugs in treating a condition is established.

There are five main groups of drugs used in psychiatry: the minor tranquillisers (such as valium, used to treat anxiety), the antidepressants (such as tryptizol or prozac, used to treat depression), the mood-stabilising agents (such as lithium, used to prevent recurrence of mood disorders), the anticonvulsants (such as phenytoin and tegretol, used to control epilepsy, and also widely used as mood-stabilising agents) and the neuroleptics. It is the latter group with which we are primarily concerned here. The neuroleptics[2] are also referred to as the major tranquillisers, or anti-psychotic agents, on the basis that they have a specific effect in controlling psychotic symptoms. For reasons that will become clear later, this is a misnomer and I shall refer to them as the neuroleptics. This group of drugs includes largactil (or chlorpromazine), serenace (haloperidol), melleril (thioridazine), stelazine (trifluoperazine), orap (pimozide), and the newer drugs clozaril (clozapine) and risperdal (risperidone). All these drugs are usually taken in tablet or capsule form. Others, including depixol (flupenthixol decanoate), modecate (fluphenazine decanaote) and clopixol (fluclopenthixol), are given as a 'depot' injection with variable frequency, from weekly to monthly. In this form the active chemical is held in an oily base, which is injected deep into the fat layers beneath the skin, from where it is slowly absorbed into the bloodstream over a period of many days. This means that you don't have the inconvenience of having to remember to take your medication.

We must also consider the methods used to show that a drug is effective in treating a particular illness. True to the scientific tradition that has dominated medicine for 300 years, doctors are not

---

2   The term 'neuroleptic' literally means that they 'seize' the neurone, a vivid description of the powerful and various effects that they have on the central nervous system.

happy relying solely on their patients' opinions as to the effectiveness of a new drug. They need to go one better and show beyond any reasonable doubt that one treatment is superior to another. Over the years the drug trial has become the established way of achieving this. There are different types of drug trials and there is little to be gained by describing each, but they share certain important features. They all rely upon comparisons of the effects of treatment in groups of patients, some of whom are given an established drug, some of whom are given the new drug, and some of whom are given inert tablets, or placebos. The reason for this is that it has been shown that the act of taking a tablet has powerful psychological effects relating to the expectation that most of us have, that tablets are going to help us to get better. Because of this a significant number of people will improve if they are given placebo tablets alone. This is true for many conditions, not just psychiatric ones. For a drug to be effective then it must be shown to be superior in its effectiveness to a placebo, or dummy tablet. In addition to this it is important that the patients taking the drugs, and the doctors who assess the patients' outcomes (whether they improve or not) are both unaware of which drug was being taken. Otherwise it is possible that bias could influence the patients' subjective response to medication, as well as the doctors' objective assessment. This situation, in which both doctor and patient are unaware of which drug is being taken, is called a 'double-blind'. The most widely used study design used to investigate the effectiveness of the neuroleptics is the double-blind, placebo controlled trial.

Following the introduction of the neuroleptics, there were many double-blind studies which demonstrated their effectiveness in controlling the positive symptoms of acute schizophrenia. For example, in one early American study (Pasamanick et al., 1964) 83% of patients on major tranquillisers were able to stay out of hospital over an eighteen-month follow-up period compared with 55% of patients on placebos. In Britain, Leff and Wing (1971) found that over a twelve-month period 35% of out-patients taking neuroleptics relapsed, compared with 80% on placebos. However, early enthusiasm for the new treatment was tempered when it was realised that many patients were discharged from hospital symptom-free on neuroleptics, only to be admitted a few months later with a recurrence of symptoms. Crumpton (1967) pointed out that this was because they had stopped taking their medication. A study by Engelhardt and Freedman (1969) found that over 60% of out-patients suffering from schizophrenia chose to discontinue their medication twelve months after discharge. In Edinburgh, Renton *et al.* (1963) found that 40–45% of people failed to take oral medication. Poor compliance on the part of patients appeared to jeopardise the prospect of keeping them out of hospital. It did not take long for the pharmaceutical industry to jump to the rescue, by introducing the long-acting neuroleptic in which compliance is guaranteed through the provision of a neuroleptic in an injectable form that passes slowly into the bloodstream. In addition, the administration of this medication by a psychiatric nurse in a continued care clinic made it possible to monitor the individual's mental state. For countless thousands of people suffering from schizophrenia, these clinics formed the mainstay of their treatment in the community, often providing an important point of social contact with others. A number of studies demonstrated the value of this new pharmacological management of schizophrenia in the short term. For example, in Britain Hirsch *et al.* (1972) found that over a nine-month period, 50% of people suffering from chronic schizophrenia had a recurrence of symptoms necessitating hospital readmission if they were taking placebo injections. Only 10% of those on active injections relapsed over the same period. There seems to be little doubt, then, that taking these drugs can help to keep many people suffering from schizophrenia out of hospital. This raises a difficult question: is there any evidence that the continued use of neuroleptics improves the long-term outcome of the condition? As we saw in Chapter 2, the classic view of schizophrenia is that it is a chronic condition with a marked tendency to relapse. Although neuroleptics do not cure the condition, it is important for a number of reasons that we try to establish whether their continued use reduces the risk of relapse in the long term. This is because continued use of these drugs is also associated with the risk of unwanted adverse effects. If we expect someone to take medication for many years in the hope that it will reduce the risks of recurrence of symptoms and possible hospitalisation, it is important that they are able to make an informed decision about this, in which they weigh up the risks of relapse against the risk of side-effects.

One way of trying to establish whether the continued use of neuroleptics influences outcome is to examine studies in which people in the early stages of the condition were either given or not given neuroleptics, and then see whether there was any difference in outcome in those treated and those not treated. Wyatt (1991) examined the results of over twenty such studies of people in the early stages of schizophrenia, some of whom received medication and some of whom did not. The important questions here are whether neuroleptics control the severity of psychosis in the early stages of schizophrenia, and whether they prevent subsequent relapse and improve social functioning later. Wyatt concluded that treatment with neuroleptics in the early stages of schizophrenia probably did increase the likelihood of a better long-term outcome. In particular the results of discontinuation studies, which establish what happens when well-adjusted patients in the community stop taking their medication, suggested that when discontinuation is followed by relapse, the patient finds it more difficult to regain the previous level of adjustment. Wyatt's review suggests that there is evidence that neuroleptic medication is not only effective in helping to control the symptoms of acute schizophrenia, but may also help to maintain social functioning if taken over a prolonged period of time.

This is all very well, but as we shall see, there are drawbacks associated with the prolonged use of neuroleptic medication. People taking them are at risk of side-effects, some of which are unpleasant, some irreversible, and some life-threatening. In this context the most disabling long-term complication of neuroleptic medication is a condition known as tardive dyskinesia (TD) which we shall consider in Chapter 6. This is a neurological disorder in which patients have abnormal movements over which they have no control, affecting the jaw, tongue and lips, and sometimes other parts of the body. Once established, the condition is irreversible. If we expect someone to take powerful medication for many years, we have a responsibility to ensure that the risk of these adverse effects is reduced as far as possible. Are there ways of reducing the risk that someone on long-term neuroleptic medication will develop this disabling condition? There is now much evidence that the risk of TD is directly related to the length of exposure to neuroleptic medication, so it would appear that the easiest way of reducing this risk would be to use only the smallest dose consistent with symptom control. This can be achieved in two ways: either through the use of continuous low doses of medication, or by intermittent medication. There are two ways of achieving intermittent medication. People taking it may have what are called 'drug holidays', such as taking medication for nine months in every twelve, with three months off. Another way is to use medication only when the individual appears to be in the earliest stages of a relapse. This demands a close working relationship between the subject and the psychiatrist, with a great deal of preparatory work to ensure that the individual is able to recognise the earliest signs of relapse and start medication immediately. The critical question in assessing the effectiveness of these strategies is whether there is a level of medication that can prevent relapse as effectively as higher doses, whilst minimising the risk of side effects. Schooler (1991) reviewed the findings of a number of studies which investigated this. Both dose reduction and intermittent treatment strategies appeared to improve the subjective feeling of well-being, as well as reduce the risk of side-effects, but there was a greater risk of relapse compared with conventional dose strategies. Some studies suggested that this risk might be greater in people whose adjustment was 'less stable' following an acute episode of schizophrenia. Despite this, there was evidence that these strategies could help to reduce the risk of TD and other side-effects. The difficulty is that most of these studies took the form of clinical trials in which subjects were followed up for a maximum of two years. Most of the evidence indicates that it takes an average of seven years of continuous exposure to neuroleptics before TD develops. Because of this, Schooler's paper may underestimate the extent to which drug reduction strategies may be effective in reducing the risk of long-term side-effects. So far no study has followed up subjects on dose reduction strategies over a ten-year period to examine the risk of TD.

The most important question that psychiatrists are asked is: 'How long should I stay on these tablets?' This is a very difficult question to answer. If you stop taking your medication, what are the chances of your having a recurrence of symptoms at a later stage? Is there evidence that neuroleptics are effective in preventing relapse in the long term? One way of trying to answer this question is to see what happens to large numbers of people who decide to stop taking their medication. Johnson (1979) performed such a study in a group of out-patients, all of whom had been doing well in the community for at least a year before they stopped taking medication. He found that 60% of those who stopped had a recurrence of symptoms on average twenty-nine months after discontinuation, whereas 17% of subjects who remained on medication had a recurrence of symptoms. The difficulty with this and similar studies is that the researchers looked back in time at people who had stopped taking their medication, so there is no way of knowing why they decided to adopt the course of action they did. It could be argued, for example, that the reason they stopped taking medication was because they were in the early stages of relapse anyway. If so, then we can hardly conclude that stopping medication was the reason for relapse. In fact, this situation would be described more appropriately as failure to respond to medication. The discontinuation of medication should never be abrupt. It is something that should be planned well in advance, and undertaken very gradually. As a general principle it is never a good idea suddenly to stop taking powerful drugs that affect the central nervous system, because of the risk of rebound anxiety and sleep disturbance. Later, we shall examine the evidence that discontinuation of neuroleptics may result in recurrence of symptoms, that are mistaken for relapse, but which in fact arise because of the long-term effects of these drugs on the brain. In order to say whether recurrence of symptoms really does follow discontinuation of medication, we must identify a group of people currently without symptoms and taking medication, plan and discuss discontinuation with each of them very carefully, reduce medication slowly and gradually, and compare what happens in this group with a very carefully matched group of people who remain on medication. As far as I am aware, there has been no such study, although there have been several prospective studies in which medication is stopped and individuals are followed up to see what happens. One such study was performed by Dencker et al. (1980). They found that sixteen out of thirty-two people experienced a recurrence of symptoms within six months of discontinuation. All subjects were symptom free and well-adjusted in the community at the start of the study. A year after discontinuation over 80% of subjects had experienced a return of symptoms. The problem with this study was that they had no comparison group who remained on medication. In a similar study, Johnson et al. (1983) did use a comparison group, and found a relapse rate in the group who stopped medication of 80% eighteen months later, compared with 23% in the control group. They also claimed that relapse in the group who stopped taking medication was more severe, which resulted in the need for more medication in the long term.

There have been hundreds of studies over the years examining the effectiveness of medication, and shortage of space and time means that it is impossible to look at them in detail. However, there is a short cut. Over the last few years there have been several studies in which researchers have pooled the data on outcome and use of medication from a large number of earlier studies. These studies, called meta-analyses, have the advantage that they are able to examine the effects of different types of treatment in much larger numbers of subjects, by pooling the results from a group of small studies. This has the advantage that the results are based on very large numbers of subjects which, theoretically, should increase the robustness of the results. The problem is that it is important to ensure that the studies whose results are pooled are broadly similar in terms of design and subject selection. If not, then the results are meaningless. Wyatt's (1991) paper included an analysis of pooled data taken from twenty-two studies in which subjects were not given neuroleptic medication during the course of their illnesses. He found that people suffering from a first episode of schizophrenia who received neuroleptics at an early stage tended to do better in the long term. He also found that following a first episode, people who were well-adjusted in the community who stopped taking medication found it difficult to regain their previous level of adjustment. In other words, they tended to do badly if they had a recurrence of symptoms. On the face of it there appears to be compelling evidence that neuroleptics are of value in preventing the recurrence of symptoms after the acute stage of the illness, but the use of medication in schizophrenia is a double-edged sword. It may help to keep people out of hospital by controlling acute symptoms, but it does not cure the illness. It may help in the long term to maintain social functioning, but it carries the risk of serious side-effects. So it is important that we consider other, non-pharmacological ways of helping people who have the symptoms of schizophrenia. In the last chapter we examined the influence of psychological and social factors on schizophrenia, so how is this knowledge used in helping people to cope with schizophrenia?

PSYCHOLOGICAL INTERVENTIONS IN SCHIZOPHRENIA

The term psychological as used here covers a wide variety of techniques. The one thing they share in common is that they are 'talking' therapies. They achieve their effect through the medium of language and human communication. They differ in regard to their content, that is the things that are talked about. Psychoanalytic approaches may focus exclusively on aspects of early life, family relationships and the relationship between subject and therapist. They may continue for two or three years at weekly or more frequent intervals. Cognitive therapies, on the other hand, may last only three or four months and concentrate only on specific aspects of the subject's experience, such as delusional ideas or hallucinations. They also differ as far as the structure of therapy is concerned, being shorter and less intense.

Psychoanalytic approaches

Psychoanalysis is the form of psychological treatment developed by Sigmund Freud. Most psychiatrists would say that Freud's theories have no influence on their practice. They would also say that they were taught that psychoanalysis and most forms of psychotherapy should not be used in schizophrenia under any circumstances. This is because it is widely believed that such approaches may make the patient's condition worse. Traditional wisdom in psychiatry maintains that in schizophrenia the subject's defence mechanisms are too fragile to endure the probing and challenges posed by psychotherapy. I myself do not believe that psychoanalysis is of any value in the treatment of schizophrenia, although I would not necessarily agree that psychoanalysis makes psychotic patients worse. I am, however, suspicious of the intentions of those who say that schizophrenia is *not* to be treated psychotherapeutically, because this view has become generalised and applied indiscriminately to any 'talking' therapy. For this reason it may be useful to examine just how the belief that psychoanalysis should not be used in schizophrenia gained ground. This can be traced back to Freud and his *New Introductory Lectures on Psychoanalysis* of 1933, in which the following passage can be found (Freud, 1973):

> The second limitation upon analytic success is given by the form of the illness ... *psychotic conditions [are] unsuitable to a greater or less extent.* It would be entirely legitimate to guard against failures by carefully excluding such cases. (p. 190; emphasis added)

This dictum appears to have been highly influential, and appears in that great codex of psychiatric authority, Slater and Roth (1977), who write as follows:

> Prolonged psychotherapy, even in mild cases, can no longer be justified. *Psychoanalysis* is, indeed, *contraindicated* in any stage or type of schizophrenia; to apply it is, as Freud commented to L. Binswanger, a professional error.' (p. 325; emphasis in the original)

and,

> ... it is a waste of time to argue with a paranoid patient about his delusions. (p. 326)

We see here a fascinating interaction of different discourses. The champions of the biological approach to psychiatry, two great academics whose opinions helped to shape the practice of a generation of psychiatrists, quote the father of psychoanalysis in the act of slapping the wrist of one of his students (Ludwig Binswanger), the man who pioneered existential psychotherapy in the psychoses. It appears that Slater and Roth have chosen to agree with Freud when it suits their purpose, for most of their references to his work are critical. These statements about psychoanalysis have since been interpreted in a broader context and taken to refer to most psychological approaches, not just psychoanalysis. For over fifty years, psychiatrists, clinical psychologists and others in Britain have desisted from talking with psychotic patients about their experiences, although there have been notable exceptions. In America, psychoanalytic models dominated psychiatry for over fifty years. In the past if you were suffering from schizophrenia then the odds were that you would be treated with psychoanalysis, provided you had money. In France, Ludwig Binswanger, a psychoanalyst trained by Freud, developed existential psychotherapy which he used to help people suffering from psychotic conditions including schizophrenia. In Britain in the 1960s and 1970s, Laing, Esterson and Cooper were helping people suffering from schizophrenia with psychotherapy. Psychiatrists in Scandinavia see no conflict between biological and psychoanalytic interpretations of schizophrenia. In their view the condition has many causes operating at different levels, so the management of the condition must reflect this. Alanen (1975) has described the use of a therapeutic community in the management of schizophrenia in Finland.

Although later in his career Freud placed an injunction on the use of psychoanalysis in the management of the psychoses, he had used it as an exploratory device earlier on, although it is important to note that Freud had never psychoanalysed someone suffering from schizophrenia himself. His comments about psychosis are largely based on his analysis of the memoirs of Schreber, a prominent judge who developed a paranoid psychosis. The effectiveness of psychoanalysis as a treatment depends upon what Freud called the transference, the feelings that the patient has about the therapist, and describes a particular set of attributes perceived in the therapist by the patient. Exploring these attributes, and discerning their origins and roots in the patient's early life, lies at the heart of psychoanalysis. Freud thought that psychoanalysis with psychotic patients was impossible because they formed no transference. They withdrew into an inner world of fantasy (delusions and hallucina-

tions) unamenable to approach by the therapist. Not all psychoanalysts agreed with this view.

Melanie Klein was trained by Freud, and spent much of her life
working with children. She noticed similarities between the primitive anxieties of small children and those found in some people
suffering from psychotic illnesses. Although she did not analyse
any psychotic patients herself, she did analyse a six-year-old child,
Dick, suffering from autism (Klein, 1930), and concluded that in
psychosis a particular type of severe anxiety made it impossible for
the individual to establish and use symbols. This has devastating
results. For example, if we are unable to form and manipulate
symbols effectively, it makes it very difficult for us to use language
and to distinguish between ourselves and the outside world. Effects
which most of us would attribute to causes outside ourselves are
attributed to self. In Klein's view, such mechanisms underlie psychotic symptoms such as delusions and hallucinations. We can see
how such a failure is descriptive of First Rank Symptoms. Although
their theoretical backgrounds differ radically, there are similarities
between Klein's explanation and the Theory of Mind model proposed by Frith. Klein's explanation also accounts for the difficulties
some people suffering from psychoses appear to have in the use of
metaphor. Segal (1975) points out that the analysis of the subject's
use of *language* is particularly important, for it is through language
that the confusion of 'you' and 'I', other and self, becomes apparent. This distinction, according to Klein, is learnt by the child in
its first relationship, that with its mother, where it has to tolerate
its frustration and fear in the face of its dependence upon its
mother for love and sustenance. The therapist's ability to contain
and endure this primitive fear is of great importance in the psychotherapy of someone suffering from schizophrenia. Segal has
described how Kleinian analysis may be helpful for people suffering
from schizophrenia. She disagrees with Freud's contention that psychotic people do not form a transference relationship. In fact she
argues that they form an immediate, intense transference. This is
because the subject, unable to distinguish between inner and outer
worlds, attempts to shed the terrified, unwanted parts of self into
the therapist. The experience here is difficult to describe, but in it,
the subject believes that he or she has immense power over the
therapist, and that the analyst has immense power over the subject. Consequently the subject may believe, for example, that he or
she is being threatened or attacked by the therapist. The metaphor
here is drawn from how we might imagine a helpless, dependent
new-born infant views its mother, as it realises that this first

other-person has the power both to frustrate it and to provide it with love. Segal believes that Klein's theory provides a psychological framework for understanding the nature of schizophrenia, as well as helping someone to recover from it. The real problem here is that this form of psychoanalysis is a lengthy, time-consuming procedure. How can we justify the expense of so much time and effort on a form of therapy whose effectiveness has never been demonstrated? Indeed, as Slater and Roth point out, psychoanalysts have been loathe to subject their treatment to the same criteria of effectiveness as pharmacological or behavioural treatments. But there is a quite different sense in which this question raises a number of difficult issues for the majority of psychiatrists who would laugh at any suggestion that psychoanalysis has any part to play in the management of schizophrenia. This relates to the implications of strictly utilitarian arguments that are used to justify the cost of treatment offered to people suffering from schizophrenia, as well as moral and ethical issues concerning the nature of psychiatry that I want to return to later.

Behavioural and cognitive approaches

The move towards community care had a considerable influence on the work of the psychologists who worked in the old asylums. Until then they had largely concerned themselves with applying behavioural techniques to help people suffering from neurotic conditions such as severe anxiety, agoraphobia and obsessions. As attempts were made to move long-stay patients out of hospital, they became interested in trying to help this group, whose lives had been devastated by years of institutionalisation. Was it possible to devise psychological interventions to help improve their level of activity so that it would become possible to engage them in more active programmes of rehabilitation that would eventually assist in their discharge from hospital? At that time, in the 1950s and 1960s, behaviourism was at its zenith. The principles underlying behaviourism were simple enough, and extended back to classic conditioning and the work of the Russian neurophysiologist Pavlov, and the more recent theory of operant conditioning and the American psychologist B.F. Skinner. Pavlovian conditioning had provided a theoretical and experimental foundation for much early work in understanding animal and human behaviour. It proposed a system whereby the behaviour of an animal could be changed experimentally by environmental stimuli. In his classic experiment Pavlov showed that dogs salivate when they are shown a bowl of food; in other words there was a simple link between an environmental stimulus (food) and behaviour (salivation), a link that applies to ourselves just as well. But the important thing that Pavlov did was to show that it was possible to change the behaviour, so that salivation occurred with new stimuli. This he managed to do by ringing a bell a few seconds before the animal was fed. At the start of the study the animal would not salivate when it heard the bell, but after a number of trials in which the bell was followed by food, the animal came to associate the bell with food, and its behavioural response (salivation) occurred in response to the new stimulus. In other words its behaviour had been changed. There are many interesting aspects to Pavlov's theory, not the least of which is the importance he ascribed to the association between stimulus and response. The idea of associationism is an ancient one. Bertrand Russell (1961) notes that it can be traced back to Classical Greece. It represents a particular feature of Western thought that seeks to understand the world and ourselves deterministically in terms of cause and effect. Behaviourism, the linking of (causal) stimulus with response (effect) is a form of associationism, which in turn forms part of the wider field of biological determinism.

One of the main criticisms of Pavlov's work was that although it provided an excellent model for understanding behaviour in experimental situations, it fell down when it came to explaining the behaviour of animals or humans in natural situations. The real world simply does not rely on elaborately constructed experiments in order to shape and change behaviour. It was partly this that led Skinner to develop the theory of operant conditioning. Skinner was also influenced by ethology, the science of animal behaviour in natural settings. He became fascinated by aspects of animal behaviour that appeared to be random and devoid of any obvious explanation. In order to study this he set up a series of experiments using pigeons in a cage. The cage was specially constructed so that it was possible to deliver a pellet of food through a chute in the wall. Skinner found that by delivering the food at random, it was possible to shape the birds' behaviour. For example if the bird was pecking at a particular point on the floor of the cage each time the food was delivered, then it would go on repeating this behaviour over and over. It was as if the animal believed that tapping that particular spot had caused the food to appear. In this way Skinner found that it was possible to get the birds to perform a great variety of novel behaviours. Skinnerian, or operant, conditioning forms the basis of techniques used by people who train animals for films. All it requires is a great deal of time and a large sack of 'treats'. You observe the animal carefully and whenever it shows the sort of behaviour you want it to develop, you reward it with a treat. Operant conditioning also provides a neat way of explaining superstitions. Most professional sports people will admit to having minor superstitions, such as having a favourite sweatband, or going on to the field of play in a particular order. According to Skinner this happens because of a chance association between success and the wearing of that sweatband, or taking the field in that order. Like the pigeons, we believe that in some way our success is linked to the behaviour, even though it only occurred through chance. Of course, the important difference between pigeons and ourselves, presumably, is that pigeons do not *believe* that their reward is linked to their behaviour, whereas we do. In fact, Skinner didn't consider that believing, thinking and knowing were important in man either. His model sought to reduce all aspects of our experience to a great net of stimuli and responses, in which there was no room for thinking and believing. Over the last twenty-five years there has been a profound shift in psychological thought, with the emergence of cognitive science. This change has occurred partly in response to the deterministic view of human behaviour that grew out of the more extreme forms of behaviourism, and which attempted to reduce man and consciousness to the level of a blind, non-reflexive machine.

Twenty years ago the psychological management of schizophrenia in the old asylums largely consisted of so-called token economy programmes. These used behaviour modification techniques based on the principles of operant conditioning, to assist in the rehabilitation of long-stay patients suffering from chronic schizophrenia. The purpose of these programmes was to encourage patients to communicate more and become more involved with their environments. Chronically ill patients were rewarded if they became engaged in certain activities, but there were no attempts to help people who were acutely ill with positive symptoms. One exception to this was a paper by Beck (1952), the founder of cognitive therapy, a psychological method which is now widely used to help people suffering from depression. Beck suggested that in depression the fundamental problem was that individuals have a set of negative beliefs, or cognitions, about themselves. These beliefs are held despite the absence of evidence to support them, and they have a powerful influence upon the way individuals feel about themselves. In cognitive therapy the therapist questions the basis for the negative beliefs held by the subject, and in doing so helps the subject to see that the particular perspective that he or she has adopted is unreasonable. In this way the negative beliefs are challenged and gradually changed. In this early single-case report, Beck described the use of a reasoning technique to help a patient with chronic delusions. Nobody paid much attention to this pioneering work, but since then things have changed, and the last fifteen years have seen the growth of a number of psychological techniques for helping people who have positive symptoms. Kingdon and Turkington (1991) reviewed a number of studies describing the use of cognitive therapy and other types of psychological help for patients suffering from schizophrenia. They suggested that such approaches are valuable, especially when used in conjunction with pharmacological and social interventions. The problem is that these methods are in their infancy and there is a shortage of systematic studies to demonstrate their effectiveness. The situation concerning hallucinations is rather better. Slade and Bentall (1988), in Liverpool, have shown that a number of psychological techniques are useful in helping people to cope with these experiences. These include procedures based in behaviour therapy techniques, as well as a variety of novel approaches. One technique, known as counter-stimulation, encourages subjects to divert their attention from the voices by humming or gargling. Other useful techniques include listening to music or speech through headphones, using a Sony Walkman. In another approach, called self-monitoring or focusing, subjects keep diaries about the voices in which they record details of frequency, intensity and quality. Some people have been able to obtain relief from hallucinatory voices by using ear-plugs. This idea came from a neurological theory of hallucinations which suggested that they could arise through the inefficient transfer of sensory information from one side of the brain to another. The small number of studies that have investigated this approach have shown it to be very useful. Slade and Bentall have suggested that these techniques have three features in common: focusing, or directing the patient's attention to the voices; anxiety reduction; and distraction or counter-stimulation. Recent work has seen the development of focusing as a therapeutic intervention in its own right (Haddock *et al.*, 1993; Bentall *et al.*, 1994).

A recent study by Chadwick and Birchwood (1994) has shown that cognitive psychotherapy may be useful in understanding the subject's relationship to the voices, as well as having some therapeutic potential. In the first part of this study they examined the belief systems of twenty-six people who had had chronic hallucinations, and who, in the authors' words, were 'drug-resistant'. In every case, if the subject believed the voices to be malevolent, they were resisted, whereas if the voices were benevolent, the subject engaged with them. The important point here is that this was independent of the content of the voices. In other words, in these subjects it appeared to make no difference what the voices actually said. Despite the voices saying pleasant things, almost a third of the subjects believed them to be malevolent, and so they were resisted by the subject. The authors concluded that this provides strong evidence to support a cognitive model of verbal hallucinations. In the second part of the study they went on to use cognitive therapy to challenge the subjects' beliefs about their voices. The therapy consisted of three parts. In the first, the subject's central beliefs about the voices were defined, together with the evidence to support these beliefs. In the second stage the beliefs were disputed by the therapist; first through the use of hypothetical contradiction ('What would you do if ...?') and then through a verbal challenge in which the subjects were each asked to question their own beliefs about the voices, and to develop other interpretations. The final stage involved testing their beliefs, in which the therapist manipulated situations where the subjects' belief, that they were unable to control the voices, was challenged. The majority of subjects appeared to benefit from this approach, with a reduction in distress, improved coping mechanisms and a reduction in voice activity.

There are two points I want to make at this stage in relation to psychological therapies. This is a new area. Most of these techniques are in the process of evolution. Most of the scientific reports are of single-case studies (that is descriptions of what happens when they are used in one patient), so a degree of caution is justified in interpreting the results. Many psychiatrists would argue that the effectiveness of these techniques can only be shown through the use of studies whose design is similar to that of the clinical drug trial we considered earlier in this chapter. Some people would dispute this. For one thing it is difficult to provide psychological treatment in 'blind' or 'double-blind' fashion. It is also difficult to specify the features of placebo psychological treatments, although attempts have been made to follow these precepts in establishing the value of psychological therapies. There remains the question of who specifies which criteria should be used to demonstrate the effectiveness of a psychological therapy? Also, on what basis is this specification made? These questions relate to who decides that one way of looking at the world is better than another. As yet, recent psychological theories have contributed relatively little to therapy in schizophrenia. This is in direct contrast to the biochemical theories which have formed the rationale for drug therapy in schizophrenia. In recent years, I gave a talk about the new cognitive theories of schizophrenia to a group of colleagues. An experienced psychiatrist told me that she had found it interesting but she couldn't see what practical use it was. One answer is that utilitarian outcomes are not necessarily the sole arbiter of value for psychological theories. Like philosophy, they greatly extend our understanding of mind and its relationship to brain. We shall return to this theme in Part II. Cognitive science is now developing new therapies based on models of what is thought to go wrong in the mental processes of those suffering from schizophrenia. The problem with the type of cognitive approach advocated by Chadwick and Birchwood (1994) is that it offers little help to those subjects who want to understand the significance of their voices. As we have seen, content and meaning is of little importance in this work. Furthermore, the approach assumes that the subject's chosen way of understanding voices is 'wrong'. This may appeal to those who are happy to defer to the expert cognitive technician, but not everyone who hears voices is happy to do this. In the final part of this book I shall describe in detail a new way of helping people who hear persistent verbal hallucinations, which places the emphasis on understanding the significance of the voice in terms of the subject's experience.

SOCIAL INTERVENTIONS

We have seen that social factors have an important influence on schizophrenia. Stressful life events are likely to lead to relapse in those who suffer from the condition, but there is not a great deal that can be done to stop people having life events. The social environment in the old asylums influenced the behaviour and symptom status of its residents. This observation was one of a number of reasons for the closure of the old large mental hospitals and the move to community care. Once people are out of hospital the nature of their family and social environments is probably the single most important non-medical factor that determines outcome. We have seen that high levels of EE in the family of the sufferer are associated with the risk of readmission. Given the influence that family atmosphere has on the course of schizophrenia, it follows that attempts to reduce EE may be valuable. At the very least this may help to make life more bearable for family and sufferer, and, if EE is primary to relapse in the chain of causality, interventions may help to reduce relapse. It is also important to establish whether there is any value in combining social and pharmacological interventions, as both Brown's and Vaughn's work suggests. Vaughn et al. (1984) found that high levels of EE appeared to influence the course of schizophrenia in a culturally diverse group of families in California. She also suggested that high EE may be associated with poor drug-compliance. The problem is that any intervention in a family, even assessment, may be therapeutic. For this reason trials of social intervention are extremely difficult to design. Despite this, there have been several intervention studies aimed at reducing EE. Leff et al. (1982) randomly allocated twenty-four subjects from high EE families to standard out-patient care or social intervention, consisting of education sessions for patient and relatives, a support group, and 'eclectic' family sessions. At a nine-month follow up, only 9% of the experimental group had relapsed, compared with 50% of the control group. Tarrier et al. (1988) obtained similar results using a behavioural intervention with high EE families. The reduction in EE in their experimental groups was associated with lower relapse rates, suggesting that EE plays a causal role in relapse. Falloon et al. (1985) also found fewer positive and negative symptoms in their experimental group, who also required less medication. Hogarty et al. (1986) investigated the interaction between drug treatment and social intervention in high EE homes. No patient who took medication, and whose family received family education and social skills training, relapsed. The absence of relapse in any home which went from high to low EE also supports the importance of EE in causing relapse. These studies differ considerably in the methods they have adopted in working with relatives to reduce EE, so it is difficult to know whether one method is superior to another. Lam (1991) categorised intervention studies into family education (the use of educational techniques such as videos, discussion groups and so on, to aid in the recovery from the disabling effects of mental illness) and family intervention (the use of psychotherapy, behaviour therapy or family therapy in an attempt to reduce EE). Educational approaches, whilst not showing any substantial benefit in reducing EE, did help to alleviate relatives' burden and distress. The value of intervention studies aimed at reducing EE in preventing relapse in the first nine months' post-discharge was established repeatedly. Such approaches are cost-effective compared with in-patient treatment, and benefit patients by avoiding repeated hospital admissions.

It seems that the value of family intervention is established beyond doubt. There are problems, however. Some have suggested that the use of these techniques means that expensive resources are selectively focused only on high EE families. Consequently we are at risk of ignoring the needs of those from low EE families. Because they have low levels of expressed emotion we assume that they need no help in adjusting and coping with having a member who suffers from schizophrenia. Their distress, although not as obvious, is no less significant. Is it fair to neglect this? Clearly not. My own clinical experience in working with families in which a member suffers from schizophrenia has thrown up another problem, for although these interventions may be effective in helping in the earliest stages of schizophrenia, they seem to be less so in families who have had to cope for years. It is as if there is a narrow 'window of opportunity' for changing potentially maladaptive coping mechanisms before they become established within a family. Nevertheless, social interventions point to the importance of the relationship between the individual and his or her social environment in understanding schizophrenia. The interface between biology, psychology and society, how we understand this and the value we attach to it, forms a major part of my argument in Part II.

Part II ANTITHESIS

5 The Fall of the House of Kraepelin

In Chapter 1 we briefly considered the difference between signs and symptoms, both of which play an important part in the way doctors think and act in relation to illness. Here, I want to examine concepts of illness and disease in some detail, and then apply them to schizophrenia. For some time now the medical model of schizophrenia has been under attack from different quarters. Psychologists have argued that it is an unscientific concept, sociologists that it is a way of labelling people who show deviant behaviour, and some (anti)-psychiatrists that it is a sane response to insane families, or an insane society. I shall not be disputing any of these claims. Each has its merits. Each has its weaknesses. So does the medical model, but alternative views of schizophrenia have had little impact within psychiatry. The main purpose of this book is to examine the implications of the use of different languages in talking about schizophrenia. Some languages are more powerful and are accorded greater significance than others. Nowhere is this more true than in the field of mental health. The single most important consequence of the power of psychiatric thought (and action) is that it determines how people with schizophrenia (and mental health problems in general) are treated. It shapes and controls much of the experience of this group of people. For this reason I make no apology for subjecting the dominant psychiatric paradigm to a detailed and critical review. After Part I of this book, we are now in a position to do so, but first I want to delve in greater detail into some basic concepts relating to medicine. These include health, illness and disease.

HEALTH, ILLNESS AND DISEASE

Most of the time we are unaware of our bodily state, the position of our arms and legs and so on, unless our attention is drawn to it. We are unaware of tiny shifts of posture, which occur unconsciously to ease a stiff joint or an aching muscle. For most of the time we take the state of our bodies for granted. We regard health in the same way. We tend not to think about it as long as we have it. We only notice it when our attention is drawn to it (for example at a routine medical check-up), or in its absence. Health is notoriously difficult to define. You might ask, is it not simply the absence of illness or disease? This definition is satisfactory until we consider someone whose blood pressure is consistently elevated. Such a person may have no symptoms of illness and no evidence of any disease process, but they are at risk of serious illnesses such as heart attacks and strokes. If you ask such a person about their health, they may well say that they feel fit and healthy, yet they are at risk of ill-health. At its inception, the World Health Organisation produced a utopian definition of health: '... a state of complete physical, mental and social well-being and not merely the absence of disease and infirmity'. Who amongst us would say they felt 100% healthy using these criteria? Most of us can find some reason to state that we are not healthy. My right ankle is still painful after an old motor-bike injury twenty years ago. If I go for a long walk it is sore the next day. It is now permanently weak and I can easily turn it if I don't wear proper walking boots. At some point in the future I might ask my doctor if there is anything that can be done about it. This does not mean that I regard myself as ill, but the problem has a significant effect upon my well-being, because I enjoy hill-walking. I don't want to get too bogged down in trying to define health. The point is that the concept is a complex one. The same applies to illness. We tend to think of illnesses as discrete entities, as if they have an independent existence. But the sociologist David Mechanic (1972) has shown that emotional and social factors have an enormous influence on the way an individual presents an illness. The situation is even more complicated if we attempt to define mental health. Disease concepts, on the other hand, are somewhat easier to think about.

Most of us will have had a chest infection at some time in our lives. When we do, we will probably notice the following changes: a bad cough producing lots of phlegm; tightness in the chest; breathlessness; chest pain, worse when taking a deep breath; and wheeziness. In addition to this we may notice other disturbances, such as feeling unwell and feverish, tired and run down. These changes may interfere with our ability to carry out our usual activities, and we may decide to see our doctor who will carry out a physical examination. The doctor will listen to your chest with a stethoscope and notice the presence of abnormal breath sounds indicating the presence of infection. She may also tap your chest with her fingers to assess the degree of resonance of the underlying lung tissue. Her suspicions that you have an infection will be confirmed if she detects an area of dullness in comparison with the resonant sound of the rest of the chest. At this point she will have decided that you have a chest infection, but she will not know what has caused it. In order to treat the condition and to be able to predict the outcome (whether you will get better or worse), she must understand the cause. This constellation of symptoms (cough, chest pain and so on) and signs (abnormal breath sounds and dullness on percussion) has many different causes. To decide which, she must perform investigations. These will include a chest X-ray, blood tests, and sending a sample of phlegm to the laboratory for bacteriological investigation.

SYNDROME

Symptoms   cough, chest pain, breathless, phlegm, wheeze, feverish

Signs   abnormal breath sounds, dull percussion note

DISEASES

| TB | Cancer | AIDS | Emphysema | Bronchiectasis | Influenza |

| homeless | smoking | i/v drugs | pollution | cystic fibrosis | old age |

PREDISPOSING FACTORS

Figure 5.1   The disease model and physical illness

Figure 5.1 reveals the important features of this process. The box at the top contains an abbreviated list of symptoms and signs associated with a chest infection. Together, these constitute what is called a syndrome. This is nothing more than a group of symptoms and signs which tend to cluster together in a recognisable pattern. We can say nothing about the cause of a particular syndrome, for there may be many. This is indicated by the second box. Tuberculosis (TB) was once a common cause of severe chest infections. Acquired immune deficiency syndrome (AIDS) can also result in severe chest infections by a variety of unusual bacterial organisms. Cancer of the lungs not infrequently presents with chest infections, as the growing tumour blocks the air passages and thus makes the affected part of the lung vulnerable to secondary infection. Emphysema and bronchiectasis both involve structural changes to the lung tissue with expansion of the air spaces. Emphysema is frequently associated with chronic bronchitis, but in this and bronchiectasis, the affected parts of the lung become vulnerable to infection. Elderly people who develop influenza are especially vulnerable to severe chest infections, partly because their immune systems may not work as effectively, making them less able to resist invading organisms. The important point here is that the same syndrome (cough, wheeze, chest pain and so on) may have a number of different causes, varying in severity and prognosis.

Prognosis is the term used to refer to the outcome of an illness. It is a prediction which establishes your chances of recovering from an illness, and what sort of treatment will help. In order to know this we must know exactly which disease process is responsible for the syndrome. In Figure 5.1 the prognosis varies depending on the disease responsible for causing the syndrome. Tuberculosis was once a life-threatening condition, but it can now be treated successfully with antibiotics. It is easy to confirm that a chest infection is caused by TB, by examining the patient's sputum directly for TB bacteria. These can be seen after the sputum has been specially treated to make the organisms visible. Once this has been done, we can be reasonably certain that the patient will make a good recovery if given a full course of antibiotics. If we establish that the reason for a patient's chest infection is AIDS, or lung cancer, then the prognosis is poor. At the moment there is no treatment or 'cure' for AIDS. The natural history of the disease is that it becomes progressively worse leading to death. The same is true of lung cancer, although here the outcome depends to some extent on the type of cancer, and how advanced it is. Some varieties may be treated successfully with radiotherapy and anti-cancer drugs, if detected early enough. The important point here is that it is not possible to predict outcome and treatment response simply at the level of a syndrome. This is because we must know which particular disease is responsible to predict outcome and response to treatment.

DISEASES AND PREDISPOSING FACTORS

Let us consider the case of a young child who develops a chronic chest infection which the family doctor has been unable to control. The child may be referred to a paediatrician who, after performing further tests, may discover that she is suffering from cystic fibrosis, a genetically determined disorder transmitted by a recessive gene. This means that there will be a significant family history, a fact which makes it likely that the GP would have made the diagnosis on this basis alone. The effect of the disorder is that the body produces abnormally thick mucous, which blocks the small air passages, leading to infection. In this case we can see that the reason for this individual developing the chest infection relates to a genetic abnormality which results in the child having a predisposition to chest infections. There is an extra dimension to diseases that I want to consider. In Figure 5.1 each disease is linked to a specific factor at the bottom of the diagram. TB is linked to homelessness, AIDS to intravenous drug misuse, cancer of the lung to cigarette smoking and so on. In the nineteenth century TB spread like wildfire through overcrowded Victorian slums. Poor housing and nutrition led to conditions that were ideal for the spread of the disease. The incidence of TB fell long before the introduction of the anti-tuberculous drugs. This was brought about through improvements in housing and in the diets of working-class people, introduced as a result of political reforms and efforts of public health medicine. Recent work (Bhatti *et al.*, 1995) shows that the disease has reappeared, especially in the poorest third of the population. This suggests that socio-economic factors have played a major role in the increase. It seems likely that this is mediated through poverty, poor diet, poor housing and homelessness. In the case of AIDS two factors increase your risk of developing the condition: intravenous drug misuse involving the sharing of syringes and needles with others, and unprotected sexual intercourse with a sufferer. There has been an explosion in the number of people who use intravenous drugs in recent times. The reasons for this are complex and to do with our culture and society, *not* medicine.

Let us consider the case of a woman in her fifties who presents to her doctor with repeated chest infections. The doctor finds out that her patient has smoked thirty cigarettes a day for forty years. A chest X-ray shows a suspicious dense shadow in part of her left lung. A bronchoscopy[1] reveals the presence of a rapidly growing cancer of the bronchus. The growth is inoperable, so the patient is referred to a physician and given a course of radiotherapy and chemotherapy. Six months later she dies. We know that there is a strong link between cigarette smoking and lung cancer. Whilst it is

---

1   A bronchoscopy is a direct examination of the air tubes of the lungs, using a tube passed through the mouth and down the trachea.

true that genetic factors may play a small part in determining the risk of developing cancer, most people would accept that the significant factor in this lady's demise was cigarette smoking. An environmental factor, cigarette smoking, accounted for the fact that she developed lung cancer, which led ultimately to her symptoms of chest infection. The point here is that medicine may explain how diseases affect the body, but it can't always explain why a particular individual is affected. The question here is why me and not you? In order to do this we must consider an interaction between the individual and his or her environment. I want to see how well schizophrenia fits this model. We already know from Chapter 2 that there is no evidence to prove unequivocally that schizophrenia is a disease with a specific cause. Can we draw conclusions about the nature of schizophrenia from the outcome and course of the condition, and what is the significance of the symptoms that psychiatrists use to diagnose it?

KRAEPELIN AND *DEMENTIA PRAECOX*

The weakness of the medical, or disease model of schizophrenia will become clearer if we consider its history. The French psychiatrist Morel (1852) provided one of the earliest descriptions of the condition we now call schizophrenia. He described a case of severe intellectual deterioration in an adolescent which he called *demence precoce* (dementia of early onset). There followed a series of descriptions in the neurological literature of the day, but the most important description came from the German psychiatrist Emil Kraepelin in the fourth edition of his textbook in 1893. Here he described an illness called *dementia praecox*, under the heading of 'Psychic Degenerative Processes'. This group of illnesses was characterised by a progressive and irreversible deterioration of intellectual function, typically in young people. He gave the following definition of the illness in the eighth edition of his book (Kraepelin, 1913):

> Dementia Praecox consists of a series of clinical states which have as their common characteristic a peculiar destruction of the internal connections of the psychic personality with the most marked damage of the emotional life and volition.

In Kraepelin's time, considerable success had been achieved in understanding the pathological basis of diseases such as neurosyphilis, which was a common organic cause of insanity. Consequently, psychiatrists believed that medical science would reveal the cause of all forms of insanity. But basic clinical sciences such as pathology, physiology and anatomy, which had been so successful in revealing the cause of neurosyphilis, failed to reveal the cause of *dementia praecox* so Kraepelin had to rely on systematic clinical observation. According to Hoenig (1983), Kraepelin's objective was to apply the clinical methods of medicine to psychiatry. This relied on the detailed description of individual cases, focusing on symptoms and the examination of mental states (signs). It was hoped that such an approach would confirm that *dementia praecox* was a disease entity with a specific anatomical basis and pathology. The important question here is, to what extent did he succeed in describing a single disease (*dementia praecox* or schizophrenia)? Another way of looking at this is to return to the description of schizophrenia in Chapter 1, and analyse it in the same way we examined chest infections in this chapter. Are the signs and symptoms of schizophrenia caused by a single underlying pathological process (in other words a single disease entity), or are they brought about by a variety of different causes. In other words is schizophrenia at best a syndrome with a number of different 'causes'? Because we cannot point to an established cause we must be very clear about the significance of symptoms, and the relationship of these symptoms in making what is a *clinical* diagnosis to the eventual outcome of the condition.

The first point to be made here concerns the great variability of symptoms to be found in schizophrenia. Even Kraepelin (1913) had to admit to this, going so far as to say that:

> Unfortunately in the field of psychic disturbances there is not a single symptom which is pathognomonic for any particular illness. On the other hand we can expect that the composition of the individual characteristics which form the total picture, and in particular *the changes which develop in the course of the illness*, will not be produced in exactly the same way by any of the other diseases.
>
> (Vol. II, p. 945, quoted in Hoenig, 1983, p. 548;
> emphasis added)

As Hoenig points out, Kraepelin fails to provide a clear description (a 'pathognomonic' symptom) of schizophrenia, and, in lieu of this, he chooses to emphasise the importance of the course of the illness. This position has been immensely influential. After Kraepelin, psychiatrists believed that a deteriorating course was a cardinal feature of schizophrenia, although Kraepelin himself described considerable variation in the rate of deterioration. Indeed, he found that complete recovery was possible in 12.5% of cases (1913, Vol. II, p. 865, quoted in Hoenig, 1983, p. 549). Deterioration here refers to the 'changes which develop in the course of the illness' in the quotation from Kraepelin above. It is this that forms the basis of the belief that schizophrenia is a poor prognosis illness. Furthermore, there is an implicit assumption that this deterioration is in some way related to the putative disease process.

In this view someone who develops symptoms of schizophrenia (delusions and hallucinations) in late adolescence will not recover fully from this or subsequent episodes. At some point this person will develop negative, which result in social and intellectual deterioration, and which, in the opinion of most psychiatrists, are inextricably linked to poor outcome. Such individuals will not regain previous levels of functioning. They will not return to work. They lose interest in their families and relationships. They become apathetic and withdrawn to the extent that, in Kraepelin's time, they received asylum care. The problem is that Kraepelin not only found it difficult to be prescriptive about the symptoms required to diagnose schizophrenia and thus predict outcome, but he was also unable to show that all of the 127 cases of schizophrenia he studied in detail actually turned out to have poor outcome and deteriorating course. Bleuler, another influential figure in the early history of schizophrenia, was not as convinced that the condition was a single disease entity, because of the diversity of symptoms and variation in outcome (Bleuler, 1911):

> Kraepelin's concept continues to be opposed by many, who because of the wide diversity of the clinical pictures, cannot accept it as a single entity, *which originally appeared to be based on the uniform course of the illness, and yet could include cases with a good as well as a bad outcome.*
>
> (p. i; emphasis added)

THE COURSE OF SCHIZOPHRENIA

We have seen that traditional psychiatric wisdom holds that deterioration is a core feature of schizophrenia, and this has played an important part in attempts to validate the diagnosis. The problem here is that because we don't know the causes of schizophrenia, there is no diagnostic test, so psychiatrists have to find other ways of confirming the diagnosis. A popular way of doing so has been to use the presence of deterioration after the condition first presents. If Kraepelin was correct in identifying a single disease, schizophrenia, then we would expect most people suffering from it to have similar (poor) outcomes.[2] What evidence is there that people diagnosed with schizophrenia fail to recover and proceed to an end-stage of psychological and mental deterioration? There have been two ways of investigating this. The first depends upon detailed long-term studies of patients over many years. The second involves smaller studies over shorter periods of time, but has the advantage that standardised diagnostic and outcome criteria are used.

In the first approach Huber et al. (1979), in Bonn, studied the outcome of over 500 people diagnosed with schizophrenia over twenty-one years. In 57% of cases outcome was favourable, although there was great complexity in the patterns of the condition over time. In Zurich, Bleuler (1978) followed up over 200 patients for twenty-two years. He found good outcome in 53% of subjects. Ciompi (1980) identified nearly 300 people admitted to a psychiatric hospital in Lausanne whose histories were documented until the age of sixty-five. The average follow-up period was almost thirty-seven years. Like Huber, he found considerable variation in the pattern of the symptoms with time. Overall, 49% of patients had a favourable outcome, and in comparison with the situation on admission, in two-thirds of cases mental health was completely or partially improved. These studies show remarkably similar outcomes for schizophrenia, with approximately 50% having good outcome, but there are weaknesses relating to the design of these studies. Patients were not assessed at the time of admission, so the researchers had to trawl through voluminous notes to search for information which may or may not have been present, in order to make the diagnosis. This casts doubt on the reliability of the diagnoses. In addition many British psychiatrists would contest the criteria used to make the diagnoses. Ciompi used Bleuler's criteria, which may be too broad to be of value in this type of research. This may result in the inclusion of some people who are not suffering from schizophrenia and who are destined to have a good outcome, thus artificially improving the apparent outcome in schizophrenia. The best way around this is to identify a group of people in the earliest stages of the illness, make the diagnosis using strict

---

2   In practical terms this means that psychiatrists are often in the absurd position of having to say: 'I don't know at this moment whether you are suffering from schizophrenia, but come back in ten years' time and I'll be in a position to let you know then'!

criteria, and then follow them up for as long as possible to see what happens. The objective here is to investigate the extent to which the presence of acute, or positive, symptoms of schizophrenia identifies a group of people who will have poor outcome.

In Chapter 2 we encountered the International Pilot Study of Schizophrenia (IPSS), one of the objectives of which was to study outcome in schizophrenia diagnosed using strict criteria. In Washington, one of nine field centres for the IPSS, a group of psychiatrists were interested in the extent to which individual schizophrenic symptoms, regardless of their diagnostic role, predicted poor outcome. Carpenter *et al.* (1978) followed up over 130 patients in the American IPSS research centre after five years, and repeated the initial clinical assessments using the Present State Examination (PSE), together with details of social functioning (work record, ability to look after self, quality of personal relationships) and duration of hospitalisation. They split their sample into two groups, based on the twenty patients with the best and twenty patients with the worst outcome scores. They were thus in a strong position to determine which symptoms of schizophrenia in the earliest stages of the condition were associated with poor outcome. Only one sign or symptom variable, restricted (or blunted) affect, discriminated between the two groups of subjects. The authors concluded that the diagnosis of schizophrenia, when based on the presence of acute (positive) symptoms, was of little value in predicting the course and outcome of the condition. This study indicates the difficulties in predicting outcome when people present with acute symptoms of schizophrenia. The main purpose of diagnosis and recognising diseases is to enable us to make such predictions. Hays (1984) has pointed out that despite the efforts of thousands of researchers over many years and the development of many different sets of diagnostic criteria, the cause of schizophrenia remains unknown. Psychiatrists must, he argues, face up to the unpalatable fact that schizophrenia as a disease entity conceived of by Kraepelin, does not exist. '[Kraepelin] is the sole, flawed, authority for this extraordinary but influential theory' (Hays, 1984, p. 6).

This forces us to the conclusion that there is little evidence to support the Kraepelinian model of schizophrenia. There is neither the evidence to support biological models of the condition, nor the evidence to justify the existence of the condition as a diagnostic category, characterised by specific acute symptoms which predict outcome. I want to make one final point concerning poor outcome. Ciompi (1980) found that in two-thirds of cases *social* outcome was either intermediate or poor. His figures suggest that the main field of impairment in schizophrenia is not symptoms, but social functioning. But in view of the fact that all the patients studied had been institutionalised for decades, this is hardly surprising, and may have little to do with the progress of an illness. Zubin *et al.* (1983; Chapter 2, p. 28) have suggested that over the last fifty years schizophrenia has become a less severe condition with a better outcome. Over this period the management of the condition has changed profoundly. People who have the condition are no longer incarcerated in institutions for years, as was the case when Kraepelin wrote about *dementia praecox*. This raises the possibility that the poor outcome described by Kraepelin was an artefact of institutionalisation. But before we write off Kraepelin completely there remains one reason for believing that he might have been partly correct. Evidence in Chapter 2 indicated that some people, those with prominent negative symptoms, may have a neurodevelopmental disorder. My view is that a small number of people diagnosed as schizophrenic may have a poor prognosis neurodevelopmental disorder. This 'narrow' definition of schizophrenia is one based on the presence of negative symptoms. Others, including Andreasen (Andreasen and Flaum, 1991) have suggested that greater importance should be attached to negative symptoms in diagnosing schizophrenia, precisely because these conform more closely to the core Kraepelinian concept. But this raises a difficult question. What exactly is the significance of positive symptoms? These are much more striking than negative symptoms and for this reason have formed the basis for diagnosis. If I argue that it is misleading to use them to diagnose schizophrenia, then what exactly is their significance?

A CASE OF MISTAKEN IDENTITY

The argument developed so far is based in the scientific and academic literature. We can obtain a view of the implications of this evidence by considering another vignette.

Jim was nineteen years old when he first presented to a psychiatrist. At that time he had just received his A-level results which were not as good as he had hoped, and he had lost his place at university where he had hoped to study psychology and philosophy. Over the course of the summer, while he was waiting for his results, he had become increasingly withdrawn, but his family and friends were not particularly worried about this because he had always been a rather anxious person, who didn't have a lot of close friends. Everybody thought he was a bit apprehensive about his results. After the results, when it was clear that he would not be going away to university, he became even more withdrawn. He spent hours locked away in his bedroom. He stopped eating regularly, and couldn't be bothered to shower or change his clothes. He lost weight, his hair grew into a tangled mess and he started to smell. His parents tried to encourage him to leave his room. They tried to encourage him to take more interest in himself. They even offered to take him away on holiday for a couple of weeks, in the hope that it might help to stimulate him into taking more interest in himself. But the more they tried, the more he withdrew into himself. He stayed awake at night, smoking and listening to records. Shortly after this they started to hear him talking to himself in his room. At times he would shout out as if he was frightened. They began to think that he was hearing voices, so they went to consult the family doctor who offered to see Jim at home. When he came the next day, Jim refused to talk with the doctor, who was so appalled by Jim's condition that he spoke to the local psychiatric hospital for advice, and later that afternoon a consultant psychiatrist visited. Jim also refused to talk with her, so she contacted the local social services and arranged for an assessment by an approved social worker, and later that evening he was admitted to a psychiatric hospital on Section 2 of the Mental Health Act. He was seen there by a junior doctor who made the following comments in Jim's notes:

> *Appears blunted in affect, flat and perplexed. At times suspicious. Very little spontaneous speech, and most responses to questions are monosyllabic. Has poverty of speech. Appears to be hallucinating, but denies AH on direct questioning. Probably suffering from schizophrenia. For stelazine 15 mg twice daily.*

Over the next few days his behaviour deteriorated. He started to shout out at what the staff assumed to be threatening auditory hallucinations. He became quite aggressive and attacked an older male staff nurse, whom he accused of being a 'bugger'. He was given more medication but he developed a lot of side-effects and didn't appear to be improving. After three weeks his condition had not improved. His Section was converted to a Section 3 because he had refused to take any more stelazine. He was started on a depot neuroleptic, clopixol, but the side-effects persisted. He started to accuse staff of trying to castrate him or turn him into a zombie.

His consultant, who had been seeing him once a week, started to see him fortnightly. She made the following entry in his notes two months after his admission:

> He remains disturbed, deluded and hallucinated. At times his behaviour can be quite threatening, and his symptoms appear to have made only a partial response to medication. In my view he has a poor prognosis schizophrenic illness, a variety commoner in men, probably associated with neurodevelopmental features. He will have to remain on medication for years because the family show evidence of high expressed emotion. Plan discharge over the next three weeks.

A year later Jim moved away from home to a hostel. He was still on large doses of clopixol. He was stiff and couldn't walk properly. His speech was slurred and he had put on three stones in weight. He kept saying to the community nurse who came to give him his injection, that he thought he had been castrated as a punishment. The nurse didn't have enough time to go into this with him. He saw his consultant once a year. She told him he had to continue with medication. In the hostel, Jim was befriended by a young care worker. Andrew was the same age as Jim, and was spending two years working as a care worker before going to university himself to study English. He became interested in some of the things Jim did and said. He noticed that Jim always avoided his attempts to strike up a conversation. He was also puzzled by Jim's statements that he was being castrated, so he started to spend more time getting to know Jim. Whenever he was on duty he arranged to spend at least an hour or so with him, encouraging him to talk about himself. The first thing that happened was that Jim told him about the voices he was hearing. He had heard them for years, he said, since childhood, and long before the psychiatrist came to see him. He heard a number of different voices, most of them his family members. They kept telling him – 'Shut up. Play the game', or 'You're a dirty little piece of shit'. Whenever he heard these voices he felt threatened and oppressed by them. After he failed his A-levels they had become much worse. He couldn't shut them out. The medication had made him slightly less anxious about what the voices were saying, but had not stopped them entirely. He also told Andrew that he thought somehow that he had been castrated by his family, and that the medication had something to do with this. Andrew looked up the effects of the medication in a book kept in the office. There, he discovered that impotence and erectile failure were common side-effects of major tranquillisers in men. He went back and told Jim, who was first reassured that there was an explanation for the distressing side-effects he had experienced, then angry that no one had told him what to expect. When the nurse came to give him his next injection, he asked him if it could be reduced. The nurse agreed to ask the consultant.

Over the next couple of months Jim began to trust Andrew more and more. He started to talk about his family and childhood, and he also began to talk about disturbing images during the day and nightmares at night. In these images he saw a bizarre and distorted image of himself as a glove-puppet being pulled on to his grandfather's right hand. He felt dreadful inside when these images occurred, like he was being torn apart inside. Gradually, he was able to explore the significance of these images. He remembered times in childhood when his parents went out for the night, and he and his brother went to stay with his maternal grandparents for the evening. To his horror he remembered being sexually abused by his grandfather, who had told him that if he ever told anyone his willy would be chopped off and his brain would be removed, turning him into a zombie. He had been terrified. He had been unable to tell anyone. At the age of nine he had turned in on himself. He lost all confidence in himself. He became an anxious, bedwetting, socially withdrawn child. His concentration had been ruined by intrusive images related to the abuse. His teachers thought he was in a daydream. His academic performance deteriorated, although he was still bright and capable. His relationship with his parents deteriorated too. There were outbursts of aggression at home, especially whenever it was suggested that he stay with his grandparents for the night. Family relationships deteriorated. He longed to get away.

Over the next six months he continued to explore the consequences of his abuse with Andrew. Because he had moved away he now had a new psychiatrist who was interested to hear what Jim made of his illness. Andrew accompanied Jim to some of his appointments, and with his support, Jim was able to tell the new psychiatrist about his childhood experiences. Although the voices persisted, he understood their origins and because of this was better able to deal with them. This psychiatrist encouraged him to start reducing his medication more. He suggested that Jim should decide how much to take and how often, in discussion with Andrew. Over the course of the next twelve months Jim himself reduced and discontinued his medication. At that stage he decided that he no longer needed to see the psychiatrist, who told him to *contact him if ever he felt he needed further help. Three years later Jim started at university. He was well and regarded himself as not having a psychiatric problem. His voices were now a part of him.*

Positive symptoms, that is hallucinations, delusions and thought disorder, have formed the basis of most diagnostic systems for schizophrenia. When a diagnosis of schizophrenia is made, psychiatrists make a number of assumptions, one of the most important of which is that the experiences reported by the patient (symptoms) or the behaviours noted at interview (signs) represent symptoms of an illness. This means that psychiatrists regard these experiences as somehow different from 'normal' experience. They believe that non-schizophrenic people never experience hallucinations or have thought disorder. They make another assumption that has serious implications for the way in which the individual's experience is responded to. In 1913 the German psychiatrist Karl Jaspers (1963) published the first edition of his highly influential book, *General Psychopathology*, in which he set out the criterion of *understandability*. In it, Jaspers argued that unlike other psychoses, the experiences of people suffering from schizophrenia – the delusions and hallucinations – are not understandable in terms of the person's life history. There is a discontinuity, or a break, in which the new 'schizophrenic' experience develops, and which is beyond explanation in terms of all the experiences and events that have taken place in the subject's life before. I shall have much more to say about this in Chapter 8, but for the moment I want to note this point because it relates to issues that we are about to consider. We can reformulate this as follows. Are psychiatrists justified in assuming that First Rank Symptoms are features of 'abnormal' experience? In other words do 'normal' people ever have these experiences? I want to examine the evidence that, at least as far as thought disorder and hallucinations are concerned, the answer to this question is yes.

Talking nonsense

Both Kraepelin (1913) and Bleuler (1911) regarded thought disorder as an important symptom of schizophrenia, a view widely held by psychiatrists both in America and in Europe. Willis and Bannister (1965) found that over 70% of a sample of 300 UK psychiatrists considered thought disorder to be the single most important symptom in diagnosing schizophrenia. Edwards (1972) found that over 80% of American psychiatrists shared this opinion. In view of this, it is not surprising that the symptom is given much prominence in standard textbooks of psychiatry. Slater and Roth (1977) regarded the presence of thought disorder in clear consciousness as a 'diagnostic sign [of schizophrenia] of the first order' (p. 316). They devote two pages to it, and place it before all other disturbances, including hallucinations. According to Slater and Roth, thought disorder consists of a variety of abnormalities of communication:

> Ordinary conversation may be interfered with by 'Vorbeireden' (talking beside the point, or allowing the essential nature of an issue to escape), blocking of the stream of thought, drifting into irrelevant sidelines of thought, narrowing of concepts, vagueness, and all the other peculiarities which have been earlier described ... If thought disorder can be convincingly demonstrated, by clinical or other methods, its presence is highly significant, and may clinch the diagnosis.
>
> (1977, pp. 316–18)

Andreasen (1979a, 1979b) has produced rigorous definitions of thought disorder in the scale for the assessment of thought, language and communication (TLC) disorders, and has shown that it occurs in a wide range of conditions, including affective disorders (such as serious depression and hypomania) and organic disorders such as dementia. These phenomena are not specific to schizophrenia. For this reason thought disorder no longer plays a part in diagnostic criteria for schizophrenia. In a recent paper (Thomas, 1995) I have argued that the concept of thought disorder is flawed and best replaced by descriptions of human communication based in linguistic science. One of the earliest linguistic descriptions of thought disorder was provided by Elaine Chaika (1974). She examined in detail a segment of speech taken from a woman diagnosed with schizophrenia and who also showed evidence of thought disorder. Chaika concluded that her speech had a number of abnormalities affecting sentence structure, as well as the phonological (sound) and semantic (meaning) features of words. According to Chaika, this indicated that the speaker was unable to apply rules which specified how linguistic elements such as phonemes, words and sentences were organised into meaningful structures. This meant that word, sentence and discourse structures were disorganised. Others contested this. Fromkin (1975) pointed out that the errors made by Chaika's patient could be seen in the speech of non-schizophrenic, non-psychiatric speakers. She gave, as examples, errors taken from speakers, many of whom were leading academics, which she had collected over many years. She also provided examples from the White House Transcripts, the recordings of conversations which took place between ex-president Richard Nixon and his aides at the time of the Watergate scandal. These transcripts provided plenty of evidence that 'normal' speech contained the same errors which Chaika claimed to be a feature of schizophrenic speech. Fromkin argued that, because the participants in the White House tapes were non-schizophrenic, Chaika's description was not peculiar to schizophrenic speakers.

This makes sense. Just think for a moment about the last time you heard a politician being interviewed on the television or radio. No doubt the interviewer wanted to get the politician to answer a particular question. No doubt the politician concerned had his or her own agenda. Consequently the politician would avoid the interviewer's questions and instead turn the discussion around to the issues that he or she wanted to cover. Under these circumstances one of two things could occur. The interviewer might ask a question which the politician would ignore. Alternatively, the politician might respond to the question, only to move away on to the topic that he or she wants to discuss. We have also heard politicians participating in debates in the House of Commons where they have been asked difficult questions, or been under considerable pressure. This most commonly occurs when they are being interviewed in front of camera by a select committee. Under these circumstances their speech often becomes hesitant, vague, unclear and repetitive. They may produce adequate amounts of speech, but it conveys little information and can be condensed considerably.

Andreasen's (1980) TLC scale defines twenty items of 'thought, language and communication' disorders, two of which are tangentiality and derailment. Tangentiality occurs where a speaker replies to a question in an indirect manner, or where the speaker even fails completely to answer a question, moving on to an unrelated topic. Derailment is a pattern of spontaneous speech in which the ideas slip off the track on to another one that is clearly but obliquely related, or on to one that is completely unrelated. The result is speech that sounds disjointed. The TLC scale also contains an item called 'poverty of content of speech'. This is defined as speech which is adequate in amount, but which conveys little information. There is much repetition, and a tendency to be over-abstract or over-concrete. The interviewer may recognise poverty of content because a person may speak for some time without conveying much information. Much of what is said lacks conciseness. On numerous occasions I have heard politicians speak with evidence of derailment, tangentiality and poverty of content of speech. To be fair, I have no doubt that my speech too has shown these features on occasions. Presumably these speakers are not schizophrenic. They are not even considered to be thought disordered. Yet their speech shows evidence of thought disorder according to Andreasen's criteria, but the reasons for this are easy to understand given the context of the interview and the different intentions of interviewer and interviewee. Thought disorder is not specific to schizophrenia and may occur in 'normal' people. It is, if you like, a feature of communication that emerges where speaker intentions differ from listener intentions (derailment and tangentiality), or in response to stress (poverty of content of speech). For this reason thought disorder is no longer included in most diagnostic criteria, but this is not the case with hallucinations, which play an extremely important role in the diagnosis of schizophrenia.

Hearing voices

In Western culture, auditory or verbal hallucinations (VHs) are widely regarded as a sign of madness. Sometimes the experience is referred to as 'hearing voices'. In Chapter 1 we discovered that there were three types of voice-hearing experiences regarded by psychiatrists as diagnostic of schizophrenia. They were hearing your own thoughts spoken aloud, hearing one or more voices commenting on your actions, or hearing two or more voices having a discussion about you in the third person. These experiences are all included in the group of First Rank Symptoms (FRSs) used to diagnose schizophrenia. Although some people who present with these experiences are undoubtedly suffering from serious mental health problems, they can also occur in a wide variety of other circumstances.

Verbal hallucinations in non-psychotic states

I use the term non-psychotic states here quite deliberately because there is evidence that VHs may occur in people who would not be diagnosed schizophrenic by psychiatrists. Usually they have experienced some form of trauma, such as bereavement or sexual abuse. Over twenty years ago, Rees, a GP in the quiet market town of

Llanidloes in mid-Wales, published a detailed survey of almost three hundred widows and widowers, the majority of his patients who had been bereaved over the period of his study. All subjects were interviewed by Rees, who had the advantage of knowing most of them personally. They trusted him. In the interview he was interested in whether the widowed person had experienced hallucinations, either seeing, hearing or feeling the dead spouse. His results are very interesting (Rees, 1971). Nearly 50% of his subjects had experienced hallucinations of one form or another. VHs occurred in over 13% of the sample. More than 10% had actually spoken to the dead spouse, because they were so convinced of the reality of the experience. There was no evidence that these people were suffering from psychiatric disorders such as depression, which are common following bereavement. The incidence of depression was the same in hallucinating groups (17.5%) and non-hallucinating groups (18%). Rees made the interesting observation that most people found these experiences helpful; in fact over 80% of those who spoke to the deceased found this comforting. Another interesting point to emerge from this study was that nearly three-quarters of the subjects had not disclosed the fact that they had experienced hallucinations, presumably because they were afraid that if they did so they would be thought of as 'mad', when they knew they were not. This is an important study which suggests that the experience of hearing voices, as well as other hallucinatory experiences, may be much more common than most psychiatrists believe, and not limited to 'abnormal' experience. It is interesting to note that Rees' work is not well-known in psychiatric circles, despite the fact that it was published in the *British Medical Journal*. The study is not without its weaknesses, however. In particular many psychiatrists would argue that Rees was a GP, not a psychiatrist. The questions he asked when interviewing his subjects were quite limited, so there is no way of knowing whether these experiences were the same as those seen in people who would be diagnosed schizophrenic by a psychiatrist. This may be true of Rees' work, but Bernadine Ensink, a psychologist working in Holland, has carried out research which raises some difficult questions for those who believe that the three types of VHs described above are symptoms of schizophrenia.

Ensink worked closely with Marius Romme, whose work with the Hearing Voices Network we shall consider later. She was interested in the long-term effects of sexual abuse and studied nearly a hundred women recruited from a number of incest survivor organisations in Holland. This was a well-designed study in which all subjects were interviewed personally by trained interviewers who used a number of interview schedules to gather information about the subjects' pasts, their experience of abuse, and the consequences of this. These included detailed questions about hallucinations as well as other experiences, such as dissociation. This was because there had been earlier reports of links between sexual abuse and dissociation, a distressing change in the experience of self.[3] Dissociation is a form of coping mechanism sometimes seen in subjects who have experienced severe trauma. Recently, interest in this area has taken off with interest in the concept of post-traumatic stress disorder (PTSD), the reaction seen in survivors of traumatic events such as plane crashes or fires.

Ensink (1992, 1993) found that all her subjects had been sexually abused in childhood, usually by their fathers, or other close male relatives. She found that 43% reported hallucinatory experiences, and 28% had had auditory hallucinations. Of the subjects who heard voices, 85% of these experiences were identical to First Rank Symptom auditory hallucinations. She provides some examples:

> ... she used to be daydreaming alone in her room for long periods of time. During these periods she heard voices. When asked to give some more specific information she said: 'When I hear discussions, it is just like if there are many people in my head and that is disturbing. I can not stop it. They used to say terrible things, that I should be punished and so on.'
>
> (Ensink, 1992, p. 127)

In general, auditory (and visual) hallucinations were more likely to occur in women who had experienced more severe forms of abuse, and in women who had been abused by their fathers. Most of the women who heard voices had done so for many years. Although many of these subjects were in therapy because of the

---

3   Dissociative states may take many forms. Subjects feel as if they are walking around in a trance, they may be very forgetful and sleep-walk. In severe states they may have fits or convulsions indistinguishable from those caused by epilepsy. Sometimes subjects may have what are called 'fugue states', in which they wander for days on end, but with no recall of what they did during this time. The history of dissociation is interesting in its own right. Both Freud and his contemporaries, for example Pierre Janet, were interested in it, but these days the concept is regarded as controversial and generally not accepted by the psychiatric establishment.

abuse, none was seeing a psychiatrist, or had received a diagnosis of schizophrenia or psychotic illness. Bernadine Ensink's work suggests that hallucinations identical to those seen in schizophrenia are relatively common in women who have been sexually abused. There is also evidence from well-designed epidemiological studies that the experience of hearing voices occurs in the general population, in people who never get to see a psychologist or psychiatrist.

Verbal hallucinations in the general population

Over the years there have been several studies of auditory hallucinations in 'normal' subjects. Johnson (1978, reported in Posey and Losch, 1983) reports a survey in 1897 by Parish in which auditory hallucinations were reported by 10–30% of 'normal' subjects. Sidgewick et al. (1894, results reported in detail by Tien, 1991) found that almost 4% of the population admitted hearing voices, in a general population survey undertaken for the Society for Psychical Research. The problem was that in 3% these experiences occurred whilst subjects were falling asleep or waking up. In general, hallucinatory experiences are much more likely to occur in states of lowered vigilance such as when we are drowsy. For example, McKellar (1957) found that over 40% of college students described hearing voices whilst drifting off to sleep. If these experiences were excluded, 1% of Sidgewick's subjects heard voices whilst wide awake. This figure is remarkably similar to that obtained in recent work by Tien (1991). This study was undertaken specifically to compare the prevalence of hallucinations in the general population in five American cities (Baltimore, New Haven, Durham, St Louis and Los Angeles) with the prevalence from the Sidgewick study. Tien specifically excluded hallucinations related to sleep. Subjects were interviewed with a diagnostic schedule devised by the National Institute of Mental Health, and widely used in psychiatric research. He found that at least 10–15% of the sample studied admitted to hallucinations of one of the senses, and around 2% of the sample admitted to hearing voices. Both the Sidgewick and Tien studies were of large numbers of subjects. Sidgewick et al. interviewed 17,000 adults (largely in England) and Tien interviewed over 18,500. We can be reasonably certain that, in Tien's study, the experiences reported were close to or identical with those experienced by people who would attract a psychiatric diagnosis. He also made strenuous efforts to establish the severity of these experiences, by enquiring how subjects had coped, and whether the level of distress or interference with function was such that they had consulted a professional. He found that the proportion of non-distressing hallucinations (for all senses) was much higher than those associated with distress or interference with function. This suggests that the majority of his subjects had not seen a psychiatrist, although we cannot be sure about this.

The idea that hallucinations can occur in 'normal' subjects is not particularly new. Forrer (1960) described what he called 'benign hallucinations' occurring in five of his friends. The most important work here though is that of Posey and Losch (1983). Their study was triggered by a book published by an American psychologist, Julian Jaynes (1976). In it, Jaynes argued that in so-called primitive people, the unconscious use of language by the right side of the brain[4] caused people to hear voices, an experience which may be regarded as an important stage in the origins of consciousness. Posey and Losch argued that if this is so, then it would be reasonable to expect to find VHs in the general population. They constructed a questionnaire to establish the presence of fourteen different types of VH and gave this to 375 college students, 249 of whom were female. They found that over 70% reported brief verbal hallucinations whilst fully awake. Almost two-fifths (39%) reported hearing their thoughts spoken out as if aloud (one of Schneider's First Rank Symptoms of schizophrenia), and over one-third (36%) said they had heard a voice calling their name when they were alone. They interviewed a small sample of voice hearers with a personality inventory to make sure they were not suffering from psychiatric disorders, but there was no evidence that this was so.

Another way of looking at the evidence concerning the occurrence of VHs in non-psychotic subjects is to say that it blurs the boundaries between 'normal' and 'abnormal' experience. It suggests that the great varieties of human experience we have considered here are located on a continuum, and that there is no point of discontinuity, or a clear boundary, between the experience of mental illness and that of 'normal' subjects. This view has been stated most clearly by Gordon Claridge in Oxford (1985), who argues that so-called abnormal experiences such as hallucinations and delusions may be more

---

4   In most of us the faculty for language is located within the left cerebral hemisphere. The left side of the brain also controls motor activity for the right side of the body. This is why people who have had strokes affecting the right side of the body often experience profound language difficulties.

closely related to the *temperament* (or personality) of those who become mentally ill, rather than a feature of mental illness itself. This in turn is related to differences in brain function thought to be associated with different types of temperament. Claridge uses the term 'schizotypal' to describe those personality features which, he argues, may be associated with schizophrenia. This approach may be regarded as a variant of the diathesis-stress model we examined earlier, and which identifies the diathesis in terms of a personality type that develops psychotic symptoms in response to particular environmental stressors.

SCHIZOPHRENIA ON TRIAL?

Where does this take us? In this chapter we started off by examining the traditional medical model in which we explored the relationship between symptoms, syndromes, diseases and outcome. In applying this model to schizophrenia we found that there is no evidence that either the diagnosis itself, or the acute symptoms used to make the diagnosis, are of any value in predicting poor outcome. The notion of poor outcome played an important role in the historical origins of the condition. In any case, we had to use poor outcome to validate the diagnosis in the absence of a diagnostic test for the condition. Only the negative symptom of blunting of affect appeared to predict poor outcome. Then we saw that some positive symptoms, such as thought disorder and verbal hallucinations, occur in people who are unlikely ever to attract a diagnosis of schizophrenia, especially those who have been sexually abused. VHs indistinguishable from First Rank Symptoms may occur in this group as well as college students who have never seen a psychiatrist. Whilst we do not know whether other FRSs, such as passivity experiences or thought alienation phenomena, occur in 'normal' and non-psychotic subjects, the fact that VHs do so must raise doubts about the specificity of other FRSs for schizophrenia, and, therefore, doubts about the value of the concept as an illness.

There is nothing new in this. Boyle (1993) points out, as I have, that there is little correspondence between symptoms or diagnosis and outcome. She also agrees that there is little in the way of hard scientific evidence to support theories of schizophrenia. She is especially critical of what she regards as the fallacious arguments used by advocates of disease models of schizophrenia in the absence of empirical evidence to support this. Psychiatrists use terms such as mental illness and the mentally ill, which in them-

selves are terms which have little utility, to justify the maintenance of medical power in this area. This is all very well, but we
may say exactly the same about psychologists and their use of their
own specialist terms. All professional groups use specialist languages as part of the processes which enable them to maintain
control in a particular area. Unlike Boyle, I do not believe we
should throw away the concept of schizophrenia altogether. The
predictive power of negative symptoms strongly suggests that there
is room for a greatly slimmed-down version of Kraepelin's all-
encompassing monstrosity, with the preservation of a very narrow
concept of schizophrenia as a neurodevelopmental disorder. The
problem with this is that it leaves unanswered the significance of
positive symptoms. If they do not predict outcome, then what
exactly do they represent? What is their significance? The only way
we can really understand this is if we move away from the use of
'schizophrenia' as a diagnostic entity and study symptoms in their
own right. This is the view advocated by Richard Bentall. In Chapter 2 of his book *Reconstructing Schizophrenia* (Bentall, 1990) he
presents detailed arguments for dropping diagnosis in favour of the
study of symptoms. He points out that for a diagnostic system to
be useful it must be reliable and valid. Reliability refers to the
extent to which clinicians can agree that a condition is present.
Validity refers to its usefulness when judged by other criteria. The
diagnosis of schizophrenia fails on both counts. It has proved very
difficult in the past to get clinicians to agree whether the condition
is present in an individual. Although the reliability of the diagnosis
has improved with the introduction of diagnostic criteria, the need
to do so indicates that the validity of the condition is very low. In
other words, the absence of a diagnostic test means that clinicians
are forced to use diagnostic criteria to agree that the condition is
present. Richard Bentall argues that the simplest way around these
problems is to cut out diagnosis completely and study individual
symptoms. This has a number of benefits. It is easier to define
symptoms, so they have higher reliability. It is also easier to relate
individual symptoms to underlying theoretical disturbances in cognition. Bentall's own research into the nature of hallucinations is
an example of this. Through the systematic study of a single set of
symptoms (it is important to remember that even a symptom such
as hallucinations consists of several different subtypes), he and his
colleagues have increased our understanding of the cognitive disturbances associated with the symptom, in a way that would not have
been possible had he stuck with diagnosis.

Reframing schizophrenia in this way is not to deny the existence of states of being in which the individual loses control to powerful thoughts, images and experiences which are communicable only with great difficulty. It is essential that the reality of these experiences is recognised as far as the sufferer is concerned, as well as the distress such states may cause the family and friends of the sufferer. I believe that the confusion surrounding our understanding of how and why these states arise has not been clarified by 100 years of research into schizophrenia. It is for this reason that I agree with Boyle and Bentall who suggest that we should now be adopting different approaches in researching the origins of these experiences. We must never forget that the purpose of research is to help people with these experiences, and we have already seen in Chapter 4 that the psychiatrist's response is to offer help in the form of medication. But what are the implications of the arguments developed in this chapter for the treatment of schizophrenia with drugs?

6 A Bitter Pill

Schizophrenia is an illness. Doctors are trained to treat illnesses with drugs. Therefore psychiatrists treat schizophrenia with drugs. Thus, somewhat simplified, runs a crude argument for the drug treatment of schizophrenia. It is widely claimed that the neuroleptic drugs control the acute symptoms of schizophrenia. But there is more to it than this. Many psychiatrists believe that there are additional benefits if people with schizophrenia remain on neuroleptic medication for many years. The view is that, used in this way, these drugs may have a beneficial effect by helping to prevent the inevitable progress of the disease to an end stage of deterioration. In Chapter 4 we examined only a small part of the huge research literature which appeared to confirm the efficacy of these drugs. In Chapter 2 we also saw that one of the properties of these drugs, their effect in blocking the transmission of dopamine in certain nerve pathways in the brain, has played a central role in supporting the dopamine theory of schizophrenia. We also found that when attempts are made to measure directly dopaminergic transmission there is little evidence that this is increased in schizophrenia, and in Chapter 5 we examined critically the concept of schizophrenia so important to psychiatry. It follows that we must now re-examine the role played by drugs in the management of the condition. Here we shall consider in some detail the problems associated with the use of these drugs. I also want us to consider the validity of drug trial evidence by examining studies that suggest that symptom control by neuroleptics is far from certain. One of the consequences of this is the use of higher doses of standard medication and the continuing search for better and 'different' major tranquillisers. These issues ultimately lead to the relationship between the medical profession (and psychiatrists) and the pharmacological industry, as well as the relationship between psychiatrist and patient on medication. But first it may be helpful if we consider the implications of long-term neuroleptic use.

Josie was in her mid-forties when she first came to see me. She had recently moved into the area from a town in the Midlands where she had lived for over twenty years, after she and her husband had come to England from the small town in County Limerick where she had spent her childhood. She was a tall, awkward lady whose angular movements had a peculiar jerkiness, reminiscent of the JCBs her husband had driven for many years. There was only a brief note from her GP saying that she was 'a known schizophrenic on depot neuroleptics', and asking me to take over her care. Over the next few weeks we got to know each other better as we met on three or four occasions. She told me that she had first started to hear voices shortly after the birth of her first child, in Ireland before she came here, following which she had her one and only admission to hospital. She had been put on injections then, and had remained on them ever since. The doctors in Ireland and the Midlands had told her that if she wanted to avoid further breakdowns she would need to remain on the injections for the rest of her life.

She told me that despite the medication she still heard voices. Perhaps they were not quite as troublesome as they had been when they first started, but, nevertheless, they were still there. I asked her to describe them to me. She told me that she usually heard the voices of her mother and a priest who had been in the village she was brought up in. She was never certain what the voices were saying, but she thought the priest was shouting at her, saying unpleasant things about her, and she could hear her mother crying. By now she had become accustomed to them and she had even developed some ways of dealing with them. If they were very troublesome they would sometimes go away if she switched the radio on. She often got up to make a cup of tea each time they started up, and this would sometimes stop them getting out of hand. Over the years she noticed that the voices would be very troublesome in a crowded room, such as a pub, and for this reason she rarely went out and spent most of the time looking after her children. By and large we agreed that she coped very well with these experiences. Her explanation for them was that they were 'part of the schizophrenia, doctor'.

The thing that concerned me was her medication. Each time she had seen a new doctor or psychiatrist, changes and additions had been made to her drugs, because, when asked, she said she still heard voices. Sadly, her doctors did not think to ask how she coped with the voices, and, even more sadly, she did not think to question the doctors about her medication. As a result she was on a combination of five different drugs. In addition to the high dose of injection (100 mg of depixol a week) she was on 10 mg of stelazine twice a day, 10 mg of kemadrin three times a day,

800 mg lithium carbonate at night and 20 mg temazepam at night. The stelazine has almost identical properties to depixol but is taken by mouth. The kemadrin was to counter the side-effects of stelazine and depixol. It was not clear why she was on lithium. Presumably one of her doctors had at one stage thought that she was suffering from a mood disorder, because lithium is widely used to treat severe depression and mania. The temazepam was to help her sleep at night.

She had been taking the depixol for twenty years or more and there was evidence that she was developing long-term side-effects. These took the form of unusual movements affecting her lips, tongue and lower jaw, which moved from side to side as her tongue protruded from her mouth. She told me that the movements had first appeared five years earlier, when she had asked her psychiatrist to reduce her depixol. At first she appeared unaware of the movements, but other people were not. Strangers avoided her and local children made fun of her. It was this that upset her more than anything. The movements were also starting to affect her arms and her back, which largely accounted for the peculiarly gauche way in which she moved and walked. She told me that when doctors in the past had tried to reduce the depixol, within six weeks both her voices and the movements would become much more severe, to the extent that she had been quite distressed by them. She did not know what the cause of the movements was, but thought that it had something to do with her medication. No one had ever discussed this with her.

This unfortunate lady's story is typical of that of thousands of people who have taken major tranquillisers for many years, and developed side-effects. At this point I want us to consider these side-effects in some detail.

SIDE-EFFECTS OF MAJOR TRANQUILLISERS

We can obtain a good idea of service users' experiences of major tranquillisers from the Rogers *et al.* (1993) study (see Introduction). More than 60% of respondents reported severe or very severe side-effects, although this figure must be set against over 57% who said that they found these drugs helpful. The major tranquillisers are complex compounds that have many different effects upon the central nervous system. We have seen that one property, their ability to block the neurotransmitter dopamine, has been widely linked to their therapeutic effect in schizophrenia, but they interfere with transmission in many neurotransmitter systems in the brain. There are two additional points to be made here. The first is that no two drugs are identical in terms of the neurotransmitter systems they interfere with. Second, there is an enormous range of *individual* responses to these drugs. These two factors make it very difficult to predict which drug will suit an individual best. In addition to this, there is much variation in the sensitivity of individuals to a given dose. For these reasons it may be very difficult to select the correct drug at the correct dose to produce an effective response with minimal side-effects. Like all drugs that have effects upon the central nervous system, the major tranquillisers also affect other parts of the body, causing low blood pressure, blurring of vision, dry mouth, constipation, interference with sexual function[1] and, occasionally, difficulty in passing water. The most significant side-effects for my purposes are those arising from effects on the central nervous system itself. I shall break these down into four types: movement disorders, muscle stiffness, restlessness, and others.

Movement disorders

It is customary to divide these into two groups: acute movement disorders which come on very soon after starting medication, and chronic movement disorders whose appearance may be delayed for many years. The acute movement disorders closely resemble Parkinson's disease, and for this reason they are sometimes referred to as drug-induced Parkinsonism. They include a generalised slowing down or reduction in the amount of movement, or bradykinesia. Affected individuals may appear slowed down, clumsy or stupid. They may not respond to things that are going on around them. There may be lengthy delays before they respond to questions. If severe the person may appear like a zombie, sitting immobile in a chair with a flat, vacant expression, not responding to things going on around him or her. Another common group of acute movement disorders are abnormal movements, or the dyskinesias. The most common of these is tremor, which is of course a common symptom of Parkinson's disease. The tremor may be barely perceptible,

---

1   These are particularly distressing, and are rarely discussed by doctors. They include difficulties in achieving and sustaining an erection, and failure of ejaculation in men.

or so severe that it may be impossible to write or hold a cup without spilling the contents. Such a symptom may be socially very disabling. Less common abnormal disturbances include writhing movements of the arms, or abnormal body posture which may be sustained for long periods of time unless action is taken. The common feature of this group of side-effects is that they come on rapidly after first starting major tranquillisers. There are three ways of dealing with them. Either the dose may be reduced, or the drug changed, or the person may be given an anti-Parkinsonian drug. These are widely used to treat Parkinson's disease and are also effective in the management of drug-induced Parkinsonism. Sadly this is not the case with the chronic movement disorders.

The most troublesome chronic movement disorder is tardive dyskinesia (TD). Its name refers to the fact that it is a movement disorder (dyskinesia) whose onset is delayed and appears many years after exposure to major tranquillisers (tardive), as was the case with Josie above. The movements appear gradually after many years of exposure to major tranquillisers. They consist of chewing and lip-smacking movements, facial grimacing, as well as movements of the tongue and jaw. These movements often become apparent when the medication is stopped or the dose reduced, and they may disappear again when the dose is increased back to its previous level. The problem with TD is that, once established, it is extremely difficult to treat, and sufferers are likely to show evidence of abnormal movements for the rest of their lives. What evidence is there to link the presence of TD to exposure to major tranquillisers?

There have always been plentiful descriptions in the psychiatric literature of neurological abnormalities in chronic psychiatric patients. Mettler and Crandell (1959) undertook a detailed epidemiological survey of neurological abnormalities in over 3000 residents of a state psychiatric hospital in the mid-1950s. They found a wide variety of neurological abnormalities, including movement disorders, but nothing resembling TD. It was seven or eight years after the introduction of the neuroleptics that descriptions of abnormal movements of the face started to appear in the literature. Crane (1968) commented that 90% of cases of TD had been reported after 1964 and that the majority of sufferers were people with chronic schizophrenia, especially those exposed to large amounts of physical treatments such as ECT, insulin coma therapy and leucotomies. His impression was that TD was brought about by exposure to large doses of drugs, but that increasing age also played a part. Kane and Smith (1982) reviewed over seventy early studies of

TD, and found that on average 20% of people exposed to long-term treatment with major tranquillisers had TD, compared with only 5% in untreated patients. Most authorities now accept that chronic exposure to major tranquillisers greatly increases the risk of developing TD. The person who articulated this view most clearly was the American psychiatrist Klawans (1973). Evidence in support of this came from a study by Smith *et al.* (1978) who found a significant association between TD and the total amount of fluphenazine (a major tranquilliser) in people over the age of fifty. Mukherjee *et al.* (1982) also found a significant association between TD and the use of high potency or depot preparations.

Although the exact mechanism of TD is not understood, it is thought to arise from changes in brain dopamine receptors brought about by prolonged exposure to major tranquillisers which reduce dopaminergic transmission. In Chapter 2 we saw that there were two main dopaminergic systems. The meso-limbic system is thought to be the site at which dopaminergic overactivity produces the acute symptoms of schizophrenia. Dopamine transmission also occurs in the striatum, an area concerned with the regulation of movements. Because these receptors are blocked, regulatory mechanisms attempt to overcome this by increasing both the numbers of receptors and their sensitivity to dopamine. When the dose of neuroleptic is reduced and dopamine blockade lifted, the effect of the increased number of supersensitive receptors is to increase the amount of dopaminergic transmission. It is thought that a consequence of this is increased dopamine activity in the areas responsible for the control of movement, causing the abnormal movements affecting the face. This explains why the symptoms usually become apparent when the dose is reduced. But there is more. One factor known for some time to be associated with TD is dementia, the organically determined illness caused by destruction and loss of brain cells. This results in poor memory, confusion, disorientation and a reduction in the capacity for new learning. There is evidence that prolonged exposure to neuroleptic medication is associated with more serious interference with brain function resulting in dementia. Famuyiwa *et al.* (1979) found that people with schizophrenia and TD performed less well on a test of new learning than those who did not have TD. There was no evidence that this was associated with brain atrophy on brain scan. Some years ago Ralph McGuire and I examined the relationship between TD, memory impairment and medication in a group of forty-three people institutionalised for many years with schizophrenia, or serious personality disorders (Thomas and McGuire, 1986). We estimated the total lifetime dose of major tranquilliser by going through their records in detail, noting how long they had received medication and at what dose. The best predictors of TD score were the subject's age and the total amount of medication he or she had received. These relationships were largely independent of each other, indicating that the total dose of medication predicted TD score independently of its obvious relationship with age. Subjects with high TD scores also showed evidence of memory impairment.

Sadly, TD is generally irreversible. Once it has started there is no really successful way of controlling it. Movements often become worse as the dose of neuroleptic is reduced. The condition constitutes a serious hazard associated with the prolonged use of neuroleptics. In America psychiatrists are now facing law suits filed by patients whose lives have been seriously affected by the condition, and the associated intellectual impairments. We might have expected that the severity of this side-effect would result in psychiatrists becoming cautious about the long-term use of neuroleptics. This does not appear to be the case. As we shall see there has been an identifiable trend towards the use of even higher doses of these powerful drugs, and for longer periods of time. The use of extremely high doses is associated with an even more serious risk, that of sudden death. But before we turn our attention to this, there are other serious and distressing side-effects associated with the use of neuroleptics.

Akathesia

One of the commonest acute problems associated with the use of the neuroleptics is akathesia. It may affect up to 20% of people on neuroleptics (Braude et al., 1983). This is an intensely distressing sensation of restlessness and inability to keep still. When it occurs the affected individual feels compelled to get up and walk around. Usually it comes on shortly after starting medication, but occasionally it becomes apparent when the person has been on medication for some time, and the dose has been changed. Paradoxically, this may even occur when the dose has been reduced. The symptom mimics agitation, and so the psychiatrist may be fooled into thinking that the person is experiencing a deterioration in mental state. If this happens the doctor may increase the dose of medication, making the symptom even worse. Usually, akathesia responds well either to a dose reduction, or to the addition of an anti-Parkinsonian drug. Sometimes the symptom may be so severe that individuals feel that something must be done to rid themselves of this intensely distressing symptom, even to the extent of suicide.

It has been recognised for many years that severe depression can occur in people receiving depot neuroleptic medication (De Alarcon and Carney, 1969). There have also been reports that the suicide rate in people suffering from schizophrenia may be up to fifty times greater than that expected in the general population (Markowe et al., 1967). A number of explanations have been put forward to account for this. A popular explanation is that the patient must be acting under the instruction of hallucinations, or has decided that life with schizophrenia is not worth living. What is less widely appreciated is that sudden suicide may occur as a result of akathesia and the intense dysphoria[2] that is sometimes associated with it. Singh (1976) was one of the first to point out that dysphoria could arise from treatment with neuroleptics. He noticed that its presence was associated with a less favourable response to treatment, both in the short and long term. Drake and Ehrlich (1985) reported two cases of impulsive suicide attempts associated with akathesia. Suicidal ideation in both cases appeared concurrently with akathesia and went when the akathesia was treated. We have no way of knowing what proportion of suicides in people taking neuroleptics arises as a result of this side-effect, but there is no doubt that it is responsible in a number of cases.

It is worth my commenting briefly here on my own experience of taking neuroleptic medication. Some months ago I took 5 mg of haloperidol as part of an experiment run by my colleague, David Healy, into the effects of neuroleptic medication on psychological performance in 'normal' subjects. The experiment ran for about two hours, during the course of which I had to sit in front of a computer to perform some simple tests of attention and concentration. After an hour I felt terrible. The last thing I wanted to be doing was to be seated in front of that computer. Although I did not feel suicidal, I felt restless inside, as if I could not settle. On several occasions I had to get up to walk around. If I had not done so I don't know what would have happened. On two or three occasions I came close to putting my fist through the screen, because I was so intensely frustrated and bored with what was going on. This sensation was a real physical sensation located somewhere

---

2 Dysphoria is an extremely unpleasant and distressing subjective change in mood. This may have features of severe anxiety and agitation, as well as depression and irritability.

in the pit of my stomach. I felt irritated by everything that was going on at the time. The feeling persisted well into the next day, to the extent that I found it difficult to concentrate at work.

Neuroleptic-induced deficit syndrome

One of the most distressing side-effects of neuroleptic medication is the feeling of apathy and disinterest these drugs can induce. This problem occurs to a greater or lesser extent in the majority of people who take them. Since the earliest days pharmacologists have recognised a neuroleptic syndrome in animals and humans consisting of disinterest, emotional apathy, lack of initiative and a slowing of thought processes. These changes are just as apparent in healthy volunteer subjects as they are in people suffering from schizophrenia (see for example Dimascio *et al.*, 1963; Magliozzin *et al.*, 1989). These side-effects may be so unpleasant that they may be one reason (of many) for people deciding not to take their medication. Van Putten (1974) estimated that up to 45% of people suffering from schizophrenia failed to take their medication. One recent study (Windgassen, 1991) found that distressing subjective side-effects, including akathesia, dysphoria and emotional flattening, occurred in 47% of patients taking neuroleptics. Others such as Hermanzohn and Siris (1992) have suggested that depression, Parkinsonism and negative symptoms may be related, the common underlying feature being a reduction in dopamine turnover in the brain. There is evidence that both Parkinson's disease and some forms of severe depression may be related to a reduction in the amount of dopamine activity in certain areas of the brain.

You will probably already have noticed that the list of symptoms above, which included emotional apathy, was familiar. They are remarkably similar to the description of negative symptoms of schizophrenia we encountered in Chapter 1. Lewander (1994) has compared these side-effects of neuroleptics with negative symptoms. In fact the two are so similar that they are almost impossible to distinguish. Schooler (1994) has also pointed out that such descriptions are identical to those of negative symptoms. For this reason, when they are thought to be caused by neuroleptics, they are sometimes referred to as the neuroleptic-induced deficit syndrome (NIDS). Table 6.1 compares NIDS and negative symptoms.

As Lewander points out, the existence of NIDS and its similarity with the negative symptom syndrome in schizophrenia requires

Table 6.1: Side-effects of neuroleptic medication and negative symptoms

	Symptom	
Psychological	**Neuroleptic Side-effect**	**Negative Symptom**
Vigilance	Drowsiness	Attentional impairment
'Will'	Apathy Lack of energy 'Weak, tired'	Apathy Lack of purpose
Mood	Flat affect Indifference	Affective blunting Restrictive affect
Emotional responsiveness	Lack of feeling Dysphoria 'Dead inside'	Reduced emotional range
Motivation	Reduced drive Reduced initiative	Asociality Reduced curiosity

Source: Lewander (1994)

further investigation. In one recent study, Johnson *et al.* (1994) found that the dose of neuroleptic medication was significantly related to the total score for negative symptoms, whereas there was no relationship with positive symptom score. This suggests that negative symptoms may be induced by neuroleptics. The point here is that although the presence of negative symptoms has long been associated with poor prognosis schizophrenia, we cannot assume that their presence in a particular individual means that that person will have a poor outcome. The evolution of negative symptoms and their relationship to the course of schizophrenia is extremely complicated. Some people present with negative symptoms early in the illness. In some of these individuals the negative symptoms are not present at later stages. Other people show no evidence of negative symptoms in the early stages, but develop them later on. It is misleading to assume that their presence is an integral feature of schizophrenia. It seems likely that in a number of people neuroleptic medication may be the main determinant of negative symptoms (a full discussion of these issues is presented by Somers in her 1985 paper). We require a better understanding of the relationship between negative symptoms and NIDS, depression and other drug-induced side-effects of neuroleptics before we can assume that what appear to be negative symptoms are just that.

SYMPTOM CONTROL AND OUTCOME

In Chapter 4 we found that research indicates that 60–80% of subjects whose symptoms are controlled by depot neuroleptics experience a relapse and hospitalisation if medication is discontinued. Such evidence provides strong support for the role of neuroleptics in the long-term management of schizophrenia. Those who stop taking their medication appear to be at a much higher risk of re-hospitalisation. The difficulty is that there is also much evidence that medication fails to help many people diagnosed with schizophrenia. There are four issues at stake here. The first concerns the efficacy of neuroleptics in controlling positive symptoms of schizophrenia. The second concerns their claimed effect in favourably changing the long-term outcome of schizophrenia. The third concerns the validity of this evidence, much of it drawn from specially designed research protocols (drug trials), in relation to the reality of the day-to-day practice of psychiatry. Finally, and most worrying of all, there is evidence that relapse, should it occur, arises through a supersensitivity reaction similar to that thought to be responsible for TD.

Despite the euphoria in the years following the introduction of the neuroleptics, there were early reports of people whose symptoms did not respond to these drugs. Davis and Caspar (1977) noticed that 25% of people continued to have psychotic symptoms despite taking neuroleptics. The persistence of their symptoms was not explained by the presence of physical health problems that might cause them to be suffering from organic brain disorders.

Davis et al. (1980) reviewed a large database of clinical trial data from the 1960s generated by the National Institute of Mental Health Psychopharmacology Research Branch in the USA. About 30% of subjects in these studies were rated as either minimally improved or clinically worse, following treatment with neuroleptics. Kane et al. (1988) suggested that a conservative estimate indicates that the symptoms of one-fifth of all patients suffering from schizophrenia fail to respond to neuroleptic drugs. The most striking evidence of a group of people whose psychotic symptoms failed to respond to neuroleptic medication came from a British study. Curson et al. (1988) were interested in examining the characteristics of people who remained on long-stay wards. They pointed out that over the previous thirty years the move to close the old asylums had concentrated on the least disabled residents, leaving behind those with the most serious impairments. This, they argued, had serious implications for the proposal to end asylum care by discharging these people into the community. They examined the symptoms of a group of 222 long-stay patients diagnosed with schizophrenia, using a standard psychiatric rating scale to provide detailed measures of psychiatric symptoms. A few subjects were too ill to participate in the study, so they had full data on almost 200 subjects. They found that 46% had persistent delusions, and 32% had persistent auditory hallucinations. The important point to remember here is that this was a group of people who had been and were still being exposed to what the authors described as 'energetic pharmacological ... treatments'. Many psychiatrists will of course point out that this was a highly selective group of patients with the most severe forms of schizophrenia. This is obviously the case, for if they had no symptoms these patients would presumably have been discharged from hospital years before. Whilst it is true that we can draw no conclusions from this study about the frequency of non-response to medication in all people suffering from schizophrenia, this is not the point. This study, like the Davis and Caspar paper, indicates that some people with the condition do not respond to neuroleptic medication. This has a number of important implications. First, it is yet another nail in the coffin of the dopamine theory. If the symptoms of all people suffering from schizophrenia were due to increased dopamine activity, then we would not expect to find any 'non-responders'. And why is it that these people are described as non-responders anyway? It would be more sensible to say that these people cannot be suffering from schizophrenia.

In general, psychiatrists, prompted by the pharmacological industry, have believed that maintenance medication taken for many years has a beneficial effect not only by controlling positive symptoms, but also through improving social function. Claims have been made that this helps to prevent deterioration, the hallmark of poor prognosis Kraepelinian schizophrenia. In Chapter 4 we saw that Wyatt's (1991) work reviewed data from over twenty different studies in which some people had taken medication early in their illnesses, and others had not. Wyatt concluded that the results of these studies supported the idea that continued use of medication improved social functioning. The problem is that there is conflicting evidence and a number of authorities disagree. Ciompi, whose work we examined in the same chapter, was also interested in the extent to which neuroleptic medication influenced the course of schizophrenia. In his study (Ciompi, 1980) he divided his subjects into three groups by date of first admission, corresponding to the period prior to the introduction of ECT (pre-1933), the period prior to the introduction of the neuroleptics (1933–53), and the period following the introduction of neuroleptics (post-1953). If neuroleptics have a beneficial effect on outcome, then we would expect the latter group of people to fare better. Ciompi was surprised and disappointed to find that over very long periods of observation, no statistically significant differences could be found in outcomes of people admitted in these different therapeutic eras. He concluded that people admitted with schizophrenia in the 1950s, following the introduction of neuroleptics, did no better in terms of social adjustment than those admitted in the first three decades of the century. There were of course serious weaknesses with Ciompi's study, but there is other evidence that casts doubt on the belief that these drugs improve long-term outcome.

Kane and Freeman (1994) have reviewed the advantages and drawbacks of neuroleptic treatment. They make the point that a number of authorities have doubted whether neuroleptics have a beneficial effect on outcome: '... it remains debatable whether or not long-term neuroleptic treatment substantially alters the course and outcome of this disorder ...' (Kane and Freeman, 1994, p. 22). Karl Leonhard in Munich was critical of psychiatrists for blindly following the Kraepelinian concept of schizophrenia, which resulted in anyone who experienced delusions or hallucinations being placed on long-term neuroleptic medication, in the hope that the drug would prevent 'deterioration'. He argued (Leonhard, 1980) that psychiatrists should only consider using such therapy once it was established without doubt that the condition from which the individual was suffering was a *phasic* disorder, that is a condition characterised by recurrent episodes of positive, or other acute psychotic symptoms. This was based on his view that such a symptom pattern tended to respond to neuroleptics, whereas the defect state did not. Schooler (1991), in her study of dose reduction, commented that the results of *naturalistic* long-term follow-up studies in schizophrenia show clearly the great diversity of outcomes of the condition. Despite long-term medication, some people appear to have a very poor outcome. On the other hand, some people do very well with little or no medication.

The evidence reviewed so far is in conflict with widely accepted teaching about the value of medication. Why is this so? Perhaps one clue is to be found in the adjective *naturalistic* used by Schooler. The use of italics emphasises the importance of this word, because she is referring to an important distinction between two types of studies as far as assessing the effectiveness of neuroleptic medication is concerned. In Chapter 4 we saw that the drug trial was the standard way in which the pharmacological industry, in collaboration with the medical profession, assessed the effectiveness of new drugs. Such studies follow rigid procedures taking the form of a strict protocol with criteria for patient selection and assessment. They also include procedures for ensuring that both patients and the research staff who make assessments are unaware of which medication is being taken. These studies therefore involve specially selected patients who undergo detailed research assessments, made by specially employed research staff. They are expensive to run, and for this reason usually only take place over relatively short periods of time, varying from several weeks to several months. Such studies can hardly be regarded as *naturalistic*. I take this word to indicate the extent to which a study is representative of the day-to-day use of these drugs in real clinical practice, as you might encounter if you followed a typical psychiatrist around in the community, out-patient clinics and in-patient units, over the course of a year or so.

The most naturalistic study in this sense was undertaken by Johnstone *et al.* (1986) working at Northwick Park in London. This study was designed to answer a number of important questions about the nature and management of first-episode schizophrenia in a busy urban setting. They recruited patients admitted to hospital with a first-episode psychotic illness. Patients were under the care of forty psychiatrists working within a thirty-five-mile radius of Harrow. Over 460 patients met the criteria for inclusion in the study over a period of almost two and a half years, yet 14% of these patients could not be assessed for a number of reasons. These included refusal of either patient or consultant to consent to study, self-discharge before assessment could be made, administrative problems such as patient not admitted, or 'conversation' barriers. These problems are typical of those commonly encountered by psychiatrists in their day-to-day work. Of the patients who could be assessed, almost 55% fulfilled the criteria for first-episode schizophrenia, and of these, only 120 (47% of the 55%) could be entered into a randomised placebo-controlled drug trial of maintenance neuroleptic medication (Crow *et al.*, 1986). They found surprisingly high rates of relapse in the two years following discharge both in the placebo group and, surprisingly, in the group who received active medication. Although 70% of patients on placebo relapsed, 58% of those taking active medication did so over the same period. Overall these results suggest that, at best, the benefits of neuroleptic medication in preventing relapse are marginal. This brings to mind George Brown *et al.*'s (1972) study of expressed emotion, in which 46% of patients on medication in high expressed-emotion homes relapsed over a twelve-month period.

These studies suggest that, although neuroleptic medication may be effective in the short-term control of psychotic symptoms, its value in preventing relapse or improving outcome in the long term is much less clear. In addition to this, 25–50% of patients on these drugs continue to experience symptoms including hallucinations and delusions. The situation is summarised well by Kane and Freeman (1994):

> Thus, current neuroleptics, despite their great value in controlling schizophrenic symptoms, have a number of major drawbacks. They are far from consistently effective, and a substantial subgroup of patients derive little if any benefit from them. They remain ineffective against negative symptoms. They cause adverse neurological effects which may interfere with psychosocial and vocational rehabilitation and are associated with major problems of drug compliance. (p. 29)

It is worth pausing at this point to consider an important assumption present in much of the research that we have considered here. When psychiatrists talk about the relationship between relapse and discontinuation of neuroleptic medication, the relapse has always been viewed as a function of the illness process which, in some way or another, was being dampened down or held at bay by medication. Nobody has ever produced a satisfactory explanation of how this might happen. But there are psychopharmacological models that can explain the appearance of abnormal mental states following discontinuation of drugs. Most people are familiar with accounts of what happens when someone stops minor tranquillisers after taking them for any length of time. In such circumstances minor withdrawal symptoms such as anxiety, insomnia and mild depression are very common. Similar, but more severe, disturbances occur after stopping alcohol or barbiturates, when hallucinations and delusions are not uncommon. Withdrawal states such as these are usually rapid in onset, and start almost immediately on stopping the drug. Given the fact that most psychiatrists are familiar with this scenario – the appearance of a disordered mental state in response to the discontinuation of a drug that has powerful effects on the brain – it is perhaps surprising that this model has not been proposed as an explanation for the relationship between the reappearance of psychotic symptoms on stopping neuroleptics. To put it more directly, under some circumstances, could the 'relapse' of schizophrenic symptoms on stopping neuroleptics in reality be a neuroleptic withdrawal syndrome rather than a true relapse of the illness? The model of tardive dyskinesia is pertinent here. This condition is thought to arise because of an increased number and sensitivity of dopamine receptors in the striatum. Presumably there is no reason why such a mechanism should not occur in the meso-limbic system, the pathway thought to be important in relation to the symptoms of acute schizophrenia. If this is so, then reduction or cessation of neuroleptic medication in the presence of increased receptor sensitivity in this area should result in a relative increase in dopaminergic transmission in this system with the appearance of acute psychotic symptoms. In these circumstances the occurrence of 'relapse' is hardly an intrinsic feature of the disease process, but an iatrogenic (brought about by medical intervention) phenomenon arising as a consequence of the effects of dopaminergic blocking agents on the brain.

There is evidence that this indeed may be the case. In 1980, Chouinard and Jones published a paper in the *American Journal of Psychiatry*, which, in its day, was widely quoted as evidence in support of the dopamine theory of schizophrenia. In it, they described in detail the drug treatment histories of ten patients treated with neuroleptic drugs. In each case a recurrence of psychotic symptoms was noticed almost immediately following reduction or discontinuation of medication. This runs contrary to expectation. There is nothing in our knowledge of the course of schizophrenia that would lead us to expect a sudden reappearance of symptoms on discontinuing medication. All the subjects had had lengthy periods of exposure to neuroleptics, and in addition, most had evidence of tardive dyskinesia. As with Josie, whose story started this chapter, the dyskinesia became more apparent on discontinuation of medication, and with the appearance of psychotic symptoms. The authors note that:

An implication of neuroleptic-induced mesolimbic supersensitivity is that the tendency toward psychotic relapse in such patients is determined by more than just the normal course of the illness.
(Chouinard and Jones, 1980, p. 16)

Further evidence in support of the supersensitivity psychosis comes from one of the most thorough reviews of neuroleptic withdrawal ever made. Gilbert *et al.* (1995) reviewed sixty-six studies of neuroleptic withdrawal in schizophrenia involving over 4000 patients. She found that amongst other things, 'relapse'[3] was more likely to occur in people who had been taking higher doses of neuroleptic medication prior to discontinuation, or in people who had experienced rapid discontinuation (over two weeks) as opposed to gradual discontinuation (over eight weeks). These are exactly the features we might expect to find in a disturbance that occurs simply as part of a drug withdrawal state. Severe alcohol withdrawal symptoms are much more likely to occur in people who have been drinking very heavily (higher dose) or who stop drinking rapidly. Further evidence comes from a commentary on Gilbert's review by Baldessarini and Viguera (1995) in which they compared the outcome in neuroleptic withdrawal studies in schizophrenia with that of withdrawal studies in affective disorder. Baldessarini and Viguera point out that the clinical states observed in relapses following neuroleptic withdrawal in affective disorder are not identical to those seen during the natural course of the condition. This suggests that what they call pharmacological stress factors may follow neuroleptic withdrawal, especially if the withdrawal has been abrupt. In other words, in affective disorders there is some evidence to support the view that disturbances occurring after neuroleptic discontinuation may be regarded as drug withdrawal states, and not simply the re-emergence of the disease. They suggest that some of the evidence revealed in the Gilbert review in schizophrenia is consistent with such an explanation.

The difficulty here is that so far, no research study has seriously addressed the possibility that symptom recurrence in schizophrenia on stopping neuroleptics is effectively a drug withdrawal syndrome. To examine this possibility one would have to examine the symptoms of a large number of people in their first episodes of schizophrenia, and then compare these symptoms in great detail with those seen in the same people after discontinuing neuroleptics. Such a study has yet to be performed. It is interesting to note how the drug withdrawal explanation for 'relapse' has been overwhelm-

---

3   There are enormous difficulties in undertaking a study such as this. For example, there are different ways of defining relapse. For some people, relapse is defined simply as the reappearance of psychotic symptoms. For others, it is necessary for the patient to be readmitted to hospital. This makes it very difficult to compare the outcome in different studies.

ingly neglected in the psychiatric literature. Descriptions of drug withdrawal states dominate clinical accounts of the effects of psychoactive drugs and substances. All doctors are familiar with the phenomenon of drug withdrawal syndrome, and although Chouinard's work has been in the literature for sixteen years, this explanation for the link between relapse and medication has been glossed over. The implications of this are too frightening for psychiatry to contemplate. It means that for many patients, 'relapse' may be iatrogenic, a consequence of drug treatment and not an inevitable part of the process of a disease.

UPPING THE STAKES

Earlier we considered a study by Curson *et al.* (1988), in which all the patients had been taking medication, largely by injection and under direct hospital supervision, for many years. Despite this, almost 50% continued to experience active and severe symptoms. What are the consequences of this? Most psychiatrists regard schizophrenia as a brain disease caused by increased dopamine activity in certain areas of the brain. This belief is the justification for the treatment of the condition by neuroleptics. If an individual patient fails to respond to medication it is tempting to increase the dose. Indeed, in the standard guide to drug treatment, the *British National Formulary* (BNF), which lays down guidelines and advice to doctors on the use of all drugs, the maximum safe daily dose for neuroleptic drugs is often not clearly defined. This means that there is a temptation for psychiatrists to go on increasing the dose to heroic levels in an attempt to control symptoms, if this has not happened in response to conventional doses. Another possibility is that the patient may be placed on a combination of two or more neuroleptic drugs. This has the same effect as using so-called 'mega-doses'. There has been considerable anxiety lately, both outside the profession and within, because of the considerable risks associated with the use of medication in this way.

There have been recent reports of sudden death in young people treated with very high doses of neuroleptic medication. These include a report from the USA by Simpson *et al.* (1987; quoted in Thompson, 1994), and one from Finland by Mehtonen *et al.* (1991). The latter study not only showed an association between sudden death and high doses of neuroleptics, but also found a small association between sudden death and routine doses of thioridazine. In the UK there have been thirteen reports of sudden death in patients on pimozide (a neuroleptic) to the Committee on the Safety of Medicines (CSM).[4] In response to this the CSM (1990) recommended that the maximum safe dose of this drug should be reduced from 60 mg to 20 mg a day. We do not know what caused these deaths, but it is thought that they occurred because of the effects that these drugs have on the heart. We know that they can influence the conduction of electrical activity responsible for regulating the contraction of heart muscle fibres. They are also known to cause a dramatic fall in blood pressure, as well as depressing activity in the brain centres which regulate breathing. In addition to this, there have even been reports that the use of very high doses of medication has been associated with violent behaviour (Barnes and Bridges, 1980 and Herrera *et al.*, 1988; both reported in Thompson, 1994). In such circumstances the temptation is for the psychiatrist to increase the dose even higher in an attempt to control violent behaviour caused by high doses of medication in the first place.

Concern about the use of high doses of neuroleptic medication has focused on two areas in particular. Many psychiatrists and psychiatric nurses working in in-patient units feel that the conditions found in these units contribute to the need to use high doses of medication. Particularly important here is the number of trained nursing staff on duty. It is self-evident that on well-staffed units nurses feel more confident about their ability to deal with the difficult circumstances which may occasionally arise. My own experience indicates that junior doctors are called more frequently by nursing staff to sedate or tranquillise difficult patients when there are fewer staff on duty. The second worry concerns the use of high doses of medication in particular groups, particularly young Afro-Caribbean men. This has almost certainly contributed to the sudden death of a number of young black men in hospitals over the last ten years. In 1991 Orville Blackwood died of heart failure after being forcibly injected with a combination of promazine (a neuroleptic drug similar to chlorpromazine) and fluphenazine decanoate (a widely used depot neuroleptic, also called modecate). The dose of both drugs was over the maximum level recommended

---

4   The Committee on the Safety of Medicines is the statutory organisation which monitors the safety of all drugs in Britain. All doctors must report adverse or untoward side-effects, or sudden death of patients taking medication on 'yellow' forms. This enables the CSM to monitor risks associated with particular drugs.

by the BNF. This was the third death involving Afro-Caribbean males given large doses of neuroleptic drugs in special hospitals. An inquiry (Special Hospital Service Authority, 1993) suggested that the use of powerful drugs in this way reflected crude stereotypes that black men were potentially dangerous. White health professionals often find it difficult to conceal the fact that they perceive young black men as 'dangerous' or 'violent', and it is for this reason that this group is liable to receive higher doses of neuroleptic medication.

In an attempt to allay fears about the misuse of medication in this way, the Royal College of Psychiatrists established a panel of experts in 1992 to consider the use of high doses of neuroleptic medication and to produce a statement about the use of medication in this way (Thompson, 1994). The panel reviewed evidence concerning the effectiveness of so-called 'mega-dose' treatment for people whose psychotic symptoms had failed to respond to conventional doses. They examined eight studies which compared the use of high doses with conventional doses. None of the studies showed that high-dose regimes conveyed any benefits in terms of control of symptoms. In many cases all that was required was a longer period of time on lower doses. Despite this, the use of mega-doses of medication persists. Surely the fact that the symptoms of 25–50% of people with schizophrenia fail to respond to medication would raise doubts about the validity of a disease concept of schizophrenia, predicated on the notion that symptoms arise from increased dopamine activity which is supposedly reduced by neuroleptics. This is obviously not the case. Many psychiatrists are committed to the belief that schizophrenia is a brain disease, so if your symptoms don't respond to medication the dose must be increased. The response of the pharmaceutical industry to 'non-responders' is to pursue new, better, more selective and more expensive neuroleptic drugs.

A young person presents to a psychiatrist in a confused and frightened state of mind. Perhaps he has doubts about his sexual identity. Perhaps he has been sexually abused. He hears voices, experiences that we know from the last chapter may occur in people who have had these experiences. But he is *not* suffering from schizophrenia. Despite this, the psychiatrist concludes that this is what is wrong with him and so starts him on neuroleptic drugs. His symptoms fail to respond. The psychiatrist increases the dose. The young man becomes strapped to a wheel of fate, each revolution of which binds him ever more tightly to a self-fulfilling prophecy, because whenever attempts are made to reduce the dose of medication, a withdrawal state is induced, in which he manifests further abnormal experiences (intensification of anxiety, intensification of voices and so on) which are interpreted by the psychiatrist as a relapse of schizophrenia. There is no way out of this situation. He is told that he must stay on medication for longer and longer periods because of the 'dangers of relapse'. The longer he stays on medication, the more likely he is to experience 'relapse' if the dose is reduced. When this happens the psychiatrist's opinion that his patient is a schizophrenic in need of long-term maintenance is simply reinforced. Under these circumstances the truth will never out, a situation which David Healy and I (Healy *et al.*, 1997) have likened to that which exists between abuser and victim.

AN UNHOLY GRAIL

Over the last ten years the pharmaceutical industry has marketed a series of 'new' neuroleptic drugs, such as clozaril and risperidone. These developments have been driven by a number of factors, including the fact that significant numbers of patients appear not to respond to conventional neuroleptic medication. Another important factor is a change in the nature of psychiatry itself, an important theme which we shall examine in the next two chapters. Of greatest importance, though, is the relationship between the medical profession and the pharmaceutical industry. It is this that I want finally to examine. There is a popular and romantic view that sees scientific discovery and progress arising out of the selfless and dedicated efforts of women and men who undertake painstaking work in the laboratory. In doing so they follow a tradition that is hundreds of years old: observation and description, theory formation, hypothesis formation, experimentation and measurement. The purpose of this approach is to establish whether the facts observed in experiments fit the hypothesis. If not, the hypothesis must be rejected or modified, and a new set of experiments established to test the modified or new hypothesis. The reality is quite different, for if this is indeed what happened, the dopamine theory of schizophrenia would have been thrown out years ago. We have seen that there is no convincing evidence to support it. There is no evidence that the chemical breakdown products of dopamine are increased in the brains of people diagnosed with schizophrenia. Nor is there unequivocal evidence that dopamine transmission is actually increased, using the latest generation of brain imaging techniques. This is not surprising when we find that not everybody who has positive symptoms responds to neuroleptics. Is there not sufficient evidence here to reject the dopamine theory and start searching for something which fits the observations better? Apparently not. Rather than throw the theory out because of lack of support, we saw in Chapter 2 that it is continually elaborated and modified. We are now presented with descriptions of different varieties of dopamine receptors (D_1, D_2, D_3 and D_4), each of which may have special significance in relation to schizophrenia. David Healy (1991) has argued that there are two ways of looking at these developments. Either they represent genuine attempts to further our understanding of the biology of schizophrenia, or they represent attempts to salvage a disreputable theory. Why is it that rather than ditch the theory altogether, pharmacologists and psychiatrists continually modify it and refine it? To find out why this is the case we must examine the relationship between the pharmaceutical industry and psychiatry.

For some years Healy has questioned the scientific and objective basis of much research into psychopharmacology.[5] In doing so he points out that the influence of cultural and political factors on scientific developments in psychiatry is widely neglected (Healy, 1990a). The first thing we must understand is that the discovery that chlorpromazine, the first neuroleptic, was useful in psychosis was entirely serendipitous. Once it was established that the drug appeared to have an effect on the symptoms of psychosis, the marketing side of the industry took over, and its anti-psychotic effect was trumpeted. It was only some years later that laboratory work established that one of many effects that chlorpromazine had on the brain was dopamine blockade, and only years after this that the strength of this effect was related to the potency of the drug as an anti-psychotic agent. Popular conceptions of science might lead us to expect that these events occurred in reverse order: that the introduction of the neuroleptics followed years of laboratory research in which the dopamine theory of schizophrenia was explicated. In his book *The*

---

5   Psychopharmacology is that branch of pharmacology concerned with the effects that drugs have upon the mind. David Healy makes a particularly important point when he says that psychopharmacology is more concerned with effects of drugs on the *brain*. He argues that much confusion about the effects of drugs would be cleared up if we did in fact pay serious attention to how drugs affected the mind, phenomenology, or individual subjective experience.

Suspended Revolution, Healy (1990b) points out that there are many gaps in our understanding of the causation of schizophrenia, gaps which have been exploited by the pharmacological industry. Nowhere is this more clearly shown than in the response of the industry to the fact that significant numbers of people diagnosed schizophrenic gain little or no benefit from neuroleptics. If psychiatry was a rational science, such observations would spawn intensive investigations to find out why this was so. Instead we witness the pursuit of newer, 'better', 'more selective' neuroleptics such as clozapine, marketed specifically at so-called 'non-responders'. Psychiatry is clearly not rational in the scientific sense, or at least its interface with the pharmacological industry is not. But looked at from a different angle, that of the market and profit, the relationship is highly rational. Healy (1990a) points out that there are many instances where clinical experience in the use of psychotropic drugs appears directly to contradict the theoretical assumptions on which the use of the drug in question is predicated. For example, there is evidence that antidepressant drugs are effective in hypomania, just as ECT has been used to treat both very severe forms of depression and hypomania. But because popular psychiatric opinion holds that antidepressants can *cause* hypomania, the pharmaceutical industry refused to fund a study to investigate the anti-manic properties of antidepressants. Such a study might have had fatal implications for the predominant biochemical theories of mood disorders, which, in turn, might have had negative effects upon the industry's marketing strategies, ultimately placing profits at risk. Here, the motivation for the industry is clear: money. David Healy's analysis is an important one in that it lays open the extent to which commercial, financial and ultimately political factors have a powerful effect on what is supposed to be a scientific domain. I shall examine some aspects of this in the next two chapters. But there is something missing from his analysis, and that concerns psychiatrists' motivation, for there is no doubt that the pharmacological industry and the profession of psychiatry have an intimate relationship. In its *Twenty-second Annual Report*, the Royal College of Psychiatrists (1995) acknowledged the support of a number of organisations which had helped sponsor meetings, campaigns and other activities. Over two-thirds of the organisations cited were drug companies. The college is less clear about the total amount of funding it receives from them.

David Healy (1991) also argues that during the twentieth century, psychiatry has lost contact with its most powerful tool, phenomenology.[6] The flowering of psychiatry towards the end of the nineteenth century was based upon an approach which sought to establish the exact nature of subjective experience with great precision. The driving force behind this came from psychoanalysis, early psychology – especially that of Wundt and the introspectionists – and philosophy. As biological science came to dominate psychiatry, particularly in the latter half of the twentieth century, phenomenology withered and all but disappeared. As we shall see, I believe that our interest in the nature of experience, let alone our attempts to understand it, has become subservient to the needs of biological psychiatry, for 'quick fix' ways of measuring aspects of subjective experience that are regarded simply as symptoms, which are merely the targets of control by drugs. Before I can develop these ideas, there is an important element missing from this critical examination of psychiatry, and that is its relationship to the society and culture within which it is embedded. My argument is that it is impossible to understand the true significance of recent developments and trends within psychiatry, especially the move to what is widely called neuroscience, without considering the nature of recent political changes in our society.

---

6   Strictly speaking, phenomenology is that branch of philosophy concerned with the description of experience. The German philosopher Edmund Husserl used the term 'descriptive psychology'. This approach had a great influence on German psychiatrists at the end of the nineteenth and early twentieth centuries, as witnessed by the work of Karl Jaspers, whose book *General Psychopathology* (1963) is an influential synthesis of psychiatric symptoms and phenomenology.

7 The Tower of Babel I:
On Individuals or Societies

There is no such thing as Society. There are individual men
and women, and there are families.
(Margaret Thatcher, *Woman's Own*, 31 October 1987)

In Chapter 2 we found epidemiological evidence that schizophrenia
appears to be more common in people from the lower socio-
economic groups, and more common in the centre of large cities.
Two theories have been proposed to explain this. The 'breeder'
hypothesis holds that the circumstances of the lives of poor, working-class people living in the inner city are associated with high
levels of stress, and it is this that is responsible for causing schizophrenia in 'vulnerable' (that is genetically predisposed) individuals.
This is a good example of the so-called 'diathesis-stress' model of
mental illness. The occurrence of mental illness is to be understood in terms of an interaction between environmental (stress)
and individual factors. On the other hand, the 'drift' hypothesis
holds that the apparent concentration of people with schizophrenia
in the inner-city areas is an artefact, brought about by the drift of
people suffering from schizophrenia into these areas from outlying
ones. Such a view goes hand in glove with the Kraepelinian view of
schizophrenia as an illness with a poor prognosis which leads to
intellectual and social deterioration. The problem is, as I argued in
Chapter 5, that the Kraepelinian understanding of schizophrenia
has been applied uncritically in British psychiatry. We also know
from Richard Warner's work (1985), discussed in Chapter 3, that
economic and cultural factors have an important influence on the
outcome of the condition. These arguments about the nature of
schizophrenia require contextualisation – we must understand their
significance in relation to the society in which we act. In this
chapter, I want to reconsider the nature of schizophrenia and so-
called 'deterioration' in the light of its relationship with poverty.
First, I want to examine the links between unemployment, poverty,
and homelessness with mental illness in general and schizophrenia

in particular. From there, I want to step back to examine the relationship between our health and our living conditions, before finally setting this within the context of recent social and political changes. Finally, I want to juxtapose these issues against recent changes in the nature of psychiatric discourse.

There was something about Betty that made her stick out from the crowd. She was familiar to everybody who lived in the bleak streets cowering in the shadow of the urban motorway. Her slight figure with its jerky, bird-like movements was often to be seen scurrying from her third-floor flat to the nearby shop. She had moved there two years before, after a long admission to a large mental hospital to the north of the city. In fact she had spent a total of twelve out of the last twenty years of her life in the hospital, in which her life had bled away. Her husband divorced her, taking the children and leaving her homeless. Her family had forgotten her. Nobody wanted to know her or employ her. She was left friendless, homeless, lifeless. That was one of the reasons why it had been so hard to get her out of hospital. Several attempts had been made, but each time things went wrong. Betty could not cope, and she was readmitted in an agitated state. Because she was unable to describe how she felt inside (she had always found it difficult to talk about how she felt), and because she appeared to be talking to herself, the psychiatrists thought she was hallucinating and thus diagnosed her schizophrenic. In fact she felt miserable. She often felt like ending her life, but her faith (she had been brought up a Catholic) forbade her from doing anything about it. The injections she was given in hospital simply numbed her feelings, making it even more difficult to say how she felt.

On the occasion of her last admission in the early 1980s, she had the benefit of a period of rehabilitation. This involved moving to a special unit where she was paid a small sum of money for getting up each day and going to the industrial therapy unit where she made coat-hangers by twisting pieces of wire on a jig. After several months she was moved to a hostel in the community where she lived with a group of twenty-two patients. She hated it there. She was bullied for cigarettes, and the male residents often made sexual advances. Somehow she managed to fight her way out, and persuaded her social worker to find her a flat of her own. It was then that her troubles really started. Her new flat was in another part of the city, which meant that the team who had been responsible for helping her was no longer involved. Although she was referred to a new team, the referral slipped through the net and she was left without support. She stopped the injections and a few weeks later she developed odd chewing movements affecting her face.

Living alone, with only the constant roar of traffic shattering the silence, started to get her down. Most of the flats in her building were empty because nobody else would live there. There were some families nearby, but most were being moved out to a large estate miles to the south. She was frightened to go out by herself because of the risk of being mugged, but she had to go out to get her benefits and do some shopping. Then one day a group of youngsters approached her on her way back from the Post Office. They laughed at her because of the movements affecting her face which made her look different. They jeered and laughed at her, calling her 'Mrs Nutter'. They jostled her and demanded cigarettes and money. She was terrified. She dropped her bag, leaving her purse and money, and ran home. This started to happen regularly. Each time she went for her benefits they would be waiting for her and she would end up either losing her money or having it stolen. One night two youths broke into her flat and terrified her, shouting abuse at her. They raped her.

She was in a terrible state. She had not eaten for weeks because she had no money, and had lost a lot of weight. Her self-esteem was so low that she roamed the streets picking up cigarette ends to make roll-ups out of what little tobacco they contained. It was impossible for her to lock the front door to her flat which meant that people wandered in whenever they wanted to. Her furniture was stolen, the central heating system was damaged, and on at least two occasions children started fires. The neighbours thought that she was either a junkie or a prostitute, or both. Mothers shouted abuse at her, children threw stones at her. People avoided her. They were frightened. She wandered about the neighbourhood in a dazed, dejected state, not knowing who to turn to for help, not even thinking that she might be helped, until at last she was beaten up and raped again and taken to the casualty department at a nearby hospital. After her physical state had been sorted out she was admitted to a psychiatric unit where she stayed for three weeks. She benefited from regular meals and put weight on, and was also started back on injections. She was also allocated a new community nurse who visited her regularly at home to give her injections.

But as soon as she got back home the same things started to happen again. She was robbed, reviled, raped and beaten. The nurse arranged for her to go back to the psychiatric unit, which she did for a few days, until exactly the same thing happened there. A young male patient promised her a cigarette if she would have sex with him. At that point she took her own discharge and went home, only for the cycle to start over again. Her nurse tried to persuade her to go back but she refused. Over the next twelve months she had a cycle of readmissions, often on a Section of the Mental Health Act. The situation was finally resolved when her social worker involved the housing department. Betty was referred to a team of housing officers who specialised in helping single homeless women. She left hospital to go to a women's hostel some miles away from where she had lived before. There she settled down, and gradually her self-confidence and self-esteem returned. She made new friends and a year later moved into a shared home with three of them. This time she stayed out of hospital for good.

POVERTY, UNEMPLOYMENT AND MENTAL ILLNESS

Another way of looking at Richard Warner's link between outcome in schizophrenia and socio-economic factors is that at times of high unemployment, people who have the condition of schizophrenia will find it much more difficult to find work, so they will be judged as having poor outcome, if we assume (like Freud) that successful adaptation at work is one criterion of mental health. In fact, the ease or otherwise of finding work has a powerful effect on mental health in general, independently of any relationship between employment and schizophrenia. In addition to this, we have to remember that the last fifteen years or so have seen great changes in the nature and availability of employment, so it is important for a number of reasons that we consider this. From 1979–86 unemployment in the UK rose from just over one million to three million, following which the figure fell to around 1.6 million in 1990. The increase in the early 1980s occurred as a result of major changes in British industry. The traditional heavy manufacturing and production industries of steel and coal, the foundations of the industrial revolution, were inefficient, and the Conservative government of the early 1980s believed that the country's industrial base required a radical overhaul. The majority of jobs lost were in the north of England, parts of the Midlands, South Wales and the industrial heart of Scotland. The subsequent fall in unemployment occurred partly through the creation of work in service industries, such as retail and financial services, and partly because of changes in the definition of unemployment. Many of these new jobs were part-time. The old idea that you had a job for life was replaced by a fluid work market, where workers moved from job to job, and many had a number of part-time jobs. These changes have implications for the significance of work as far as the individual is concerned. For many working-class men, self-esteem was identified with work which involved the use of hands and body in strenuous physical activity, or in the application of manual dexterity in skilled trades. Traditionally, such work was found in the construction industry, or heavy industry such as coal, steel and engineering, but this has largely been replaced by office work. The keyboard has replaced the hod. The telephone has replaced the trowel. Linguistic, not physical, prowess is now required for success in the labour market. What evidence is there that changes in the nature and availability of employment have repercussions for mental health?

Unemployment and mental health

The link between unemployment and mental illness in general has been established for many years, at least as far back as Faris and Dunham's study (1939). The difficulty lies in knowing how to interpret the relationship. Does the presence of mental illness make it more likely that you will be unable to function effectively at work, making it more likely that you will lose your job, and experience 'drift' down the social scale? Or do the stresses and strains of job loss and unemployment cause mental illness? Or are the two unrelated, but linked together through some unknown mediating factor(s)? Clearly the nature of these relationships is complex, but for my purpose it is sufficient to say that they exist. Some studies have found that a move into unemployment can result in a definite deterioration in an individual's mental health (for example Banks and Jackson, 1982), with improvements in health associated with re-employment. This suggests that mental illness does not necessarily cause unemployment in the first place. There is also considerable evidence linking unemployment and suicide or parasuicide (sometimes referred to as self-poisoning). Jones et al. (1991) found a strong association between unemployment and self-poisoning in a sample of sixty-four people who had taken an overdose, compared with a carefully matched comparison sample taken from the community. There was, however, no direct evidence to support the idea that unemployment *caused* the self-poisoning. A group in the Department of Social Medicine in Bristol have investigated a number of aspects of the relationship between socio-economic deprivation and mental health. In one study, they examined the relationship between suicide, parasuicide and socio-economic deprivation (Gunnell et al., 1995) in twenty-four localities in Bristol, with an average population of 34,000 each. Over a four-year period from April 1990 there were over 6000 hospital admissions for parasuicide, and almost 1000 suicides from this area, total population 817,000. There were wide variations in admission rates from different localities, and a strong correlation between suicide and parasuicide rates and a widely used measure of socio-economic deprivation in the localities. This leads us to the next piece of evidence.

The geographical distribution of mental illness

It is here that we gain some of the clearest evidence relating serious mental illness to socio-economic factors. In the period immediately before the dramatic socio-economic changes of the 1980s, Ineichen et al. (1984), also in Bristol, examined the geographical distribution of psychiatric admissions from the city for the three years up to 1981. The highest admission rates were found in the inner-city areas characterised by low social class and a high proportion of immigrants. There were particularly high rates of compulsory admissions to hospital from electoral wards with a high proportion of West Indian people. Another Bristol study (Kammerling and O'Connor, 1993) found a strong relationship between unemployment and rates of psychiatric admissions for serious mental illnesses such as schizophrenia. They correlated data on psychiatric admissions to hospitals over a two-year period starting in April 1990, with the unemployment rates in the electoral wards from where these admissions were drawn. They found that for people under the age of sixty-five years, 93% of the variation in the admission rates was explained by the unemployment levels in the local authority wards. This indicates that unemployment rate is an extremely powerful predictor of the rate of serious mental illness requiring hospital admission. Similar findings have emerged from studies in Nottingham and London. Giggs and Cooper (1987) classified the 800 census-enumeration districts of Nottingham into twelve neighbourhood types, on the basis of social and housing attributes. People admitted to hospital with a diagnosis of schizophrenia clustered in the inner-city areas characterised by low social status. Perhaps the most convincing evidence of a relationship between serious mental illness and social deprivation has come from a study by the Team for the Assessment of Psychiatric Services (TAPS) in London (Thornicroft et al., 1992). They carried out a detailed survey of over 200 patients admitted with chronic and serious mental illnesses to two hospitals near London, over a four-year period. The most striking finding was a fourfold variation in admission rates in the seven health authorities who admitted to the two hospitals. The most socially deprived district, Islington, accumulated patients at a rate of 11 patients a year, per 100,000 population, compared with a figure of 2.5 for the least socially deprived district, West Essex. There was a significant correlation between the rate of accumulation of people with chronic illnesses and measures of deprivation, especially overcrowding, unemployment and social class V.

Poverty and mental illness

These relationships suggest that poverty may play a mediating role, and there is convincing evidence that poverty and psychiatric status are closely related. Bruce et al. (1991) at Yale University examined the relationship between poverty and psychiatric status in almost 4000 residents chosen at random in the town of New Haven, Connecticut. This was a carefully designed study. They took great care to make sure that they excluded people who were already suffering from mental health problems, because they wanted to find out whether people living in poverty at the time of assessment were at greater risk of becoming mentally unwell subsequently, as well as to examine the effects of poverty on people who had already experienced a problem. The study also used state-of-the-art sampling techniques, psychiatric interviewing protocols and federal guidelines to classify people as poor. They found that poverty occurred much more frequently in women, the elderly and black people. In fact, poverty was six times more common in black people than white. People who met the poverty criteria had a significantly increased risk of mental ill health. At follow-up interview six months later, people living in poverty were almost twice as likely to have developed some form of mental health problem than those not living in poverty.

Poverty, as defined in this study, refers to more than just personal income. It includes references to the environmental conditions and socio-economic status of an entire household. The most devastating environmental conditions in this context are to be found in the experience of homelessness, a condition which, for many years, has attracted the interest of psychiatrists.[1] We are familiar with the psychiatric interpretation of homelessness in schizophrenia through 'drift' and 'deterioration', but in my view this grossly oversimplifies what is an extremely complex situation. Scott (1993) has pointed out that serious mental illness in the homeless is associated with a wide range of associated problems, such as alcohol (and drug) misuse and physical illness. Of particular importance here is the significance of personal histories of family disruption, early socio-economic disadvantage and poor educational attainment. These features were described in a recent study of homeless men suffering from schizophrenia by Caton *et al.* (1994), in which the co-occurrence of schizophrenia, substance misuse and personality disorder were rooted in family settings characterised by:

> ... changing parental figures, poverty, residential instability, family violence, and mental illness, substance abuse, or criminality in a parent. Triple disorder subjects emerged from the most deprived backgrounds .... (Caton *et al.*, 1994, p.687)

What does this tell us about schizophrenia and homelessness? More important still, what does it say about the way psychiatric language is used to understand the relationship? At the very least, the relationship between poverty, homelessness and mental illness is much more complicated than the 'drift' hypothesis would have us believe. The ubiquitousness of poverty, its increase over the last fifteen years, and how this relates to recent changes in the nature and structure of society must influence our understanding of mental health problems. As Bruce *et al.*'s (1991) paper concludes:

---

1 This discussion disregards the changes in patterns of service delivery, such as the closure of the old asylums and the move to community care. Many psychiatrists argue that this has contributed to the increase in homelessness in the mentally ill. Others argue that this is a spurious argument, and the increase simply reflects a general reduction in the availability of good quality, affordable housing in private and public sectors. Shortage of space here precludes a full discussion of the complex problem of the definition of homelessness.

... an important goal of [future] research is *to understand the linkages between the social phenomenon of poverty and individual experience*. Studies of individual processes are needed, for example, to determine the extent to which poverty increases the risk of mental disorders by increased exposure to negative events. (Bruce *et al.*, 1991, p. 473, emphasis added)

If we slightly modify Bruce's expression to 'the linkages between all *social phenomena* and individual experience' we have our first glimpse of what I consider to be the real problem of the language of psychiatry which I shall examine in the next chapter. But in the meantime I want to justify my statement about the importance of social context in relation to individual experience. To do this, I want to examine the social and political contexts which influence health in general, before going on to consider the significance of recent political changes in our society.

POVERTY AND HEALTH

Both popular and professional opinion holds that the most important advances in medicine accrue from science. This is true to a point, but some of the most significant medical developments over the last 150 years have passed by unnoticed. Spectacular advances in therapeutics, the introduction of new drugs and 'high-tech' medicine, grasp popular imagination, but the area of medicine that has achieved most in terms of the reduction of disease and illness is public health medicine. To understand how, we must consider the origins of this speciality at the end of the Industrial Revolution. The 100 years from 1750 to 1850 brought the most profound changes in the nature of society. The growth of industry led to urbanisation and a massive influx of people from the country into the towns where the factories proliferated. We have some idea of the appalling living conditions endured by ordinary people from this extract of Sir Edwin Chadwick's *Report of the Sanitary Conditions of the Labouring Population* (1842):

That the various forms of epidemic, endemic, and other disease caused, or aggravated, or propagated chiefly amongst the labouring classes by atmospheric impurities produced by decomposing animal and vegetable substances, by damp and filth, and close and overcrowded dwellings prevail amongst the population in every part of the kingdom ... That the annual loss of life from filth and bad ventilation is greater than the loss from death and wounds in any wars ... That of the 43,000 cases of widowhood, and 112,000 cases of destitute orphanage relieved from the poor's rates in England and Wales alone, it appears that the greatest proportion of deaths of the heads of families occurred from the above specified ... (Chadwick, 1842, pp. 133–4)

Conditions such as these took their toll on the health of the hundreds of thousands of workers who had to endure them, so, in 1837, the government appointed a doctor, William Farr, as the first medical statistician. Farr introduced the new science of *vital statistics*, in which he systematically collected data on the incidence and prevalence of disease in the population. These figures, together with graphic accounts by a London GP, Dr Southwood Smith, of the living conditions of the poor, resulted in the Royal Commission of 1843 to enquire into the health of the towns. Four years later the first of a series of cholera epidemics swept through the country, forcing the government to take action. In 1848 the first Public Health Act established a General Board of Health whose members included Chadwick, Southwood Smith, and the philanthropist reformer, the Seventh Earl of Shaftesbury.

In 1854 there was another cholera epidemic, during the course of which the anaesthetist John Snow demonstrated that the disease was transmitted by water, following early and inadequate attempts to deal with the problems of water supply and sewage disposal for the expanding urban population. It was not until 1868 that Louis Pasteur discovered that an infectious disease of silkworms was caused by a minute parasitic organism, and thus originated the germ theory of infectious diseases, and it was fifteen years after that that Robert Koch described the cholera bacillus. Of course, germ theory and the elaboration of the infectious diseases opened the road to antibiotic cure for most of these diseases, but public health interventions which *linked disease to the material circumstances of people's lives* achieved the earliest successes. Reformers like Lord Shaftesbury strove to improve the conditions under which the majority of the population lived, and this was echoed by cultural representations of English life. By the end of the nineteenth century the public conscience had been stirred by accounts of the plight of children in Dickens' novels *Nicholas Nickleby* and *Oliver Twist*, and Charles Kingsley's *The Water Babies*. Examination of volunteers for the Boer War revealed that over 50% of young men were medically unfit for military service, and this prompted the Chief Medical Officer to the Local Government Board, Sir Arthur

Newsholme, to make a series of studies of child health. In 1908 he found enormous geographical variations in child mortality, with the highest levels occurring in the poorest areas of the industrial north of England, the Midlands and South Wales. His third report dealt with the causes of mortality in one area, Lancashire. There were many, but most shared one thing in common: they related to the living conditions in the home. This focused political attention on the need to improve housing conditions in industrial areas, and put pressure on the government to take action to mitigate the worst effects of poverty. In 1911 Lloyd George, then Chancellor of the Exchequer, introduced a national health insurance scheme, the first political act in recognition of the fact that health is too important a commodity to be left solely to the discretion of the individual.

The final thread in this brief outline of public health medicine traces the course of our understanding of the complex relationship between the effects of poverty on diet, living conditions and health. Attempts to clear Victorian slums and rehouse the occupants in modern, better-designed houses paradoxically had a deleterious effect on their health. One survey in the north-east of England found that the combined effect of higher rent and rates, together with increased expenditure on fares to travel to work, meant there was less to spend on food. Indeed, in the economic recession of the 1930s a number of studies found that nutrition had a major influence on health, especially that of the poor. *Plus ça change!* On 21 January 1996, the *Observer* newspaper carried a leaked government report that the nutritional state of millions of Britons was at its worst since the Great Depression. The growth of out-of-town superstores which can only be accessed by car, coupled with the growth in poverty, meant that millions of people are unable to access the constituents of a healthy diet.

The history of public health medicine teaches us some important lessons. Disease and illness are, at least in part, determined by the material circumstances of people's lives. Improving these conditions through attempts to combat poverty can have dramatic effects upon the health and well-being of the population. Scientists may be able to develop successful treatments for diseases, but what point is there in treating such diseases without taking elementary steps to prevent their occurrence in the first place, by attending to living conditions? Prevention is surely better than cure. Many diseases are distributed inequitably throughout the population in the most disadvantaged groups. This, as we have seen, is especially so for those suffering from mental illness. Most important of all is the idea that some aspects of health are too important to be left to individual whim, and that we share a collective responsibility, mediated through government and state, to ensure that the disadvantaged have the right to health. How have politicians responded to these messages?

In a speech given on 27 March 1977, the then Secretary of State for Social Services, David Ennals, drew attention to the marked differences in mortality rates between the various social classes. He set up a working group to examine the evidence for inequalities in health and to offer policy advice in the light of this evidence. The group was led by Professor Sir Douglas Black, an eminent and widely respected physician with a dry, Aberdonian sense of humour. Sir Douglas had been Professor of Medicine at Manchester University[2] and, later, President of the Royal College of Physicians. In 1979, whilst the group was in the final stages of collating its response, the Labour government fell, and the final report was presented to Patrick Jenkin, the Conservative Secretary of State for Social Services in April 1980. Although the report received wide coverage in medical journals (see, for example, Black, 1981), the government appeared disinterested. The *British Medical Journal* claimed that the report had been met with 'shallow indifference' on behalf of the government. Patrick Jenkin's department made only a small number of copies available, but it was eventually published as *Inequalities in Health: The Black Report*. The principal findings (Black *et al.*, 1982) were that poor health in the lower occupational groups extended throughout all stages of life. This was seen most clearly in relation to death rates broken down by social class. They calculated that, on 1972 figures, the mortality rate of social classes IV and V (semi-skilled and unskilled manual workers) exceeded that of social class I (professional workers) by 74,000 deaths per annum, an estimate which included the deaths of 10,000 children. Over the twenty years from the mid-1950s, the death rates for men and women aged over thirty-five years had fallen for social classes I and II, whereas those for social classes IV and V had increased. The stark conclusion was depressing. After thirty years, a National Health Service committed to equal care for all, free at the point of delivery, had failed to improve the health of the poorest people of this country.

---

2   In 1969, I was priviliged to spend my first clinical placement as a third year medical student on his ward at Manchester Royal Infirmary.

The report suggested that low income, unemployment, and poor quality of housing and education, had adverse effects on lifestyle for the poor. In addition, those who most needed to use health services were least likely to do so, especially manual workers. It made a number of recommendations, which emphasised the need to improve the material quality of life of the poorest members of society, by increasing state benefits, and improving housing and work conditions. These recommendations could not have been less auspiciously timed, for here were proposals for the state to intervene with massive health and social welfare programmes costing billions of pounds, in the infancy of a government which was to become famous (or infamous, depending on your point of view) for reducing state intervention and cutting public expenditure. Oliver Twist's request for more was greeted not with incredulity, but with a frosty silence.

It is worth remembering that the Black report presented the relationship between poverty and health which applied *before* the decade of the 1980s, which, as we shall see, witnessed a deepening of the gulf between the wealthy and the poor. The period covered by the Black report, the twenty years up to the mid-1970s, was a period of relative prosperity and high employment. It included the 1950s boom, a time when Britain had 'never had it so good'. Subsequent studies suggest that differentials in health based on social class have increased. This has important implications for health targets under the Health of the Nation programme,[3] so the Chief Medical Officer established a working group in 1995 to examine health variations and offer guidance on effective interventions for health authorities (Department of Health, 1995). Again, it found marked differences in life expectancy and health by social class, sex and ethnicity. People in social class I have, on average, a life expectancy seven years longer than people in social class V. Children in social class V are four times more likely to die by accident than those from social class I. People living in the north of England have significantly higher standardised mortality ratios (SMRs)[4] than those living in East Anglia. Within

3   The Health of the Nation targets were introduced by the government in the early 1990s, as part of a series of reforms of the NHS. The focus here was on improving the nation's health by prevention and early identification of ill health.

4   The standardised mortality ratio (SMR) is a figure used by epidemiologists to compare death rates for different conditions over different periods of time. It can also be used to compare the death rate of one section of the community with that of the community as a whole.

each health region, electoral wards classified by level of social deprivation show a clear association between deprivation and SMRs for all causes of death. The inequalities in health highlighted by the Black report persist. They are deeply etched on the social structure of British culture.

Both reports searched for possible explanations of these relationships, including artefact of measurement, social and environmental factors, psychosocial factors, health-related mobility, biological factors, lifestyles, and differential use of health services. We can only be certain that the relationship between deprivation and health is extremely complex, and there is no single explanation. Biological factors are clearly important in explaining the mechanism of disease, especially if it has a genetic component. This may explain, for example, the greater risk of people from the Indian subcontinent of developing coronary heart disease (CHD). However, genetic predisposition interacts with environmental factors in determining the individual's risk of developing CHD. There are low rates of CHD in rural areas of the Indian subcontinent, but higher rates in people from these areas when they move to the UK. This presumably arises because of environmental factors, such as stress, diet and other behaviours related to lifestyle. Genetic predisposition alone is insufficient in most conditions to explain the risk of developing a disease. We are forced to consider an interaction between individual predisposition and environment. Amongst these environmental factors, there is no doubt that the material aspect of people's living conditions has considerable influence upon both physical and mental health. Income, wealth, quality of housing, diet, working conditions and air pollution, have all been shown to explain variations in health by socio-economic group and area of residence. Even material indicators such as car ownership or housing tenure (home-owner or rented accommodation) are associated with mortality rates. Psychosocial factors are also important. A study of Whitehall civil servants (Marmot et al., 1991) found that lower social status was associated with stressful life events, financial problems and poor social supports at home, and low satisfaction at work. Stress arising from separation from family and culture, language problems, and racial discrimination in all aspects of life – particularly housing, employment and education – make particularly important contributions to physical and mental ill-health in people from ethnic minorities.

There is one final, almost inconsequential, but telling, point to make about the two reports, which opens the door to a new world. The title of the Black report was *Inequalities in Health*. That of the 1995 Department of Health report was *Variations in Health*. The difference is a crude semantic shift driven by political correctness. The authors of the 1995 report were doubtless aware of the nature of the Black report's reception, and politicians' sensitivity to external interference. What a world of difference is conveyed by the change in title. It has been said that we live in a classless society. How can there be inequalities in a classless society? If we live in a classless society then we must be all the same, so there can be no inequality. *Quod erat demonstrandum*. It has even been said that there is no such thing as society. If society does not exist, social inequalities cannot exist, so poverty, unemployment or social disadvantage, such as racism, are irrelevant to health. At least this would appear to be one view. But is this really the case? At this point I want to consider the nature of recent changes in our culture, changes wrought through political forces which have redefined the nature of society and the relationship of the individual to it.

THE POLITICS OF POVERTY

Many psychiatrists reading this may be starting to feel uncomfortable. 'Psychiatry, or for that matter, medicine, has nothing to do with politics', they may say. This is a matter of opinion. We have already seen that some of the most notable successes achieved by medicine in the control of diseases occurred because the profession brought the links between disease and the socio-economic circumstances of people's lives to the attention of the general public and politicians. In any case, there is a well-known precedent for British psychiatrists to dabble in political matters. Ten years ago the Royal College of Psychiatrists played a central role in the expulsion of the former Soviet Union from the World Psychiatric Association because of the baleful political abuse of psychiatry in that country. If we are permitted to comment on the political aspects of psychiatry in a foreign country, then I believe we must be free to do the same in our own country.

In 1845, Benjamin Disraeli, the Conservative Prime Minister, published his novel, *Sybil*, in which a stranger tells the hero, Lord Egremont, that Britain is:

> two nations between whom there is no intercourse and no sympathy; who are as ignorant of each other's habits, thoughts and feelings as if they were dwellers in different zones or inhabitants of different planets who are formed by a different breeding, are

fed by a different food, are ordered by different manners, and are not governed by the same laws.

In the novel, Disraeli advocated a form of social democracy which, a hundred years later, came to form a central plank in post-war Conservative Party politics. At the end of the last war, the coalition government was swept aside by a Labour victory which promised large-scale social reforms, such as the introduction of the National Health Service, state pensions, benefits and education. In 1950 a group led by Angus Maude, Ian Macleod and Enoch Powell, published a pamphlet entitled *One Nation: a Tory approach to social problems*, in an attempt to change Conservative Party social policy in response to the reforms introduced by the Labour government under Clement Attlee. The group, who came to be known as the 'One Nation' group, were keen to protect the consensus politics which emerged during the last war, and especially keen to protect the welfare state. Although they adhered to the tenets of free enterprise, capitalism was the servant of the state, the means by which social welfare and full employment were to be maintained. Acutely aware of the divisions within British society based on old distinctions of class, they stressed the importance of consensus with the unions, and the growth of the welfare state through economic growth fuelled by free enterprise. The *laissez-faire* capitalism of the past was to be no longer. Tom Butler (1993) has examined the implications of this political philosophy for the development of mental health services. He argues that at the heart of 'One Nation' conservatism is the belief that the state has a legitimate role as a provider of health and welfare services which are free at the point of delivery. 'One Nation' economics, however, led to a gradual decline in industrial efficiency, which ultimately led to the Conservatives' 1964 election defeat by Harold Wilson. Subsequent Labour and Conservative governments under Harold Wilson, Edward Heath and James Callaghan continued to increase public spending on the welfare state, as health, education and other public services grew to meet the demands of the post-war 'baby boom'. This did nothing to increase confidence in the economy which experienced major upheavals including the sterling crisis and devaluation of 1967. Attempts to control public spending by restricting pay increases in the public sector brought the Heath government into conflict with the unions, and the election defeat of 1974, and further economic failure and attempts to control public sector pay resulted in the 'Winter of Discontent' and the failure of the Callaghan government in the 1979 election. This brought Margaret Thatcher to power.

According to Tom Butler, there are two important issues that lie at the heart of the political conflicts of the post-war period: one concerns the extent to which the state should intervene in the affairs of society; the second concerns the relationship between the rights of the individual and the power of the state. Margaret Thatcher in Britain and Ronald Reagan in America introduced policies based on philosophies which challenged directly the 'consensus' and 'One Nation' policies. Both believed that the state had become too powerful. Both took the view that the origin of social problems was not to be found in social inequality. Crime, unemployment and other forms of social problems were regarded as a form of personal deviance whose origins were elsewhere, either to be understood in terms of faulty family values, or in terms of the noxious effects of 1960s liberalism in education and social values. Parents and individuals were responsible for social breakdown, not society or the conditions of society. During the early 1980s, Margaret Thatcher introduced a string of policies which had profound implications for social policy and industry. Her belief in the importance of the individual, and repulsion at the idea of dependency on the state, resulted in changes in state benefits, the selling of council houses and the privatisation of nationalised industries. State intervention in the economy was reduced to a minimum. The 'market' was to have the major influence on the economy, a policy which worked its way into the health service and education. The reductions in public expenditure thus effected would benefit individuals through reduced direct and indirect taxation, especially at the higher levels of personal taxation.

The economic and social aspects of these changes have been described by the economist J.K. Galbraith in his book *The Culture of Contentment* (1992). This books charts the flourishing of a new age of the individual which has arisen like a phoenix out of the ashes of the state. There are many important themes in this book, but there are two in particular that I want to consider: the emphasis placed on belief in the individual, and the growth of what Galbraith calls the *functional underclass*. Galbraith argues that the reason for Reagan's (and Thatcher's) political success lies in the fact that both were faithful representatives of the constituencies that elected them. 'We attribute to politicians what should be attributed to the community they serve' (Galbraith, 1992, p. 18). In other words, their policies reflected the popular beliefs in the societies which elected them. In this sense we share a collective responsibility for the actions of our political leaders. We may feel comfortable attacking our political representatives, but we are the people who put them there. They do our bidding. Galbraith then goes on to establish the important features of the New Individualism:

> What the individual member aspires to have and enjoy is the product of his or her personal virtue, intelligence and effort. Good fortune being earned or the reward of merit, there is no equitable justification for any action that impairs it ...
>
> (Galbraith, 1992, pp. 18–19)

The most striking feature of Galbraith's view of economics and society is his perception of a deep division within society between those who have prospered economically, and those who have not. This latter group, which he refers to as the functional underclass, are to be found in the inner cities, poor farming communities and run-down industrial and mining communities. It is a heterogeneous group, including immigrants and other migrant worker groups. Indeed, a significant proportion of this group consists of people from ethnic communities, who have failed to benefit from the increase in prosperity enjoyed by the contented majority. The social experience of the underclass is characterised by social disorder, drug misuse, crime and conflict. Family disintegration is common. The economy in the areas they live in has failed to expand, and unemployment is high. They are trapped, cut off from the normal course of upward mobility in socio-economic status available to the majority. The underclass is a permanent feature of society. It has also become a whipping boy, for the contented majority fiercely resists state attempts at intervention aimed at ameliorating its plight. The provision of decent housing, education, health care and benefits simply reinforces their hopelessness, their dependence on the state. The underclass requires the spur of its own poverty in order to transcend its lot. The justification for this belief is the notion that individuals are responsible for the outcome of their own lives. Indeed, this belief motivated both Ronald Reagan and Margaret Thatcher to reduce and change the basis for the allocation of state benefits, or the allocation of student loans rather than grants for higher education. In so far as the state has to provide some support for the underclass, the majority regard it as a fiscal burden, through which the fortunate majority have to pay to support the minority. Accordingly, '... the sustaining taxes must be kept to a minimum; otherwise, *the liberty of the individual will be impaired*' (Galbraith, 1992, p. 46; emphasis added). Again, we see that the notion of the individual plays a central part in Galbraith's conception of the split within society. Again, it is important to stress that he does not apportion blame to the politicians of the New Right. He views them as responding to the democratic will of the majority.

The existence of the underclass is supported by a recent report from the Joseph Rowntree Foundation (1995), which paints a dramatic picture of social and economic changes in Britain through the 1980s. The most striking feature is the extent to which the poorest 20% of the population has failed to benefit from the increase in economic prosperity enjoyed by the majority over this period. Inequality in income has grown more in Britain than in any other industrial country over the last fifteen years. From 1966 to 1977, wages at all levels of income grew at roughly the same rate. But since 1978, wages of the lowest paid have hardly grown at all, whereas those on average incomes have grown by one-third, and those on high wages have grown by 50%. The evidence suggests that these changes have affected some groups more than others. Only 18% of the white population were found in the poorest one-fifth of the population, compared with one-third of the non-white population. West Indian people in particular have been left behind by these changes. Over 40% are to be found in the poorest group. These inequalities are to be found in adjacent neighbourhoods, with affluent local authority wards often situated next door to disadvantaged wards. In economic terms, the differences between the most and least privileged wards widened over the ten years leading to 1991. Indeed, the layout of many of Britain's larger cities results in the wealthiest wards sitting cheek by jowl with the poorest. Every day the least well off have their noses rubbed in this inequity, while the wealthy sneak off to well-paid jobs. Such a situation does nothing for the cohesiveness of society. But then there is no such thing. The Rowntree report suggests that a combination of factors may be responsible for these changes. These include the growth of unemployment, especially the long-term unemployed; an increase in the number of people living off income support, the value of which has fallen in real terms (in order to stimulate the underclass to accept responsibility for itself); as well as the differential increases in wages.

We may quibble about the causes, but the consequences are unavoidable: British society is deeply split between those who have and those who do not. Not only that, but the politics of the New Right has redefined the relationship between the individual and society. Where once the 'One Nation' group of Conservatives sought a compromise between social reform and welfare on the one hand, and a free market on the other, the state has had its wings clipped. Interventionism is anathema. Individuals are responsible for the outcome of their lives alone. The British live in a classless society, one in which the son of a circus artist may become Prime Minister. Britain needs only to cut the benefits to the unemployed to encourage them back to work. *There is no such thing as society.* The poor are kept in poverty by virtue of the fact that they receive public support, the welfare benefits that are supposed to save them from their plight. The helping hand reinforces their dependency and replaces their *individual initiative* which would guarantee their escape. It is for this reason that the politics of the Right demands that benefits should be cut. There is nothing like the spur of hunger to drive a man out, to force him onto his bike, and to look for work. But this group, the underclass, is the same group in which we find the mentally ill overwhelmingly represented. Recall, for a moment, the descriptions of homelessness and mental illness given by Scott (1993) and Caton *et al.* (1994) earlier in this chapter, and compare these with Galbraith's description of the underclass. Are we not dealing with the same group, disadvantaged by the same set of circumstances? Yet psychiatry argues that the mentally ill are to be found here because they suffer from a disease called schizophrenia. The problem is located firmly in the individual. These polarisations in our attitudes towards the nature of society, the extent to which we stress the collective or individualistic aspects of its structure, are not simply political. They are of great importance for psychiatry, for we are facing a profound gulf, a chasm, in the different languages that we may use to talk about schizophrenia. On the one hand we have the biological languages that deal with its causes in terms of disordered brain function. On the other hand we may now see that through social, economic, or political languages, we may regard schizophrenia in a completely different light. The question now becomes, how are psychiatrists setting about trying to bridge the gulf? Are they even aware of the gulf? And, even more important, what are the implications of this for those who suffer from schizophrenia? To answer these questions we must examine recent changes in psychiatric discourse.

'ECLECTICISM' AND TRENDS IN PSYCHIATRIC RESEARCH

Given the diverse models of mental illness, we have to find some way of organising them in order that they can be used. In the early stages of my training, I was told to be 'eclectic'. Most practising psychiatrists would claim that they too are eclectic, a word which the *Shorter Oxford Dictionary* defines as follows:

... epithet of a class of philosophers who 'selected such doctrines as pleased them in every school' ... That borrows or is borrowed from various sources ... Broad, not exclusive ...

According to Aubrey Lewis (1936), the medical model in psychiatry never considered mental illness narrowly in terms of disease processes, but as an interaction between environment and individual. When applied to psychiatry the term eclectic is widely regarded as being synonymous with the psychobiological approach of Adolf Meyer who attempted to integrate Freudian theory into the practice of clinical psychiatry. Meyer's approach to understanding mental illness was normalising, in that he regarded it as an understandable reaction to a set of life experiences. Although he did not deny the importance of genetic factors, his approach was significant in the importance that it attached to the *person* in understanding mental illness. His approach focused on persons not patients. Meyer's approach was a highly influential way of trying to integrate the different languages used in clinical psychiatry in an eclectic manner. His influence on American psychiatry was at its greatest during the middle of the twentieth century, and is best seen through the influence that psychoanalysis had upon the practice of psychiatry in that country (Sabshin, 1990). Meyer's influence was mediated by Karl Menninger, who articulated most clearly the psychosocial model. In his book, *The Vital Balance* (Menninger, 1963), he outlined a new view of mental illness, which was reducible to adaptive failures on the part of the individual to psychosocial stress. All types of disorders, neurotic and psychotic, could be explained on this basis. He rejected Kraepelin's disease model, and regarded the most important task of psychiatry as follows:

We must attempt to explain how the observed maladjustment came about and what the meaning of this sudden eccentricity or desperate or aggressive outburst is. *What is behind the symptom?*
(Menninger, 1963, in Sabshin, 1990, p. 1268; emphasis added)

This approach, coupled with changes in mental health and social policy in America, particularly the growth of the community mental health movement and the introduction of Medicaid health insurance for the poor, had a number of implications. The broad definition of mental health, or lack of it (failure of adaptation to psychosocial stress), implicit in the psychosocial model resulted in an enormous expansion in the problems dealt with by psychiatrists. Costs rocketed, and the insurance companies who were footing the bill demanded to know which conditions their money was being spent on, what therapies were involved, and what was their effectiveness. Psychiatrists working in the psychosocial model found it difficult to answer these questions because they did not make diagnoses. It was impossible to count the number of people receiving psychiatric care. A small, but increasingly powerful minority within the profession added their voice, claiming that the psychosocial model was unscientific, and failed to generate any meaningful research in the field of mental illness. A number of articles by academic psychiatrists appeared in the literature, arguing the case for the medicalisation of psychiatry (see, for example, Kety, 1974; Engel, 1977; Klerman, 1977; Ludwig and Othmer, 1977). The general thrust of the argument was that psychiatry, being a branch of medicine, should recognise and reinforce its links with the biological sciences. The medical model, with its emphasis on the role of diagnosis and recognition of disease entities, had much to offer psychiatry. In 1974 Robert Spitzer was appointed by the American Psychiatric Association (APA) to lead a task force on nomenclature and statistics. The outcome, DSM-III (*Diagnostic and Statistical Manual*, APA, 1980), was a victory for biological psychiatry over the psychosocial movement and psychoanalysis in particular. Its detailed prescription of criteria for the diagnosis of mental illness has had international implications. It provided a firm basis for diagnosis which generated a new impetus in biological research. It reaffirmed the Kraepelinian tradition of classification and nosology, reinforcing the notion that psychiatry deals with identifiable mental illnesses. In America it provided the insurance companies with a diagnostic handbook in psychiatry, which provided the justification for treatment. If your condition wasn't in the DSM, you weren't paid. The delineation of discrete mental illnesses made it possible to compare the economic effectiveness of different treatments. It became an accountant's dream. Over a period of twenty-five years the landscape of American psychiatry changed beyond recognition. Biological psychiatry overwhelmed psychoanalysis and the psychosocial model in a bloodless coup. It became the predominant language used to understand mental illness in America and Britain.

The effect of these changes can be discerned in the nature of papers published in the psychiatric journals. Pincus *et al.* (1993) examined articles published during one year of each decade from 1969 to 1990. They classified all published articles in the *American Journal of Psychiatry* and the *Archives of General Psychiatry*, two widely read journals which are influential not only in the USA but in other countries, including the UK. The *American Journal of*

Psychiatry is the academic journal of the American Psychiatric Association, the equivalent of the *British Journal of Psychiatry*, published by the Royal College of Psychiatrists. The *Archives of General Psychiatry* has a reputation for being a more rigorously scientific journal. It is probably the single most influential scientific journal in academic psychiatry. In the Pincus *et al.* study, every article was coded to identify, amongst other things, the field of research covered. This included basic biological sciences, behavioural and cognitive science, social science, clinical psychobiology, diagnosis and classification, epidemiology, psychopharmacology, psychosocial treatments and mental health services. They found a significant growth in papers reporting research on clinical psychobiology and psychopharmacology over the 1970s, associated with a fall in articles relating to behavioural and cognitive science, social science and mental health services. There was also a trend away from general categories towards more clearly defined specific disorders, or illnesses. For example the 1970s witnessed a substantial increase in the number of articles published specifically about schizophrenia. These trends reflect the biological revolution in American psychiatry and the publication of DSM-III. What are the implications of this growth in biological psychiatry?

MINDLESS PSYCHIATRY

British psychiatry has picked up the threads of this revolution with great enthusiasm. This can be seen in the work of the special interest groups which flourish within the Royal College.[5] Recently the Biological Psychiatry Special Interest Group (SIG) considered a position paper which proposed a change of name and a radical new agenda to take forward the cause of neuroscience. The discussion document went under the heading 'Proposal for a Special Interest Group for Neuroscience in Psychiatry' (Goodwin, 1995), and outlined a radical new agenda which would have important implications for the training and teaching of psychiatrists in Britain. It argued that neuroscience is a new discipline which '... promises to

---

5   It is, perhaps, worth noting that in the late 1980s the Biological Psychiatry SIG voted to disband itself and amalgamate with the then newly constituted General Psychiatry SIG. What follows in the main body of text represents an attempt to give biological psychiatry a much clearer voice within the college.

lie naturally at the heart of reliable knowledge in general psychiatry' (Goodwin, 1995) and has its origins with the scientific disciplines of neuroanatomy, neurophysiology, neuropharmacology and
psychology. Psychiatry presents neuroscience with particular problems the resolution of which has important outcomes in terms of
the discovery of new pharmacological interventions for schizophrenia and other psychiatric conditions. This in itself may seem inno-
cent and worthy enough, but the document continues:

> *This effort to overcome competing, tangential formulations of a
> given problem has important implications for psychiatry.* How
> long can we go on attempting to accommodate biology, psycho-
> analysis, anthropology, social science, learning theory and cog-
> nitive psychology as equally contributing views of mental illness
> *without any effort at synthesis or pruning.* (Goodwin, 1995,
> p. 2; emphasis added)

and:

> ... support of neuroscience in psychiatry will imply a stand against
> non-scientific discourse. In particular the claims for some anthro-
> pological, psychosocial or post-modern 'explanations' in psychiatry
> appear to reject hypothesis testing as it is commonly understood
> within the natural sciences. Such approaches are likely only to
> bring discredit *to the intellectual standing of psychiatry and fur-
> ther confuse its practice.* (Goodwin, 1995, p. 2; emphasis added)

So much for eclecticism. This document presents a set of beliefs
that are gaining in popularity within the profession. First, the
scientific approach is established in clear opposition to what is
regarded as 'non-scientific discourse'. The opposition includes
anthropology, psychosocial and post-modern accounts of psychiatry,
although these are not defined, and no account is given of their
strengths and weaknesses. Second, they are dismissed on the
grounds that they 'reject hypothesis testing' as used by the natural
sciences. There are important assumptions implicit within this
text, that scientific discourse alone is rigorous and is the only
approach capable of understanding mental illness. Finally, non-
scientific discourse must be removed from the psychiatrists' cur-
riculum, on the grounds that there is insufficient room and priority
must be afforded to scientific discourse. In one sense, the outcome
of this arrogant discussion document is irrelevant, because it represents an influential view within psychiatry which will out, come

what may. There has been a recent trend for larger academic departments of psychiatry in Britain to rename themselves as departments of clinical neuroscience. Most of the large academic centres in Britain are led by psychiatrists whose orientation is biological. These are the people who control the training of under and postgraduate students. They determine the explanatory systems used by future psychiatrists and general practitioners. Not all of them would agree with Goodwin's hard line on the need to expunge 'soft' science from psychiatry, but the threat remains either through intention or default. We glimpse a future landscape inhabited only by brain technocrats; a world in which psychiatrists can explain the cause of everything but the meaning of nothing.

There can be no doubt that the biological transformation in the US is influencing psychiatry in Britain. My intention here is not to attack the biological transformation itself, but rather to describe what the implications will be if we jettison social, anthropological and 'post-modern' approaches to psychiatry. What will happen if psychiatry becomes an exclusively biological discipline, shunning the psychological, social and political realities that the great majority of psychiatric patients have to face? There are three questions in particular that we have to consider if we are to answer this: What are the origins and features of the biological approach to psychiatry? What are the implications of these features for our understanding of mental illness, particularly for those who are subject to this experience? What are the implications if it should be allowed to dominate and exclude other languages in the field of mental illness? Perhaps we may be permitted a final glimpse of the way ahead before we are flattened beneath a biological behemoth.

8 The Tower of Babel II: On Brains or Minds

There is no cell or group of cells in the brain of such anatomical or functional pre-eminence as to appear to be the keystone or center of gravity of the whole system.

(William James)

When you get there there's no there there.

(Gertrude Stein, on visiting a nondescript American town)

If we are to answer the questions posed at the end of the last chapter we have to consider the origins of science as well as its underlying philosophy. Indeed, the history of science, medicine and philosophy are inextricably linked. The unpalatable fact for those who advocate a 'hard' science, culture-free approach to psychiatry is that science and philosophy were spawned out of a great cultural revolution, the Renaissance, and it was during the course of the Renaissance that the foundations were laid for the most important problems facing psychiatry and neuroscience, especially in the work of the French philosopher, René Descartes.

THE ORIGINS OF SCIENCE AND PHILOSOPHY

The origins of medicine and science can be traced back to that period of cultural turmoil and change we call the Renaissance. It is important to remember that this movement was rooted in European culture, and was driven by the arts, as two fourteenth-century Italian poets, Petrarch and Dante, argued for the rediscovery of classical culture, its art, poetry and philosophy. Theories of disease in the early Renaissance were grounded in astrology and alchemy. Although Galen in the second century AD had extended knowledge of human anatomy through dissection, medical knowledge had changed little from the ideas of Hippocrates. Dissection was a risky business. It was forbidden by the Catholic Church, who regarded the structure and function of the human body as God-given, sacred and not for men's eyes. The revival of interest in the art of Classical Greece and Rome stimulated curiosity about the structure of the human body. At the end of the fifteenth century, Leonardo da Vinci published his famous series of anatomical sketches, which influenced the Belgian anatomist Vesalius, who had been taught a tradition of anatomy unchanged since Galen. Vesalius, who studied medicine in Paris, was eventually appointed as lecturer in anatomy in Padua where he published his famous work *De humani corporis fabrica* in 1537. His observations of the structure of the human body challenged ideas sacred to Christianity, such as the belief that women had one more rib than men. He also argued against the Aristotelian theory that the heart was the centre of the mind, claiming that the brain was the seat of the mind. Vesalius' work marks the origins of biology as a science.

Before the Renaissance the Church had been the prime controller of knowledge, and had exercised its power to maintain belief in the sanctity of man, his supreme position in Creation, and his relationship to God. The Renaissance challenged this in two ways. Galen had overstepped the mark when he noted the similarity between pig and human organs, and for this reason the Church had forbidden human dissection for over 1000 years. The work of da Vinci and Vesalius challenged this. Anatomy symbolised the secularisation of Adam, a second Fall in which the human body lost its sanctity and became an open book, a text for science. The second challenge came from the new understanding of the structure of the universe born out of detailed observations of the motions of the stars. The old model of the universe had stood two millennia and was reasonably practical. Matter consisted of four elements (earth, water, fire and air) with four qualities (heat, cold, moist and dry). The earth was at the centre of the heavens, which consisted of a series of concentric spheres sliding past each other under the influence of the four qualities. In this model everything was safe and predictable. Farmers planted their crops by it, sailors navigated by it and physicians treated their patients by it. The organisation of the Universe and man's place in it, indeed man's very nature, were intimately related. The situation of the earth at the centre of a Universe created by God symbolised man's closeness to his Creator.

This safe, predictable and controlled view of the nature of the Universe and man's place in it was shattered in 1543, when the Polish astronomer and physician, Nicolaus Copernicus, published *De Revolutionibus Orbium Coelestrum* (The Revolution of the Heavenly Spheres). He had calculated that the sun, not the earth, lay at the centre of the solar system in 1530, but such ideas were heretical. Sixty years later, the Neapolitan scientist and philosopher Giordano Bruno was an enthusiastic supporter of Copernicus' ideas. Bruno entered the Dominican order of monks in 1563, but his sceptical attitude to Catholic doctrines forced him to flee Italy in 1577. He was arrested by the Inquisition in 1593 in Venice and burned at the stake for his adoption of Copernican astronomy and his heretical religious views. It is also worth noting that Bruno was a voice hearer. Copernicus' system still held that the heaven consisted of a series of concentric spheres following perfectly circular orbits, but this was challenged by Johannes Kepler in 1609 who described the laws of planetary motion, in which the planets rotated around the sun in elliptical orbits. Kepler, with some modifications, provided us with the description of the Universe with which we are familiar today. These ideas presented an enormous challenge to belief in the divine and spiritual nature of man. Anatomy, which enabled the early scientists to think about man as a material being, and astronomy, which challenged his central position in Creation, made it possible to consider man as an object to be measured and placed in relation to the rest of nature and the physical world. These shifts in thought were reinforced by further developments in science, particularly those of Galileo, the founder of the scientific method, in which laws were deduced on the basis of careful observations made in the course of experiments. Galileo invented the telescope, with which he discovered four satellites orbiting Jupiter, and studied the Classical work of Euclid and Archimedes, extending mathematics in the service of scientific enquiry.

The rise of science is, as Russell observes (1961), closely related to the origins of modern philosophy. Copernican astronomy had important implications for philosophy and knowledge. Scientific truth is based on painstaking observations, and established traditional beliefs may be false. The invention of the telescope, thermometer, barometer and microscope in the seventeenth century provided the means by which the early scientist philosophers could delve ever more deeply into the material properties of the natural world. This reinforced the observational basis of science, which in turn influenced philosophy. Although Newton, who perfected the scientific method of experiment and observation, accepted that the hand of God had thrown the planets into motion, his own laws of motion rendered further intercession on the behalf of the Almighty unnecessary in keeping the system up and running. If God's role in the Universe and Creation had changed, so had man's. Newton's use of the word 'force' is interesting, because it signifies a lingering belief that nature is driven by a divine agency. Increasingly, mathematics and science permitted the replacement of such concepts by mathematical formulae, abstract representations further removed from the agency of God. If science challenged established beliefs in the nature of knowledge and man, then it was up to philosophy to take these arguments further.

PHILOSOPHY AND THE MIND

René Descartes is generally regarded as the founder of modern philosophy, and his ideas charted out a part of the territory which forms the battleground I shall describe shortly. The scope of his work was enormous. He was the originator of co-ordinate (or Cartesian) geometry, and also worked in optics and algebra. For Descartes, the bodies of men and animals were machines, but animals were automata because they lacked consciousness. Man was different because he possessed a soul located in the pineal gland at the base of the brain. It was here that soul and body interacted through the 'vital spirits'. It is important that we examine Descartes' view of body and spirit in some detail (the following account is largely taken from Russell, 1961). Descartes was interested in the interaction between the physical world and mind. How could non-material mind be responsible for physical action? If I decide to move my arm the physical laws of motion determine the movement, but my will which initiates the action is a feature of my mind, and thus non-material. If we assume that mind and matter are different entities incapable of interaction, then why does my body act as if my mind had controlled it? One way around this problem was the theory of the 'two clocks'. If we imagine two clocks keeping identical perfect time, then whenever one strikes the hour the other will do so. If you saw one and heard the other you could believe that one had caused the other to strike. This, it was argued, is the situation that applies to mind and body. The two were like identical clocks wound up by God, each in perfect time. If my mind willed my body to perform an action then purely physical laws ensured that my body would move at the precise instant that my will determined it. It turns out, of course, that there are serious problems with this analogy. If the physical world is determined by rigid natural laws, then the mental world must be equally rigidly determined (otherwise the two clocks would not keep the same time). If this is so, then there must be some means by which events in the brain (it was accepted by then that the brain was the seat of consciousness and thought) could be equated to mental events. The problem here is that such a view of human activity and experience is difficult to reconcile with Christian ethics and moral values. These appeared to have been written out of human experience. On the other hand, scientists and philosophers at the time considered that Descartes' model had the advantage that the soul or mind became entirely independent of the body. The two concepts, mind and matter, were entirely separated in such a way that any interaction seemed impossible. This dualism, the separation of mind and body, has had enormous influence on Western thought, but there is one other feature of Cartesian thought that I want to emphasise, concerning the nature of knowledge. After the growth of science Descartes was concerned with the problem of knowledge in the face of uncertainty about the role of God. He started with scepticism about the nature of the information we gain about the world through our senses, and argued that it was possible that our entire experience of the world could be nothing more than illusion. The only thing of which we could be certain was our power of reflexivity, our ability to think about ourselves as sentient beings.

> While I wanted to think everything false, it must necessarily be that I who thought was something; and remarking that this truth, *I think, therefore I am*, was so solid and so certain that all the most extravagant suppositions of the sceptics were incapable of upsetting it, I judged that I could receive it without scruple as the first principle of the philosophy that I sought.
>
> (Descartes, cited in Russell, 1961, p. 547;
> emphasis in the original)

This statement, Descartes' *Cogito ergo sum*, lies at the heart of his system of knowledge, and has subsequently influenced many epistemological[1] systems. It sets out the principle that mind is more certain than matter, and that in my experience, my own mind is more certain than the minds of other people. This opens the way for subjectivism, the idea that we can only gain knowledge of the physical world by inference through mind. Of particular importance here is the emphasis that Descartes' *cogito* places on the experience of the individual. Our understanding of the world is located in internal experiences, in the mind of the individual. The twin peaks of Cartesian thought, mind/body dualism which opened the way for the materialistic study of human behaviour, and belief in the foun-

---

1   Epistemology is that branch of philosophy concerned with the nature and scope of knowledge.

dation of knowledge through the experience of the individual, has had a potent effect in shaping psychological thought. In particular, it has stimulated scientific approaches aimed at understanding the internal mechanisms of mind, and their relationship to brain. The problem is that it has led to the neglect of the relationship between the individual and the other(s), for, as Russell observed, morals and ethics, those aspects of philosophy that understand the values that govern our individual and social relationships, had little or no place in Cartesian thought.

A SCIENCE OF BODY AND MIND?

It was not until the nineteenth century that developments in natural science, particularly the scientific method of observation, measurement, experimentation and hypothesis testing, came to be applied to medical science. It was the work of the French physiologist Claude Bernard who established physiology as a separate discipline from anatomy, firmly rooted in the scientific method. Bernard, although qualified as a doctor, never practised medicine, and chose instead a life in experimental physiology. He undertook a famous series of experiments on digestion, particularly the nervous control of gastric secretion. He was also interested in the effects that drugs such as curare and opium had on the nervous system. Bernard was a devout materialist who was driven to show that the function of the human body could be understood in exactly the same terms as the function of chemical and other physical systems:

> I propose, therefore, to prove that the science of vital phenomena must have the same foundations as the science of the phenomena of inorganic bodies, and that there is no difference in this respect between the principles of biological science and those of physico-chemical science.
>
> (Bernard, 1957, p. 60)

Vital phenomena were driven by the laws of chemistry and physics, not the spark of life granted by God. This was set out most clearly in the concept of homeostasis which Bernard regarded as essential in the maintenance of the *milieu interior*, a series of regulatory mechanisms by which the body maintained a constant internal environment. His work established two principles. The first was that science, and especially the scientific method, could be used to explain human experience and affairs. In philosophical terms, this is a form of positivism. The second principle was that materialism, in the form of the laws of physics and chemistry, was most appropriate to the positivistic principle. This led directly to attempts to understand the function of the mind in material, or physico-chemical, terms. It was from this that experimental psychology grew. The important link here lies in the work of the German physiologist Helmholtz, who held chairs both in physiology (at Heidelberg where, later, Kraepelin worked) and in physics (in Berlin). The scope of his work was enormous. He did pioneering work in thermodynamics, hydrodynamics and acoustics, and his work on colour perception and vision laid the foundation for the psychological study of perception. During the latter part of the nineteenth century his work dominated medicine, and helped to establish materialism and determinism as the dominant philosophical approaches to understanding the function of body and mind. Three of the most influential figures in early twentieth-century psychology, Freud, Pavlov and Wundt, studied with men who had worked alongside Helmholtz (Brücke, Ludwig and Du Bois-Reymond respectively). The influence of materialism and determinism on psychology and psychiatry can be traced back directly to the work of Helmholtz and Claude Bernard. Freud's dynamic theory of mind, modelled on thermodynamics; Wundt's development of experimental psychology in laboratory settings; and Pavlov's attempt to understand behaviour in terms of reflexes – a psychology devoid of consciousness and reflexivity – these are the origins of the scientific approach to psychiatry.[2] Perhaps the most influential figure, though, was Wilhelm Griesinger, who, in 1860, became director of the Burgholzli in Zurich, where Bleuler and Jung were to work. Although some aspects of his work presaged the dynamic psychology of Freud, his influence is widely recognised in relation to the development of psychiatry as a natural science. He believed that mental diseases were in effect brain diseases, and that a full understanding of mental illness would come only through an understanding of neuroanatomy and pathology. Griesinger founded academic psychiatry as we know it today, and it was through his teaching and writing (he wrote one of the first textbooks of psychiatry) that his influence spread. At this point I

---

2   There were, of course, other features of both Freud's and Wundt's work which cut across the argument that I am developing here. These include the importance of psychoanalytic theory as a hermeneutic system, or the significance of Wundt's method of introspection for phenomenology. The point I want to make here is that of understanding the philosophical basis of biological psychiatry.

want to examine the implications of this history for the neuroscience approach to psychiatry.

A CASE OF MATTER OVER MIND

A fundamental assumption which characterises neuroscience is that the symptoms of psychiatric disorders arise from underlying disorders of brain function. This position is stated clearly by Trimble (1988) in his textbook of biological psychiatry:

> Mental disorders are neither more nor less than nervous diseases in which mental symptoms predominate, and their entire separation from other nervous diseases has been a sad hindrance to progress. (p. 11)

And psychiatry is:

> ... concerned with behaviour in its widest sense, and has continually searched for knowledge of brain-behaviour relationships and *somatic underpinnings of psychopathology*.
>
> (p. 11; emphasis added)

Such statements are typical of the neuroscience approach to mental illness, but they make a number of assumptions that are rarely made explicit, and which require detailed consideration. We may state these as follows: first, that mental disorders are simply forms of brain disorder; second, that brain events determine mental events, and that this direction of attribution only ever occurs in that direction.

Mental disorders are simply forms of brain disorder

Strictly speaking, there is no logical basis in which we can say that this assertion is true. Whilst it is true that Trimble presents a great deal of evidence in his textbook that a wide variety of psychiatric disorders have a biological basis, for his assertion that mental disorders are brain disorders to be true, he must be able to show that there are no psychiatric disorders that do not have an underlying brain disorder. This is nonsense. There are many mental disorders which have a psychological, or even social basis, such as post-traumatic stress disorder or induced psychosis. Induced psychosis is a particularly good example. Sometimes referred to as *folie à deux*, the condition has been recognised for well over 100 years, and was originally described by the French psychiatrist Jules Falret. It occurs in specific social situations where a dominant member of a family develops a paranoid psychosis, which other members come to share. Such families are often quite isolated and have few social contacts. The psychosis which is induced in the other family members may be regarded as a means of coping with the exigencies of living with an overbearing person who has paranoid delusions. Once these members are removed from the influence of the psychotic relative, their paranoid beliefs usually disappear. Although the condition is relatively uncommon, it is well recognised in the literature. It is widely regarded as having a psychosocial explanation. Whilst it may be possible to argue that the abnormal beliefs in the dominant member may have a biological basis, it is difficult to argue that this is so for the other members. Common sense and human nature dictate that for them, the apparent sharing of the abnormal beliefs is a coping strategy. The point here is that there are circumstances where people present with mental disorder in the absence of brain disorder. Trimble's assertion is not true.

Mental events are brain events

It is this statement that really underpins the neuroscience position. Its origins extend back to the dualistic position stated by Descartes, honed and refined by 300 years of natural science research. In this context it is represented by Trimble's assertion that psychiatry is concerned with the search for links between behaviour and brain events. Psychopathology, or the abnormal experiences that form the basis of diagnosis of psychiatric disorders, is to be understood in terms of brain disorders. We have just seen that not all psychopathology is understandable in terms of brain disorder, but this does not mean to say that all mental events are not brain events. Our bodies are physico-chemical structures, so ultimately it must be true that all our experience, our thoughts, feelings, perceptions, beliefs, everything about us that characterises us as human beings, arises out the complex chemical and physical events that occur in our brains. Of course it is impossible to deny this, but the issue here concerns the nature of the relationship between brain and mind. Neuroscience accounts of mind require that we should be able to account for two things: that the physico-chemical properties of the brain *cause* mental events; and that the direction of causality *only ever runs from brain to mind*. The first statement is the materialist position. Materialism is the belief that everything in the Universe can be understood in terms of matter, energy and the interaction between the two. The second statement is the determinist position. In its most general terms, determinism holds that all events are effects, caused by earlier events. This implies that in terms of cause, some events are more important than others. As far as the mind–brain relationship is concerned, these two statements constitute what is sometimes referred to as the epiphenomenalist position, that is the mind is nothing more than the by-product of the brain's physico-chemical properties. As Thomas Huxley is reputed to have said, mind may exist, but it is of no more significance than the cloud of steam that hangs over a factory. This view relegates the significance of mental life to a secondary position. It is more concerned with the *causes* of experience rather than experience itself or the *meaning* of experience. In philosophy there have been many attempts to understand the relationship between mind and brain, although psychiatrists have always been suspicious about the value of philosophy in mental illness, as this statement from Slater and Roth (1977) indicates: '... attempts to solve the problems of psychopathology by the use of philosophical short-cuts, instead of the relatively slow method of investigation of natural science'. This emphasis on the value of natural science in psychiatry recalls Claude Bernard's scepticism about the value of philosophy: 'le meilleur système philosophique consiste à ne pas en avoir' (Claude Bernard, 1865).

Despite this, recent developments in cognitive science, computer theory and linguistics have forced psychiatrists to engage in discourse with philosophers, in attempts to re-examine the mind–brain problem and Cartesian dualism. One of the most influential reformulations of the mind–brain problem in recent years is Mind–Brain Identity Theory (MBIT) associated with Churchland (1986). MBIT, or neurophilosophy,[3] requires that there is a one-to-one relationship

---

3   To avoid confusion over the use of terms, I shall use the word neuroscience to refer to the approach advocated by Goodwin and others as a set of values to be adopted in regard to the study of mental illness. These values imply that only the sciences of neuroanatomy, neurophysiology and neuropharmacology are useful in understanding mental illness. The word neurophilosophy is used to refer to a particular theme in recent philosophy, associated with the work of Churchland and the mind–brain identity problem. The two are thus not the same, although, as will be seen, they share much in common.

between brain events and mind events. There is an equivalence between physical and mental events. It is, if you like, a digital, rather than a clockwork, version of Descartes' two-clock theory. The neurophilosophical view holds that mind–brain problems of cognition and perception will be resolved by advances in cognitive neuroscience. In fact, it goes further by claiming that all 'folk' psychologies will be replaced by neuroscience. 'Folk' psychologies here refers to explanations of human behaviour based in our understanding of human intentions, beliefs, desires and reasons. Such approaches are considered naive by neuroscience. They are primitive, not proper, sciences. Neurophilosophy's ability to excise radically all 'soft' science from understanding of mind is sometimes called eliminativism and can be seen clearly set out as a subtext in Goodwin's (1995) article at the end of the previous chapter. Such 'soft' sciences include much of psychology, sociology, anthropology, psychoanalytic theory and aspects of philosophy such as phenomenology, all of which share one thing in common: their purpose relates to understanding rather than causes. This is interesting, for, as Smythies (1992) points out, neurophilosophers appear not to apply the approach to their own consciousness, choosing instead to rely, like the rest of us, on 'folk' theory. Smythies has pointed to a number of serious flaws in the MBIT/neurophilosophy approach. Again, these relate to the assumption, underlying all materialist constructions of the mind–brain problem, that there is a one-to-one causal relationship between mind events and brain events.

Visual fields and stimulus fields

The visual field is that aspect of our subjective experience located in our consciousness that is filled with our visual sensations. The stimulus field is objective and consists of the physical objects located in the external world that our visual fields represent. As Smythies points out, we examine the stimulus field through our perceptions. We examine our visual field by introspection.[4] The two sets of experiences occur in different arenas.

---

4   Introspection is sometimes regarded as a form of perception in itself, through which we examine and establish our own, inner, mental states. Although its status in philosophy is controversial, I want to assume for the moment that it is a valid method of reporting our subjective experience.

Stimulus fields occur in physical space, whereas visual fields occur in phenomenal space.[5] This distinction is related to the Cartesian split between mind and body. Just as physical objects in the external world are located in space, so too are visual images represented in phenomenal space. Consider, for example, the after-image of a bright light seen in the dark. Such an image is not located in external space, but in internal, phenomenal space. It hangs and hovers, approaches and recedes, and moves up and down or from side to side. It does these things with, or despite, our intentions. All phenomenal images and events occur in internal phenomenal space, not external space. Descartes held that mental elements, being non-material and therefore different from physical elements, could not thus be represented in space. Introspection reveals that this is not so. The neurophilosophy approach to the mind–brain problem says that the more information we have about brain, the more we shall understand mind. But this is not to say that brain *is* mind, or that brain can *replace* mind. We may be able to represent the visual field through patterns of neuronal activation which may represent information in the brain, but we are left with no understanding of the nature of the experience as we are aware of it in phenomenal space as a content of consciousness, a problem raised by Lord Brain over thirty years ago (1960). This is relevant to the attempts of Cohen and Servan-Schreiber to relate PDP systems and dopaminergic function (Chapter 3, pp. 46–7) to the symptoms of schizophrenia. The more sophisticated the neuroscience attempt to model the putative disturbances in the brain which are presumed to underlie the symptoms, the further we seem to get away from the nature of the symptoms themselves.

The nature of consciousness

Some of the most penetrating investigations of the mind–brain problem have been proposed by Dennett (1991). He points out that the Cartesian distinction between mind and brain can result in absurd positions on the part of those who attempt to justify

---

5   Phenomenal space refers to that aspect of our consciousness in which external events are represented, or recreated as we recall an event to consciousness.

it. He develops the idea of a Cartesian 'theatre', located in the pineal gland, the point at which mind and body interact, in which the mind sits like an audience observing that which the senses portray of the external physical world. This is the central point at which it 'all comes together' for the observer (mind). The problem then arises as to how exactly mind becomes aware. Is it possible that the observer has an inner centrum, where everything from outside is brought together yet again for this observer? Of course not, for we descend rapidly into a tautological spiral from which there is no way out. Dennett points out that although brain events representing environmental events may be precisely located in time and space within the brain, the *onset* of brain events does not necessarily mark the onset of our consciousness of their content. This is most clearly demonstrated by experiments using the *phi* phenomenon, the perceptual mechanism responsible for the apparent motion of movie pictures and television screens. In its simplest form the *phi* phenomenon may be experienced if we observe two white spots separated by about 4° of visual angle in a dark room, which are lit for a short period in rapid succession. In these circumstances, the subject has the experience of seeing a single spot of light move to and fro between the position of the two spots. The Harvard philosopher Nelson Goodman asked psychologist Paul Kolers what would happen if the two illuminated spots were of different colours. What would happen to the colour of the spot as it 'moved'? Would the illusion of movement be lost entirely to two different coloured spots of light simply flashing on and off? Or would the spot change gradually in colour from, say, green on the left, through an infinite series of intermediate hues, to red on the right? When Kolers and von Grünau performed the experiment (1976) the results were astounding. Subjects in their experiment experienced the spot to start moving in one colour, but when it reached the halfway point, it suddenly changed colour whilst smoothly continuing its journey to the position of the second spot. The problem here was, how was it possible for the subjects to predict the trajectory of the spot between two points when they did not know in advance where the location of the second point was? Dennett dismisses precognition as an explanation. He points out that the illusory switching of colour at the midpoint cannot occur until after the identification of the second spot's position by the brain. But then, would it not be too late to impose the illusory colour change? How does the brain–mind manage to achieve this *léger de main*? Dennett's explanation indicates that for this to happen, there can be no one-to-one equivalence of brain and mind events.

> But then since what you experience is *first red, then red-turning-to-green, and finally green*, it ('surely') follows that your consciousness of the whole event must be delayed until after the green spot is (unconsciously?) perceived.
>
> (Dennett, 1991, p. 115; emphasis in the original)

The two clocks are not always keeping the same time.

There are further problems with MBIT. It follows from the theory that particular mental events will be associated with activity in particular areas of the brain. It is far from clear that this is the case, as the history of the aphasias, the speech disturbances often associated with strokes, demonstrates. In 1861, the French neurologist Paul Broca presented the case of 'Tan' to the Anthropological Society of Paris. Tan was named after the only syllable that he could utter. Examination of his brain after death indicated that he had a frontal lobe lesion. Two years later Broca had presented a further eight cases similar to Tan's, all of whom had lesions in similar positions. He concluded that lesions in the posterior of the third frontal convolution on the left side were associated with severe disturbances of expressive language. This created a considerable amount of interest in the localisation of language function in the brain, and, shortly after this, the neurologist Wernicke presented a series of patients in whom lesions of the temporal lobe were also associated with language dysfunction. The difference between Wernicke's series and Broca's, was that the former were able to speak fluently, whereas the latter found it extremely difficult to produce any speech at all. Following these studies, debate continued as to the precise nature of the localisation of language. Despite this early work, the relationship between anatomy and functional deficit in the aphasias becomes less clear if we consider the exact boundaries of lesions responsible for aphasic defects. Classically, the abnormality in Broca's aphasia is located in the posterior portion of the third frontal convolution, the so-called 'Broca's area'. Recent work by Mohr (1976) suggests that Broca's aphasia may arise from lesions much larger and more extensive than originally thought. The same applies to Wernicke's aphasia. We now know of the existence of a variety of aphasias that do not fit readily into the traditional descriptions. We are concerned here with the possibility of identifying a particular mental or psychological function with a specific brain area. Although the classic accounts of aphasia indicated this was possible, it is has become difficult to sustain a one-to-one relationship between function and localisation. In fact, the evidence suggests that mental operations are related to the co-ordinated activity of a number of different brain areas, rather than operation of a single area in isolation. This flaw in neuro-philosophical thought arises from reductionism.

Causes for concern

Here, we are concerned with what is known as theory reduction, that is the extent to which one theory may be reduced to an-other theory which, for some reason, is regarded as more basic or fundamental and thus more important. The natural sciences of physics, chemistry and biology are generally regarded as more basic in this sense, whereas psychology, sociology and anthropol-ogy are not. Reductionism can occur in many different ways, thus there are social, psychological or political reductionists. Many so-called 'anti-psychiatrists' use social or political reduction-ism in seeking to explain *all* mental illness only from a socio-logical or Marxist perspective. However, here we are concerned with the reductionist features of neurophilosophy, which emerge explicitly in the claims of Trimble and Goodwin, both of whom seek to reduce explanations of mental illness to neuroscience terms. But we have already seen that there is more to it than this. In the claims of neurophilosophy we can discern a very clear purpose to *replace* sociological or psychological concepts with neuroscientific ones. We may describe this purpose as elimi-nativism. There is an additional feature of the reductionism of neuroscience: its view of the relationship between mind and brain is not simply that there is an *equivalence* between mental and brain events, but that mental events are *caused* by brain events, and brain events alone. In fact, this is a restatement of the epiphenomenalist position. It implies that causal effects *only* occur in the 'bottom-up' direction, that is to say that the more 'basic' science events (brain events) are solely responsible for the 'higher level' (mind) events. The problem with this view of the mind–brain relationship is that it disregards evidence that causal effects can work in the opposite direction. The narrow preoccupa-tion of neuroscience with reductionism is ignorant of current interest in what is called 'downstream' causality. A recent study by Pardo *et al.* (1993) examined the relationship between brief changes in mood and brain activity. They measured regional cerebral blood flow (rCBF) using the method of positron emission tomography[6] in two situations: first, with subjects at rest; second, by the experimental situation in which they were asked to recall or envisage a situation which would make them feel very sad. Activity in brain areas associated with the experience of sadness were then calculated by subtracting the results of brain activation in the first condition from those of the second condition. Significant differences in brain activity were detected in the two conditions, with the experience of sadness being associated with increased activity in the frontal lobes, more prominent on the left in men. The precise localisation of activity is less important than the observation that, in this experiment, *mental events cause brain events.*

A recent study by McGuire *et al.* (1995) is of even greater significance in relation to schizophrenia. They examined rCBF in three groups of subjects: people with schizophrenia who heard voices when acutely ill; people with schizophrenia who did not hear voices; and control subjects with no psychiatric history. Cerebral activity was measured in all subjects during three tasks: a control situation in which subjects were asked to read silently from a list of words; an 'inner speech' task in which they had to recite mentally a sentence ending in a given word; and an auditory verbal imagery task, similar to the second task, but in which they had to imagine the sentences being read by an unknown neutral voice. They found that brain activity in people with a propensity to hallucinate differed from the other two groups only in the third experimental condition, that is when asked to imagine the sentences being spoken in a strange voice. Of course, this study provides evidence in support of Frith's and Hoffman's theory that verbal hallucinations may be understood in terms of a failure of monitoring (Chapter 3, pp. 48–51). But the study also demonstrates that mental-state events, in this case intentional mental-state events

---

6   This involves giving subjects an injection of water labelled with ^{15}O, a mildly radioactive isotope of oxygen, which is taken up preferentially by active brain tissue. The distribution of cortical activity is then computed tomographically (that is by measuring the radioactivity in a series of 'slices'), and the results, when fed into a computer, can be shown mathematically or, more pleasingly, in the form of a coloured picture of the brain, with different colours representing different levels of activity.

representing inner speech, produce brain events. In the face of this evidence, it is difficult to sustain the simplistic notion of causal determinism, that brain events only lead to mental events. Cast in this light we may need to reconsider the significance of the attributions we make to the *causative* role attributed to brain disturbances in playing a *prima facie* role in causing mental illness.

Despite my criticisms, reductionism has its advantages as well as its disadvantages. Reductionist approaches are neat and simple, and fit in well with scientific methods of thought. In any case, simply reducing what are complex areas of thought to simple categories, as I have done here, is a form of reductionism in itself, and in order to do justice to the complexity of the area it is important that we outline other aspects of reductionism. Karlsson and Kamppinen (1995), in commenting on the problems of reductionism, have pointed out that it fails adequately to deal with the complexity of the mind–brain relationships. They examine the concept of emergent materialism (Bunge, 1977) as an attempt to overcome this criticism. Bunge points out that we may consider the category H_2O simply in terms of its physico-chemical structure. On the other hand we can also consider it as the category water, the structure of which has *emergent* properties such as viscosity and fluidity. Karlsson and Kamppinen then apply Bunge's concept of emergent materialism to the mind–brain problem. Although this approach recognises that, ultimately, the basis of consciousness and subjective experience is rooted with the physico-chemical (material) properties of our brains, it allows for the unique richness and complexity of consciousness through multiple levels of organisation. Higher (non-material) levels, such as consciousness, emerge out of lower (material) levels. Higher levels are independent of lower levels in terms of their nature, their organisation and their governing laws. They are characterised by unique, emergent properties which are not found in lower levels.

Emergent materialism has the advantage that it is consistent with the view that the world is organised at many different levels and in different ways. It allows us to regard the symptoms of schizophrenia in a variety of ways, some of which may be mutually exclusive. The problem is, as Karlsson and Kampinnen point out, that there are no satisfactory theories for emergence which establish the relationships between different organisational levels. There is a more fundamental problem. Emergence fails adequately to account for intelligibility, or what counts as an explanation. This may become clearer if I reframe the problem. If we can agree that intelligibility refers to *understandability*, and that this understandability relates to subjective events in consciousness, then the problem becomes slightly different. We are not concerned with understanding, for example, how a verbal hallucination arises out of the physico-chemical properties of the brain. We have followed that route for much of this book, and spent most of this chapter examining its problems. No, understanding here refers to the possible *meanings* of a verbal hallucination. So far this is something that we have not really considered. Psychiatry appears not to be concerned with the possibility that hallucinations or delusions might have meaning, or be made intelligible (recall Slater and Roth's attitude towards talking to deluded patients: Chapter 4, pp. 66–7. That neuroscience is concerned with causes, not meaning, is patently clear from its determination to write out anthropological, psychosocial or post-modern 'explanations' in psychiatry. It seems to me that those eliminative materialists who believe that mind will ultimately be understood purely in terms of its physico-chemical properties have neglected an important area of overlap between psychiatry and philosophy. This area has played an important role in the development of psychiatry as we know it today. It is my contention that the trend to domination of psychiatry by neuroscience must be complemented by approaches that recognise the complexity, significance (both in personal and scientific terms) and potential meaningfulness of subjective experience. The counterbalance has to come from phenomenology.

PHENOMENOLOGY: TOWARDS UNDERSTANDING?

We have just examined two types of causal relationships between mind and brain. The so-called 'top-down' (or neuroscience) approach (that brain events cause mind events), and the less well-known 'bottom-up' approach (that mind events can cause brain events). The German psychiatrist Michael Langenbach (personal communication, 1996) is interested in a third set of relationships, what he calls a 'side-to-side' influence, between mind and mind. This relationship may be self-induced through memory, the subject's 'inner voice', images, or through other people and external events. This takes us right to the heart of the area that I want now to consider, that is phenomenology and our intersubjective nature. And here, although it may seem like stating the obvious, it is as well to remind ourselves that psychiatry is concerned with our mental lives, not brain activity. The difficulty is that we have no way of measuring this experience in the same way that the empirical nature of medical science can measure physical aspects of our natural functions. Empirical methods have two important features, reliability and validity. Reliability examines the extent to which observers at different times and in different places can agree upon a particular observation. Validity is concerned with the extent to which the observations made really represent those that are purported to be made. Quantitative observations, those in which measurements of some form or another are made, usually have good reliability, but may not necessarily have good validity. On the other hand, qualitative, or descriptive, observations have good validity, but are not necessarily reliable. Mental-state phenomena, which include all psychiatric 'symptoms', are subjective experiences whose properties are complex and emergent. We have no way of quantifying them, or rather, if we try to do so we end up with absurdly simplistic representations. The point I want to make here is that our knowledge and understanding of mental-state phenomena will not be achieved through measurement alone. We may gain some idea of the problems here if we consider the following example.

While I have been writing this passage there has been a piece of piano music by Ravel on the radio. It is a piece I know well, 'Ondine' from *Gaspard de la Nuit*. As I write I am gradually aware that my attention is being seduced by this music. At first I am unaware of it, but the music imperceptibly imposes itself on my consciousness. I know this cannot be true because a piece of music does not have intentionality in this sense, but that is exactly how I experience it. At first it seems to interpose itself with my thoughts concerning the task in hand – writing this page. This disrupts the flow of my thoughts which become stuck and repetitive. As each moment passes I find my self unwillingly (for I am aware of my publisher's deadline) drawn to the cascades of sound until finally, I have to stop writing completely and devote all my attention to the music itself, an evocation of a water sprite inspired by a poem by Aloysius Bertrand. As I listen I am completely submerged in its complex textures. Initially I am aware of its musical properties, the ever-shifting ostinato rhythms, tonal ambiguities, subtle changes of timbre, volume, rubato, all of which combine to create a constantly changing set of overlapping textures. But these are objective descriptions using the little musical terminology at my command. As I continue to listen, my experience shifts from these purely musical sensations to something quite different. Water. Water in all its protean manifestations, in fountains, waterfalls, rain on a summer's day. I can see in my mind cascades of rain bouncing off the stone floor outside my study, sharp needles of light reflecting the dancing sun; the river which runs at the bottom of my house, at times a calming trickle, which grows with the rain to a breathless roar. Then again, this gives way to other experiences that are almost impossible to convey through words. This music has two distinct moods. There is the calm, detached introduction conveying a sense of isolated beauty which is almost austere. Then there is a great upsurge of energy as the music liberates itself and becomes passionate, excited and almost out of control. These tensions and contrasts, beautiful beyond words, are clearly highly subjective, but at the same time I am aware that they are deeply seated in Western culture. The Apollonian and Dionysian principles were described by Nietzsche as representing two fundamental human and natural properties, the god Apollo representing order, perfection of form and control, and Dionysus representing creation, energy and destruction.

It is possible to consider the processes by which these mental events occur whilst I listen to the music. There are the physical processes that allow me to listen to a piece of music recorded in a studio ten years ago, replayed on a CD player in London, broadcast by radio transmitter, the signals of which are picked up by my receiver and turned back into physical sound. But what does that tell us about the complex set of experiences which occurred in my mind when I listened to it? Or for that matter, what would it tell us about your responses to the piece if you were sat here next to me listening to the same performance? How would we know that the two sets of experiences were the same, similar or different? The problem is that explanatory accounts relating to the occurrence of physical events in the natural world have nothing to tell us about the subjective nature of the experiences that those events may invoke in our consciousness. We must rely upon a different language to understand this. We also have to rely on quite different methods of investigation when we examine the world of mental events. We must be aware that we use language to communicate and negotiate the extent to which the boundaries of our experience are shared. The example of two people listening to the same piece of music is a very simple one. What of two complete strangers, from different social backgrounds and cultures, and with different life histories, where one is trying to judge and comment on the experience of another, trying to decide whether the other's experience is 'normal' or 'abnormal'? What possibilities are there here for achieving a shared understanding of the meaning of each other's experience? If subjectivity is problematic, then what of intersubjectivity?[7] These are the problems that phenomenology attempts to deal with.

THE NATURE OF PHENOMENOLOGY

The difficulty here is that phenomenology means different things to different people. When I was a postgraduate studying psychiatry, I was taught that phenomenology was the detailed study of the patient's signs and symptoms. But the word also refers to one of the twentieth century's most influential schools of philosophy, and here the word is used in a quite different sense. The philosophical underpinnings of phenomenology may be more apparent if first we examine the phenomenological approach in action.

Example 1: description of verbal hallucinations from PSE–10

Information on 11 aspects of hallucinations

17.1	probe for hallucinations	Yes / No
17.3	non-verbal hallucinations	Yes / No
17.4	frequency of verbal auditory hallucinations	
17.5	length of utterances	
17.6	quality of vh	
17.7	internal hallucinations (inner voices)	Yes / No
17.8	voices commenting on thoughts or actions	Yes / No
17.9	second and third person auditory hallucinations	Yes / No
17.12	special features of auditory hallucinations	Yes / No
17.13	insight into auditory hallucinations	Yes / No
17.14	prominence of auditory hallucinations	

---

7   Intersubjectivity usually refers to the possibility that two or more minds are aware not only of each other's existence, but also of the intention to convey information. This definition is inadequate for my purposes because I am also interested in the extent to which the two minds share a common experience and/or understanding of that experience.

Example 2: Voice Profile, Subject XX, Schizophrenia

Individuation of self and voices
XX hears more than one voice, three or four. The voices are male or female. She used to think she knew some of the people whose voices they were. The voices have stable identities. The voices know what she thinks. She cannot hide anything from them. Voices individuated perceptually, by analogy to different people. No names, voices are gendered. The voices are false judges.

Situational triggering
The voices, when she hears them, are continuous.

Positioning
The voices talk directly to her. The voices address her, may come together as in a chorus, or individually. No evidence that the voices talk together.

DIALOGICAL CHARACTERISTICS

Regulative dialogues
The voices do not demand actions, they do not tell her to do things, but they comment on her actions. XX reacts by asking the voices to stop talking to her. Aside from this, she does not tell the voices to do things.

Evaluative dialogues
The voices judge her. The voices say that the things that she does are wrong and they abuse her. She answers the voices, or she ignores them. She disagrees with their evaluations. She never agrees because what they say to her is lies. When she answers back, the voices may stop to 'see how she gets on'. XX also asks the voices to stop talking to her. She gets angry with the voices. The voices never say anything positive about her.

Informing dialogues
The voices inform her of events outside her experience. This typically concerns what her children do.

Arguments
She feels the voices provoke her and she gets angry with them.

(Leudar *et al.*, 1997)

Phenomenology has played an important role in the growth of psychiatric knowledge, through the work of the German psychiatrist Karl Jaspers. The majority of psychiatrists would probably say that the first example represented the phenomenological approach in psychiatry. It is from the PSE-10 (Present State Examination), the diagnostic interview which yields ICD-10 (Internal Classification of Diseases, 10th edition) diagnoses for research and clinical use in psychiatry. They would be less clear about the second, a profile taken from a detailed interview in a study by Ivan Leudar and myself with a woman who had heard voices for twenty years. The most obvious difference between the two is in the detail of the descriptions. In psychiatry we are entirely dependent upon the subjects' own accounts of their experiences. Such accounts are couched in the first-person singular, and are therefore subjective. They are also based in language, and, as Michael Langenbach (1996) has pointed out, most philosophical approaches to psychiatry, especially neurophilosophy, completely neglected the 'linguistic' turn in twentieth-century philosophy. If we rely purely on the subject's account of her experience, then such an account is descriptive, and no inferences are made about the cause of that experience. In this respect, phenomenological approaches differ from psychoanalytic approaches, which rely on interpretation of the subject's experience to reveal the explanation. Phenomenology is primarily concerned with the subject's experience. It is non-inferential and non-reductionist. It does not attempt to change or mutate the subject's experience into something which it is not. Spitzer and Uehlein (1993) have summarised the principle features of phenomenology:

Empirical (in contrast to speculative)
Detailed (idiographic rather than nomothetic[8])
Subjective (dependent on the first-person narrative)
Non-inferential
Atheoretical (as regards aetiology)

---

8   Windelband (1904) made the distinction between the idiographic and nomothetic approaches. The former is concerned with the detailed description of individual cases, as in a single case study for example. Freud relied heavily on this technique in laying the foundations of psychoanalysis, as can be seen in *Studies in Hysteria* (Freud, S. and Bonner, J. 1974). The nomothetic approach relies on the distillation of essential properties out of groups of individuals who share a common feature (such as the diagnosis of schizophrenia). It forms the basis of the scientific method in medicine and psychiatry.

Non-reductionist

In general these features emerge from Example 2 above,[9] but there are problems with Example 1. It is neither detailed nor particularly subjective. In the SCAN-10, phenomenology has become truncated in the interests of brevity and the generation of quantitative measures which can be subjected to statistical analysis. The subject's experience is of value only in so far as it can be used to turn the subject into an object of scientific study. The real value of phenomenology has been corrupted and forced into being something of no consequence. Phenomenology has become the harlot of neuroscience. This is the essence of the problem of the neuroscience approach. On the other hand we should be aware that phenomenology brings its own set of problems. Spitzer and Uehlein point out that it poses two challenges: how are mental phenomena constituted in our minds; and how can we know what is going on in other people's minds?

THE PROBLEM WITH JASPERS

These were the very issues which Karl Jaspers tried to address in his phenomenology – an empirical science of others' minds. He made clear the difference between causal explanation and understanding in psychiatry. Indeed, he developed the concept of 'understandability' as a diagnostic tool. He was aware that although mental disorders had many 'organic' causes, such as TB or syphilis, no pathological basis had been found for schizophrenia. In practical terms he concluded that if no organic cause for a psychosis could be found, then it was important to attempt to understand the disturbance in terms of a reaction to events in the individual's life history. If the psychological disturbance was not thus understandable, then Jaspers concluded

---

9   Pure phenomenologists may take issue with me on this. They might argue that the Leudar and Thomas approach to eliciting detailed first-person accounts of the experience of verbal hallucinations is, strictly speaking, neither atheoretical nor non-inferential. This is because our semi-structured interview relies on an established body of theory (pragmatics and socio-linguistics) in which we attempt to ground subjects' descriptions of their experiences. Nevertheless, I would argue that we are following the spirit of a phenomenological approach, because we do not interpret this experience and we rely exclusively on detailed first-person accounts.

that it was caused by a disease *process*, that is schizophrenia. Here, he was heavily influenced by the German neuropsychiatric tradition of Kraepelin and Kahlbaum, both of whom believed in the disease process concept of schizophrenia. The burden of proof, then, is on the psychiatrist who has to understand the symptoms of the subject's disturbance in terms of life history and events. If the psychiatrist fails to do this, and the symptoms appear not to be 'understandable', then the subject is suffering from schizophrenia. This raises many issues. What do we mean by 'understandability'? What criteria do we use to establish it? What aspects of life experience are important in establishing it? To deal with these questions we must briefly consider some features of phenomenology.

Husserl's phenomenology

These problems were central to the work of Wilhelm Dilthey, the nineteenth-century German philosopher who was concerned with the nature of hermeneutics[10] and the concept of understanding, and who was one of the most important influences on the thought of Edmund Husserl. Dilthey made the distinction between the Natural Sciences, based in explanation and causation, and what might broadly be referred to as the Humanities (*Geisteswissenschaften*) in which understanding is the main objective. 'Nature is what we explain, mental life is what we understand' (Dilthey, 1894, quoted in Spitzer and Uehlein, 1993, p. 39). Husserl set out to establish a detailed account of consciousness, or the contents of mental life, starting with a description as free as possible from any form of prejudice or assumption.

One of the most important ideas in Husserl's philosophy was the notion of intuition, a concept which had appeared in Descartes' ideas. This refers to any direct awareness that we have of something. It is a particular experience in which the object of our awareness is

---

10 Hermeneutics (from Hermes, the Greek messenger of the gods) is the art of interpretation. It developed out of the Reformation, when Protestants felt the need to attain a new understanding of the Bible, and resorted to a new, literal reading and interpretation of its text. Modern hermeneutics applied hermeneutic theory more widely in an attempt to understand human culture, mind and behaviour. The word today is even more widely used to apply to systems of thought that seek interpretation and understanding, such as psychoanalysis.

itself directly given in person. An analogy might be the sense perception that I have of an object in front of me, contrasted with my memory of the object as I recall it to memory later. In this sense, perception is intuitive whereas memory is not. Husserl argues that certain knowledge in philosophy is only possible if it arises through intuition, that is a full direct 'giveness' of the object under study. Our own mental processes and their intended objects are the only things which can be intuited (cf. Descartes' *cogito*), so to attain certain knowledge we must be concerned with mental life and the objects of mental life as they are intended by mental life. Intentionality plays an important part in Husserl's philosophy, as it expresses a direct relationship between subjectivity (the inner world) and objectivity (the outer world). In this sense, phenomenology is the study of intentionality,[11] or the direct access that the mind has to the world. This is important. Without this, the phenomenological approach could be written off as little more than a form of Wundtian introspection. The importance of Husserl's approach is twofold. First, it opposes theories of mind which reduce subjective experience to something other than it actually is. It is therefore non-reductionist. Second, it attempts to describe experience without resort to explanatory models which posit unobservable mechanism underlying mental life. Phenomenology depends on the setting aside or 'bracketing' all explanatory theories, psychological, scientific or metaphysical. Phenomenological understanding is not achieved through explanation (*eklären*) but in clarification (*aufklären*). Meaning emerges only out of detailed clarification of the experience under consideration. The difference between cognitive psychological and phenomenological accounts of consciousness is that the latter do not seek to describe experience in non-experiential terms, whereas cognitive psychology uses a meta-language (such as

---

11 Intentionality, the relationship of mind to what it perceives, leads to some very difficult problems for philosophy of mind. I can imagine something that does not exist (like a mountain made out of trifle), or believe something that is patently impossible (that the next Prime Minister of Britain will be a rabbit). In essence, this leads to a dilemma. Either it is not possible for my mind to maintain an intentional relationship with an impossible object or event, other than through some odd form of intentionality, or the impossible event must exist in order for there to be an intentional relationship. The implications of this problem are really beyond the scope of this text, but it is perhaps worth noting that the dilemma may be one reason for the predilection to materialistic as opposed to mentalistic approaches in philosophy and psychology.

information processing, or neural networks) to do so. Cognitive psychology regards consciousness in passive terms – processes take place and occur in the absence of any sense of agency. Phenomenological accounts regard the subject and the experience as inseparable. The subject is an active participant in the constitution of the experience. This is why the subject's account of the experience is pre-eminent.

At this point we are now in a position to return to Jaspers and his use of the Husserlian concept of phenomenology. There are three problems with his interpretation and use of the concept. The first point to be made here concerns his book, *General Psychopathology*. The first edition was published in 1913, but it was exactly fifty years later that an English translation appeared, and this was of the seventh (1959) edition. Some authorities (see, for example, Berrios, 1989) have questioned the extent of Husserl's influence on Jaspers, but Michael Langenbach (1995) has drawn attention to the fact that Jaspers' work developed and changed from the first, German edition, to the English translation of the seventh edition. He points out that there are close similarities between Husserl's terminology and that used by Jaspers in the first edition of *General Psychopathology*. Both writers regard phenomenology as a form of descriptive psychology, an intuitive method for the clear visualisation of mental acts and how they are experienced. But there are two important differences (Langenbach, 1995). Husserl's phenomenology was concerned with the details of 'normal' mental life, whereas Jaspers was concerned primarily with 'abnormal' states. This alone makes it difficult to generalise from Husserl's methodology to Jaspers', but Langenbach then goes on to point out that Husserl's approach was developed as a first-person method, for the exploration by the subject of his or her own experience. Jaspers transformed Husserl's method, and adapted it for his own purpose as a tool of *clinical investigation* to be used by a psychiatrist on a patient. This is clear from the following statement from Jaspers:

> 'Phenomenology sets out on a number of tasks: it *gives a concrete description* of the psychic states which patients actually experience and *presents* them *for observation*' (Jaspers, 1963, p. 55; emphasis in the original).

Jaspers is quite clear that the purpose of phenomenology is the explication and clarification of one subject's experience (the patient's) for another subject to observe (the clinician). He has transformed Husserl's subjective method into an intersubjective one. Husserl later argued that intersubjective approaches in phenomenology required a quite different approach, but nowhere does Jaspers acknowledge this. The implications of this misappropriation of Husserl's techniques are considerable.

The problem here concerns a conflict between subjectivity and Jaspers' interpretation of phenomenology. The use of phenomenology in psychiatry has always been an objective approach, which regards the patient and his or her experience as an object of investigation. Most psychiatrists appear to accept uncritically Jaspers' interpretation of Husserl's ideas. An example of this is to be found in Sims'[12] (1988) authoritative text on psychopathology, *Symptoms in the Mind*, which bears Jaspers' influence throughout. According to Sims, phenomenology is '... the study of events, either psychic or physical, without embellishing those events with explanation of cause or function' (1988, pp. 1–2), and, in addition to this, it is perfectly clear that phenomenology thus defined is to be used intersubjectively: '... understanding the subjective experiences of a sufferer ...' (Sims, 1988, p. 1).

The problem that psychiatrists generally remain unaware of, however, is that Husserlian phenomenology is simply not up to the tasks that psychiatrists set it. If psychiatry is successfully to deal with the nature of individual experience developed in Chapter 7, it must use an intersubjective approach. This is an idea developed by Pat Bracken (1995), who has described the tension which exists between positivist psychiatry, or neuroscience, and anti-positivist psychiatry (existential and hermeneutic models). We have seen that phenomenology (as a first-person method) is supposed to offer a 'theory-free' view of the phenomena under scrutiny, achieved through the process of 'bracketing aside' the world. This principle becomes even more significant in relation to intersubjective uses of phenomenology (which is how Jaspers, and all psychiatrists, use the technique). Attempts to obtain as clear a view as possible of the experiences of another are notoriously difficult to achieve, and impossible unless the observing subjects are fully aware of their own intentions, perspectives and belief systems. Only if the observers are thus fully informed about their own position is it then possible to see how this might twist and distort in any glimpse of another person's experience. But as far as psychiatrists' application

---

12 To be fair, Andrew Sims has pointed out the limitations of Jaspersian phenomenology in understanding the subjective experience of another person. I want to return to his interesting ideas on this in my conclusions.

of Jaspersian phenomenology is concerned, this is impossible. The 'understanding' that psychiatrists seek is not developed in the context of a searching of self and its own perspectives, assumptions, presuppositions, beliefs about the world and the way the world is organised.[13] Far from it. In fact they already bring in the assumption that there is a condition called schizophrenia, that this is caused by a disease process (cause *still* unknown), and that if they cannot understand the form (and probably content too) of subjects' experiences, then this almost certainly indicates that those subjects are suffering from schizophrenia. There is nothing intersubjective about this. This is nothing whatever to do with phenomenology. These processes become even more significant in the context of the differences and barriers which exist between doctor and patient, which we shall examine in Chapter 10. This has had a devastating effect on the treatment, management and understanding of those who suffer from schizophrenia. It has denied them the opportunity to be listened to, to be heard and to be understood. It has provided the justification for psychiatrists to disregard psychotic experience, to shrug it off as the meaningless noise of disordered neurones. This for me is the final, dreadful failure of psychiatry as I, and the great majority of psychiatrists, have been taught. Our minds are closed as soon as we encounter someone with a diagnosis of schizophrenia. If we are to reverse this situation we have to go back to our beginnings, and challenge many of the things we have been taught. We must find new ways of understanding the individual mind, and especially the relationship between the individual and the society in which he or she is embedded. We must learn, too, that psychiatrists are individual minds, located in the same society and culture, and that there is an important and neglected interface, an *intersubjective* interface with implications for patient and clinician. These are the issues I want to deal with in the final section.

---

13 The technique here should be analogous to the use of a fine instrument used to measure radiation from outer space. The scientist has to evaluate the effects of ambient, background radiation on the instrument's sensitivity before there is any possibility of being able to detect the object of study.

Part III SYNTHESIS

9 'Talking Voices'

We may therefore view the hearing of voices not solely as a
discrete individual psychological experience, *but as an interactional phenomenon reflecting the nature of the individual's
relationship to his or her own* [social] *environment* ....
(Romme and Escher, 1993, p. 16; emphasis added)

In Part II we witnessed an unfolding conflict between neuroscience
and the experience of the individual with a mental illness. We also
discovered that there were important social and political contexts
to this conflict. This has been mediated through psychiatry's increasing preoccupation with physical methods of treatment at the
expense of psychological and other approaches. The purpose of this
final section is to seek new ground so that the conflicts may
continue afresh. I shall present some new ways of helping people
who experience psychosis, the main purpose of which is to help
the individual to make sense out of the experience. An important
objective here is to enable people to self-manage their problems.
Self-management is now widely advocated for chronic physical disorders such as asthma, diabetes and chronic pain. Many people
who experience long-standing mental health problems have been
practising self-management for years and are now starting to con-
solidate their ideas.[1] Perhaps the single most important idea that I
want to develop in this chapter is that we cannot hope to help
people suffering from schizophrenia unless we consider the relationship between the person and the disorder. In Chapter 10 I shall
take this a stage further by examining another relationship, that
between the individual and the expert who helps. But for the moment the relationship between person and illness can best be illus-
trated by the following incident.

---

1   A good example of this is the work of the Manic Depression Fellow-
    ship in the UK, whose recent booklet, *Inside Out*, provides an intro-
    duction to self-management for sufferers, by sufferers.

A couple of years ago I was talking at a meeting in East Anglia, organised by the Hearing Voices Network. Over 100 people gathered together on a miserable November day hoping to start a group for voice hearers in the city. The audience largely consisted of voice hearers, the majority of whom had been long-term users of the psychiatric system; their carers and a smaller number of professionals. Towards the end of the proceedings there was a plenary discussion where everybody had an opportunity to comment on what had taken place, and what should happen in the future. A gentleman in his early sixties stood up and spoke about his own experience of hearing voices. His voices first started when he was in his late teens, and as a result he spent the next thirty years of his life in the local asylum, until he was moved out into a group home, where he still lived with two or three friends. In over forty years of contact with psychiatric services he had experienced just about every form of treatment: insulin coma, ECT, long-term neuroleptic therapy, lithium, behaviour therapy, a lengthy period of time on a token economy ward, psychosocial rehabilitation, psychotherapy and counselling. Despite this, the voices persisted. They defiantly resisted every professional intervention. Until the year before, that is, when something very interesting happened. He had always heard three or four different voices, but he identified the most persistently troublesome one as the choirmaster of a church choir he sang with as a young lad. He remembered this man in particular because he had always picked on him for not singing the right notes. Throughout his years of contact with psychiatrists, nobody had ever asked him to talk in detail about the voices, let alone suggest that he might engage in conversation with them. But on this particular day he decided that he was going to talk to the choirmaster. He addressed the man saying that he had always enjoyed singing as a youngster, and he often wished to join a choir again. That could be arranged, replied the choirmaster, and the next day he started to hear a choir singing his favourite hymns and chorales, so he joined in. After a couple of days' membership of this hallucinatory choir, he suddenly decided to stop singing, and he angrily told the choir to go away. The following day the choirmaster returned, demanding to know why he hadn't been turning up for rehearsals. The gentleman replied that he had decided to leave the choir because he was fed up with the other members who were singing out of tune. He added that as far as he was concerned he was fed up with the choirmaster's criticism over the years, and he too could get lost.

He never heard the voice again.

This account raised more than just a laugh from the audience, it raised some extremely important issues which set me thinking for some time after. It shows that people who have been hearing voices for many years develop relationships with their voices. These relationships are not fixed and static, but may change over time. It also suggests that issues of power and control, which are so much a feature of our daily relationships with others, are just as much a feature of the relationship between the individual and his or her voices. If this is so then there is much to be gained from a detailed study of the interactions between voice hearer and voice(s). Later in this chapter we shall consider recent work which examines these interactions in great detail. I left the meeting in East Anglia chastened, because it made me aware of the enormous gulf that existed between my own understanding of the nature of hallucinatory voices, and the nature of that experience as it affects the life of the person who has to deal with it. This chapter tries to deal with ways of bridging that gulf.

THE HEARING VOICES EXPERIENCE

About ten years ago, the Dutch psychiatrist Marius Romme was struggling to help a patient who had been hearing voices for many years. Medication had had little effect on these experiences other than to reduce her anxiety, and she was becoming increasingly desperate, to the extent that she was talking about ending her life. She mentioned that she had been reading Julian Jaynes' book (1976), proposing that voice-hearing experiences played an important part in the evolution of consciousness as we understand it. She found this comforting, and it helped her to feel less distressed about her own experiences. She challenged her psychiatrist, saying that he had been unable to help her to cope with her voices, so Romme thought it might be valuable if she shared her experiences with other voice hearers. There followed a series of meetings in which he was impressed by the extent to which voice hearers were able to recognise each others' experiences. Difficulty in coping with voices was common, so Romme and his patient appeared on a popular Dutch TV 'chat' show, with the purpose of establishing contact with other voice hearers. Following the broadcast 450 voice hearers phoned in, of whom 300 said they were unable to cope with the experience. All the respondents were sent a questionnaire to find out more about their coping mechanisms. The results of the questionnaire are revealing (Romme and Escher, 1993). They categorised coping mechanisms as follows: distraction, ignoring, selective listening and setting limits. Table 9.1 compares the use of these techniques by those who were able to cope and those who were unable to do so. Copers were more likely to use selective listening and limit setting than non-copers. Selective listening involves paying attention only to positive voices and disregarding negative or hostile voices. Limit setting describes a process in which the voice hearer sets aside a period of time each day for the voices. The subject pays attention to voices only during this period and not at any other time. Romme and Escher concluded that the

Table 9.1: Coping strategies of copers and non-copers

Technique	Copers (%)	Non-copers (%)
Distraction[1]		
Yes	26	43
No	74	57
Ignoring[2]		
Yes	56	25
No	37	39
Sometimes	7	36
Selective listening[2]		
Yes	46	14
No	53	85
Setting limits[2]		
Yes	48	30
No	51	70

Notes:
1. Statistically significant difference between copers and non-copers at the 5% level.
2. Statistically significant difference between copers and non-copers at the 1% level.
Source: Romme and Escher, 1993.

nature of the individual's social environment was the single most important factor related to coping style. Those who coped well with their voices had more supportive social environments, whereas those who found it difficult to cope had more threatening social environments.

Following this, they organised a conference in which twenty 'copers' were invited to talk about their coping methods. Nearly 400 voice hearers attended. Subjects' adaptation to the experience of hearing voices fell into three stages. The first, or 'startling' stage was associated with the (usually sudden) first appearance of voices, and consisted of fear, alarm and anxiety. Subjects were usually able to recall this experience vividly. The second stage, a phase of organisation, involved a struggle to find a way of living and coping with voices. Subjects would try some or all of the mechanisms described above, with varying degrees of success. In general, ignoring voices and distraction techniques were rarely successful. The final stage, of stabilisation, involved the integration of the voices into the individual's life, as a part of self. Here, subjects were free either to follow, or disregard things that the voices said. Romme was particularly interested in the subjects' explanatory systems, because his own patient had been able to cope with her voices once she had established her own explanatory system based on the work of Julian Jaynes. The questionnaire respondents described a variety of explanatory models. Psychological systems used a number of academic sources, from Jung to Putnam,[2] and often involved psychodynamic models. Other psychological mechanisms included mystical explanations based on meditation and transcendental experiences, and parapsychological explanations, including sensitivity to the spiritual world and mediumship. Non-psychological explanations included those derived from biological psychiatry in which medication played an important part, natural medicine and religious explanations. It appeared that an explanatory system was an important prerequisite for the establishment of coping mechanisms, and that the *meaning* of the voices was of particular importance: 'Unless some meaning is attributed to the voices, it is very difficult to begin the phase of organising one's relationship with them in order to reduce anxiety' (Romme and Escher, 1993, p. 25).

Since then, Marius Romme and Sandra Escher have helped to

---

2   Frank Putnam is an American psychiatrist well known for his research into the significance of the mechanism of dissociation in psychiatric disorders.

develop an international self-help network for people who hear voices. In Britain the Hearing Voices Network, with its headquarters in Manchester, has established over thirty groups, led by voice hearers for voice hearers. They offer an unofficial network of support for members, seven days a week. The work of these groups represents a non-medical approach in which the participants' experiences are accepted at face value. Explanations are not imposed on members, who are free to choose that which most suits them. Many of these explanations are normalising, in that they regard the experience as one of a wide range of possible forms of human experience. Psychiatry's insistence that hallucinations are symptoms of mental illness forces voice hearing into a pathological framework which isolates subjects from their experience and the rest of society. This is particularly important given that subjects frequently locate the origins of these experiences in the world of social relationships, such as the loss of a partner, an abusive relationship, a sexual trauma. Personal understanding of the nature of the experience may take its place alongside biological explanations of voices, but it is a prerequisite for successful self-management and coping.

The work of Marius Romme and Sandra Escher constitutes a form of social action. It acknowledges the existence of a group within society (people who hear voices) who are regarded as 'different', and who are discriminated against on the basis of this difference. Their experiences are likely to be interpreted by the majority in a negative way, invoking fear and suspicion. Ron Coleman, a voice hearer who, for the last five years, has played a leading role in the development of the Hearing Voices Network in the UK, has compared the challenge of voice hearers to the 'coming out' of the gay and lesbian movement in the 1960s. Romme and Escher (1993) point out that psychiatrists can assist in this process by accepting the validity of subjects' attempts to make sense of their experiences. They can also help by encouraging voice hearers to come together in groups. The real difficulty here, though, is that the explanatory framework used by most psychiatrists renders them incapable of exploring their patients' experiences. Psychiatric knowledge generates models of voice hearing that are couched in terms and constructs which are remote from the experiences they are supposed to describe. We might be able to provide a detailed cognitive or neuropsychological explanation of voices, but this would be meaningless to the person who had the experiences. On the other hand, we must beware of the dangers of reinterpreting the experience, which, to my mind, is the flaw of psychoanalytic models. These are just as deterministic as neuroscientific models. We need a new way of thinking about the nature of verbal hallucinations if we are to be able to help the subject make sense out the voices. This is a difficult and demanding task. But there is more. I started this chapter with a quote from Marius Romme and Sandra Escher's book, *Accepting Voices* (1993), in which they pointed out that 'voices' reflect the relationship between the individual and the social environment. Our detailed examination of psychiatry and society in Chapter 7, and the nature of mind in Chapter 8, indicates the need for a radical revision of the model of mind that informs psychiatric research and practice. This revision must make it possible to address Romme and Escher's point about the nature of voices, as well as the following question: How are we to understand the representations of self and other, the individual and the social world in which we all exist? Is there a way of thinking about mind that makes it possible to ask these questions? This is the question that I now want to address.

VOICES, MIND AND SOCIETY

There has been one overriding perspective shared by all the approaches to schizophrenia that we have examined. This perspective is so all-pervasive, an assumption which penetrates deep into our thought about the nature of mind and our human state, that it constitutes an inescapable cultural landmark, an escarpment which constrains the horizon of our understanding. It is to be found in the neuroscientific and cognitive explanations of schizophrenia, and even some social models. The thing that binds these models together is their preoccupation with processes which are an intrinsic property of the individual. These include constitutional factors, such as the nature of the genotype and phenotype,[3] and the cognitive and behavioural processes which are considered important in understanding psychosis, and which in turn have grown out of faculty psychology. What they fail to convey is the significance of the relationship between the individual and

---

3   Genotype and phenotype are terms from genetics, widely used in medicine to distinguish between the genetic constitution of the individual (genotype), and the physical expression of that genetic constitution (phenotype) in the physiological and other biological characteristics of the individual.

the social world in which the person is embedded. There are, however, two streams of twentieth-century thought which make it possible for us to step beyond the inward-looking, individualistic constructions of self that feature so prominently in thinking about schizophrenia. Both of these developed contemporaneously in the first half of the twentieth century, one in the US, the other in the former USSR. Both try to relate the individual mind with the society and culture in which the individual is embedded. I want to see what can be gained from the insights of the American pragmatist George Herbert Mead, and the Russian psychologist Lev Vygotsky.

Self and society – the work of George Herbert Mead

Mead's work is associated with the Chicago school of philosophy, social pragmatism, led by Charles Peirce, and which included William James, which flourished in the early part of the twentieth century. The relevant account of Mead's philosophy is to be found in his book *Mind, Self and Society* (Mead, 1934), from which the following summary is taken. Mead is concerned with the relationship between society and the individual self, arguing that we can only understand the development of self through the processes of socialisation that occur in childhood, and in which language plays a central role. He is particularly interested in the outcome of socialisation which establishes the relationship of self as an object to itself. This relationship is *reflexive*, meaning that self can take the position of both subject and object. The question here, though, is how can a person get outside his or her own experience so as to become an object to self? This is the essential question facing theories of reflexivity, and the answer has profound implications for psychiatry. Mead argues that the solution is to be found in the fact that we participate in social acts with other selves, and that such action is impossible unless we adopt an objective attitude to self, in other words we become objects to ourselves. In these circumstances, self is mirrored by the others in our social world. We experience ourselves indirectly, only from the viewpoints of others. Communication plays an important part in this process, for language is directed not simply at others, but also to self.

> But it is where one does respond to that which he addresses to another and where that response of his own becomes a part of

his conduct, *where he not only hears himself but responds to himself, talks and replies to himself as truly as the other person replies to him*, that we have behaviour in which the individuals become objects to themselves.

(Mead, 1934, p. 139; emphasis added)

Here, Mead's ideas come very close to those of Vygotsky, who argues that language has a mediating role on our behaviour. In this way we are able to respond to self as another would respond to us, and participate in our own conversations with others. According to Mead, these processes lie at the heart of self-awareness, processes which involve the planning, organising and monitoring of our social relationships with others, through our use of language. In this way we encourage, censure, warn, console, cajole, love and hate ourselves, and at the same time we engage in all these features of relationships with other people. We use what Mead calls significant speech to talk to ourselves as we would talk to another person. Language, self and reflexivity are thus intimately bound together. Significant speech is the tool whereby we are able to address ourselves as an other. Language is the lever of our social world.

The ideas of Mead and Vygotsky share much in common. Both stress the role of play in childhood. For Mead, children play *at* being someone else, for example parents, teachers and so on. In doing so, the responses of others determine one's own role – the simplest form of being an other to one's self. It is through play that we are able to establish a notion of the unity of self, through the formation of what Mead calls the Generalised Other, that is the representation of the whole community of social relationships. It is the integration of this common social activity into self that leads to the fullest development of self. Society would not exist were it not for our capacity to establish the Generalised Other, and it is this that enables us to exercise self-control and self-discipline (conscience). It also enables us to participate in the universe of discourses that constitutes society. Mead maintains that there are two stages in the development of self. First, self is constituted out of the various dispositions of others towards the self, in self's social environment. Then follows the establishment of the Generalised Other, with the social attitudes and values of the various groups to which the individual belongs. There is an important distinction, though, between that aspect of self whose origins are to be found in these social relationships, and what Mead describes as subjective experiences of self (for example, pain and mood states):[4] 'We cannot identify the self with what is commonly called consciousness, that is, with the private or subjective thereness of the characters of objects' (Mead, 1934, p. 169). This distinction becomes clearer when Mead develops the relationship between the 'I' and the social 'Me'. He is not concerned with the metaphysical aspects of this relationship, such as how can I be an 'I' and a 'Me' at the same time, but more with the practical implications of this division for our conduct. The 'I' is not social, it never seeks the limelight. I may talk to myself, but I never see myself. Instead, the 'I' '... reacts to the self which arises through the taking of the attitudes of others' (Mead, 1934, p. 174).

There is a shifting relationship between 'I' and 'Me', one replaces the other each minute. The 'I' is never fully aware of itself because it is only through action that we become self-aware. The 'I' is partially disclosed through memory, as the spokesperson of self of the second, the minute or the hour. It is a historical figure (of narrative), and can only come into being historically and through narrative, as action remembered. But it is also my response to others' dispositions towards me (for example 'What do I think of them?'). Me, on the other hand, is the organised set of dispositions of others which I assume (for example 'What do they think of me?', or 'What do they expect of me?'). Self-awareness rises from '... the individual's ability to take the attitudes of these others in so far as they can be organised that he gets self-consciousness' (Mead, 1934, p. 175). Only then am I able to ask: 'What do I think of me?' Although Mead separates 'I' and 'Me', it is important to remember that they are parts of a whole, the self, which is constituted through a conversation (or dialogue) between the 'I' and the 'Me'. We are thus presented with an account of self which provides a framework for describing the dialogical organisation of experience, but we have no indication as to how this operates, or the characteristics of this experience. We can see this more clearly in the work of Vygotsky and Bakhtin.

---

4   There are, of course, a number of serious objections to statements such as this. These are dealt with in detail by Wittgenstein (1953) in *Philosophical Investigations*. Unfortunately, shortage of space means it is not possible to go into this in detail.

The Russian school – pedagogues and literary critics

Lev Vygotsky was born in Russia on 5 November 1896, and trained in psychology and medicine after the Revolution of 1917. In his tragically brief life (he died of tuberculosis in 1934) he struggled to develop a theory of the human mind consistent with Marxism, but his ideas were unpopular with Stalin and so were suppressed. It is only over the last thirty years, with the gradual easing of tensions between East and West, that his ideas have begun to influence Western thought. His work is complex and covers an enormous area, but his ideas about the role of language as a tool in the psychological and social development of the child are seminal here, for it leads to the concept of 'inner speech'. Vygotsky sought a comprehensive psychology capable of describing and explaining higher psychological functions. This included the neurological mechanisms associated with a psychological function, a detailed account of the developmental history of simple and complex forms of behaviour and, most important, a specification of the *social context* in which behaviour originates. He was one of the first psychologists to suggest mechanisms by which culture and society become a part of us, and in this respect he was heavily influenced by Marxism. In his theory of society, Marx maintained that changes in society and material life produced changes in human nature (consciousness and behaviour). Vygotsky tried to relate this to psychology, by extending the concept of mediation in human–environment interaction to the use of signs (language) as well as tools. Marx believed that societies created tool systems and throughout history these systems changed as society and its cultural development progressed. For Vygotsky, the internalisation of language, a culturally determined sign system, brought about behavioural transformations which established a bridge between early (or simple) and later (complex) forms of individual development. In other words, in the tradition of Marx and Engels, the mechanism of individual developmental change was rooted in society and culture.

Vygotsky (1978)[5] was highly critical of approaches to mind which regard mental processes as static, and occurring in isolation

---

5   This account of Vygotsky's work is taken from *Mind in Society*, a collection of essays edited in 1978, at the suggestion of his pupil, Luria.

of interpersonal, social and cultural worlds. This covers just about all the approaches to mind that we have considered so far in this book. We may trace this back to the importance he attaches to the role of speech in children's problem-solving activities. When presented with a new problem, a child will be seen to talk to him- or herself in the process of trying to solve it. He uses the term private speech to describe this phenomenon. For the child, speech and action are 'part of *one and the same complex psychological function*, directed toward the solution of a problem at hand' (Vygotsky, 1978, p. 25; emphasis in the original). The role of speech in problem solving interacts with the child's development. The child uses private speech to guide and plan his or her activities in the process of problem solving. An important part of the child's psychological and social development involves the internalisation of private speech and thus the establishment of inner speech, which is used to direct our behaviour and activity more purposefully, through the formation of intentions, plans and goals. As a result, the child's behaviour becomes mediated and thus less impulsive. For Vygotsky the internalisation of private speech is a process which results in the child's being able to appeal to him- or herself, rather than to adults: 'language thus takes on an *intra-personal function* in addition to its inter-personal use' (Vygotsky, 1978, p. 27; emphasis in the original).

In childhood, play – and the origin of our ability to use signs – is particularly important. The most significant change in a child's capacity to use language as a problem-solving tool occurs later, when socialised speech (previously used to address an adult), is turned inward. Language assumes an intrapersonal function in addition to an interpersonal one. The crucial stage occurs when speech accompanies the child's actions and reflects problem solving in a disrupted form. At a later stage speech moves more to the start of the process so that it comes to precede action. It then functions as an aid to a plan that has been conceived but not realised. Subsequently, speech guides, determines and dominates the course of action. A good example of the collaborative social function of language in problem solving can be seen in an example from research in child cognitive development referred to by Wertsch (1991). A six-year-old child has lost a toy and asks her father for help. The father asks where she last saw the toy and the child says, 'I can't remember.' He then asks a series of questions – did you have it in your room, outside, next door? To each question the child answers, 'No'. When he asks: 'In the car?', she says, 'I think so' and goes on to find the toy. In such circumstances it is very difficult to answer the question, 'Who did the remembering?' An analysis of this interchange would reveal that the functioning of remembering has occurred as part of a dyadic system.

The role played by language in individual and social consciousness is a particular feature of Mikael Bakhtin's work. Bakhtin was a literary critic who published work on Dostoevsky's novels. He stressed the dialogical nature of language, claiming that linguistics alone (the grammatical structure of language and its logical properties) is incapable of conveying the significance of language between two speaking subjects. Through his analysis of Dostoevsky's novels he charted the threads of discourse between author and characters. The point here is that although the characters are creations of the author, they are born out of dialogues located in the external world of social relationships in which the author has participated. Bakhtin developed the notion of *heteroglossia* (literally 'multispeechedness'), referring to the great variety of languages in which we participate each day as members of different groups (professional, religious, political and so on) within society. These languages stand in tension with the concept of a national language, and every utterance we make is realised through its location within one of these languages. This leads to a powerful vision of pragmatics, that each word we use is already marked by its history, bearing the accent of its previous uses. Each time a voice speaks, it places itself in a position in relation to these previous uses of the words uttered. This allows a powerful social analysis of the use of language, in which there is no such thing as a 'neutral' language, and meaning can only be established through the social 'accenting' of language. This idea emerges in a collection of essays, *Speech Genres and Other Late Essays* (Bakhtin, 1986) in which he distinguished between sentence and utterance. Linguistics may study the former, but the latter is the basis of human communication. Each time we speak, our utterance exists only in relationship to what has been said before, within both the immediate context and past contexts. From this position, Bakhtin developed a theory of speech genres, which tries to establish the constraints on how we may speak in certain circumstances. The concept of speech genres has much in common with Wittgenstein's (1953) account of language games. Speech genres are important in that they establish a link between individual utterances and the history of society. Utterances only exist, and have meaning, in that speakers occupy different positions in networks of social relationships. If we apply this principle to the voice of verbal hallucinations, we may see that such utterances may be contextualised and located within the history and narrative of the individual voice hearer. Verbal hallucinations may thus represent, in some form or another, particular aspects of the social relationships in which the individual has participated. Bakhtin's work suggests that it may be possible to use the pragmatic features of verbal hallucinations as a means of explicating these social relationships.

WHAT CAN VOICES DO WITH WORDS?

This work has important implications for the way we think about voices and how they fit in with our notion of selfhood. Although Wertsch (1991) acknowledges the value of 'individual' psychologies, he points out that they are restricted in that they fail to take into account the fact that human mental processes occur in cultural, historical and institutional contexts. 'Individual' psychologies regard self as an isolated, discrete phenomenon. This is of great importance in relation to the mental states that characterise schizophrenia, where self is fragmented or broken down. Individual psychology seeks explanations of these disturbances in terms of disordered mental structures (cognitive, neuropsychological or behavioural) in the individual's mind, but it disregards the content of these experiences. We have seen that Mead's work offers a different way of thinking about 'self', its structure and its relationship to the social world. Vygotsky's work and inner speech opens up the possibility of a dialogical model of mind and thus a new way of thinking about the 'voices' of a voice hearer. Bakhtin's work locates *all* utterances in cultural and historical contexts, providing the possibility of a narrative framework for experience. There are two consequences of this. First, if hallucinatory voices are a form of inner speech shaped by the dialogical organisation of human experience, then it should be possible for subjects to provide descriptions of the pragmatic properties of these voices, in just the same way that we may be able to describe the properties of conversations in which we engage on a daily basis. Second, it should be possible to use these dialogical properties, assuming that they exist, to help the subject understand the significance and meaning of voices in the context of his or her life experience.

Over the last five years, Ivan Leudar and I have been interested in the idea that verbal hallucinations are a form of inner speech. There is quite a lot of circumstantial evidence that this may be so. For example, many years ago, Gould (1949) found that verbal hallucinations were accompanied by subvocal speech. It was as if subjects who were hallucinating were whispering quietly to themselves, almost imperceptibly. She was able to detect this speech using a throat microphone, and found that there was close agreement between the content of the voices and the subject's own subvocal speech. Inner speech and subvocal speech are not the same, although the two may be related. The problem is that in order to show that verbal hallucinations are a form of inner speech, we must be able to demonstrate that the interactions between the voice hearer and the voices share features in common with the interactions that occur between conversational partners. To investigate this we constructed a semi-structured interview to make it easier for subjects to describe in detail the pragmatic properties of their voices. Pragmatics is that aspect of linguistics concerned with the description of the day-to-day use of language between conversational partners in social situations. It covers a wide area and draws on other disciplines, including social anthropology, social psychology and philosophy. Our interview (Leudar and Thomas, 1994) helps the subject to construct a detailed description of the conversational features of hallucinatory voices. The important point about the interview is that although it uses pragmatics to help structure the subjects' descriptions, in doing so it elicits a detailed account of the content of the voices. In this respect it may be loosely described as a phenomenological approach, in that it tries to preserve the subjects' experience without interpretation or other forms of distortion. It is solely concerned with describing the complexity of the experience. The role of pragmatics in this will become clear if I describe the type of interactions between voice and voice hearer that we want to describe.

Individuation of voices

Here, we are concerned with how the voice hearer identifies particular voices as individuals with stable identities. This may be established through features such as the quality of voice, gender, accent, knowledge and ignorance, the style of verbal behaviour, and by comparison to people who are well-known to the subject. If voices are dialogically organised (and thus a variety of inner speech), we would expect the voices to be aligned with significant individuals in the voice hearers' social and interpersonal environments.

Participant positioning

Hierarchical positioning of participants in dialogues occurs when one participant directly addresses and targets another participant. A variety of 'participant formats' are possible. Voices may, for example, talk to each other, with the voice hearer being situated as an overhearer but still the target of comments (as is the case in the First Rank Symptom of third-person verbal hallucinations). Voices may be understood as speaking for other fictitious or actual agents. Alternatively, voices may be isolated from each other and only address the voice hearer individually. In addition, voices may or may not attempt to participate in the voice hearer's dialogues with other people. Nothing is known about these features of verbal hallucinations, but if they are a variety of inner speech, the main function of which is the regulation of the subject's activities, then we would expect voices to be dialogically focused on the voice hearer rather than on others.

Sequential characteristics

In pragmatics, everyday dialogues (conversations) can be analysed in regard to their sequential properties, such as question–answer, request–refusal, assertion–agreement. These interactions, called adjacency pairs, can be initiated by either party (a reversible adjacency pair), or by one party only (a non-reversible adjacency pair). We are interested here in the type of adjacency pairs which characterise voice–voice hearer dialogues, for example, whether voices or voice hearers are restricted to initiations or responses. Our aim is to determine the general dialogical properties of voice hearers' dialogues and any constraints in these sequential properties. The expectation is that, as in ordinary inner speech, the voice dialogues will be focused on everyday activities, with voices evaluating and directing planned and actual actions.

Causal influences of voices on voice hearers' actions

It is widely assumed that most voice hearers cannot resist commands issued by voices. This raises some very interesting problems. For example, do voices take control of the voice hearer's body causing him or her to act without willing it and placing the subject in the role of a passive observer of self, as occurs in passivity experiences and dissociative disorders? Other types of influence are seen in dialogues. If I make a request of someone, this does not force the other to act, but provides a reason for them to act in the way requested. Whether or not you act on a request depends on how good you consider the reason to be, as well as on the authority of the person initiating the request and the trust between the participants. Here, we wanted to establish how the voices influenced voice hearers' activities. How do different voice hearers formulate such influences? Do they experience voices as forcing them to act without offering any resistance, or do they see voices as advising, requesting or commanding? Under what conditions do voice hearers perceive their voices to be responsible for their actions? The prediction of the dialogical model of verbal hallucinations is that voices do not mechanically impel actions. The influences are predicted to be the same as those observed in everyday social interaction where our behaviour is a function of both intent and mediated influences of others.

We (Leudar et al., 1997) interviewed twenty-eight individuals, fourteen of whom were voice hearers with a diagnosis of schizophrenia, and fourteen of whom were students who heard voices, but did not use psychiatric services. We found that the voices of these subjects were indeed focused on the regulation of mundane, everyday activities. They were typically focused on the voice hearer, and when there was more than one voice the voices did not have access to each other. This means that the voices appeared independently of each other, and did not appear to have access to each other. This arrangement was independent of the presence or absence of schizophrenia. These verbal hallucinations had the same dialogical structures found in ordinary speech and the activities regulated were mundane. For example, over 80% of subjects reported voices attempting to regulate their activities through directives (for example 'Do x', 'Don't do x', 'You could do x', and so on). The kinds of directives involved included advice to carry out a particular course of action, instructions to carry out a course of action, and directives not to carry out a course of action. Voice hearers were not usually compelled to carry out actions under the voices' influence, but any influences were cognitively mediated, that is the subjects thought through the request or directive for themselves. Voices were rarely bizarre, and they were usually aligned to significant individuals in the voice hearers' lives. All this is consistent with verbal hallucinations being a form of inner speech. They are, however, an unusual kind of inner speech, because subjects experience it without speaking and the degree to which it is considered ego-alien is exaggerated.

The participant positioning described by our informants is relevant to the significance of First Rank Symptoms of schizophrenia (Schneider, 1957). It seems common for voices to comment directly on subjects' thoughts and actions, and this happens in informants with and without schizophrenia. Third-person hallucinations (voices addressing each other, with the voice hearer being the subject of their talk and an overhearer) were rare in our sample. There were few differences between the voices of the two groups of informants. The voices of informants with schizophrenia were less often aligned with their family members. Their voices more often instigated violence and, irrespective of this, the voice hearers with schizophrenia tended to consider less often the worth of what the voices said. These are not, however, radical differences in structure and function of voices. Overall, our results supported the idea that verbal hallucinations may be regarded as a form of inner speech which has pragmatic properties. The dialogical properties of voices indicate that cognitive models of verbal hallucinations which focus on the planning and monitoring of actions are unable to account for all features of these experiences. It also reveals the potential value of a phenomenological approach to verbal hallucinations, in which the subject's own detailed description of experience is at the centre of attention. But, in practical terms, the real value of the phenomenological approach may be found in its ability to help the subject to clarify the meaning and significance of voices. This, as we shall see, is an essential part of the process of being able to cope with the experience.

DIALOGICAL ENGAGEMENT

This work stems directly from the idea that voices are a form of inner speech with pragmatic properties. A detailed phenomenological account of the voices lies at the heart of this approach, although additional work is necessary before it can be used to help someone. It can only take place in the context of a trusting relationship between the person who hears voices and the person who is trying to help. The voice hearer is expected to accept increasing responsibility for voices, through keeping a daily diary of their severity. In some respects, the technique shares features in common with focusing, but its theoretical perspective is unique, based in the model of VHs described above. Dialogical engagement implies that one natural mode of cognitive focus on the voices is to engage them in dialogues.

This emerged in the course of work with a fifty-seven-year-old single retired lady, Peg Davies, who had a long history of schizophrenia, controlled by depot neuroleptic medication for nearly twenty years. At the age of twelve months she had been adopted after her biological mother had abandoned her. Her adoptive parents were strict, middle-class, middle-aged professional people, and she described herself as being a 'difficult child', disobedient and naughty. She completed normal schooling, attended Teacher Training College and then worked as a teacher in a school for physically handicapped children. Her early career was very successful, and a few years later she was promoted to Head Mistress of a residential school for maladjusted children. She was first admitted to psychiatric hospital at the age of thirty-nine after she had tried to give her elderly, ill mother an overdose of tablets in response to imperative auditory hallucinations. At the time she was under considerable stress dealing with the impending loss of her mother, and pressures at work. A diagnosis of paranoid schizophrenia was made, and she was treated with depixol which damped the voices down, although she continued to experience them most days. She returned to work but was readmitted two years later, after she had broken into her local church and stolen the Host from the tabernacle, again in response to imperative auditory hallucinations. Her medication was increased, the voices appeared to settle, and on discharge she decided to take early retirement and moved to the countryside where she shared a house with her friend, Sheila. At the time of initial assessment her ICD-9 diagnosis was schizophrenia (residual), with persistent second-person auditory hallucinations. Her friend's observations indicated that over the twenty or so years since her illness first appeared, Peg had changed to a remarkable degree. Whereas she had previously been a confident, outgoing person, a first-class teacher and leader, she became withdrawn and shy. She avoided company wherever possible, and stopped driving through lack of confidence. She would not think of going anywhere unless accompanied by her friend.

Before starting work, Peg made it clear that she had always been puzzled by her voices. She was frightened of them because they had overwhelmed her in the past, but she had decided that it was important that she tried to make sense out of them, so that she might understand them. She was also concerned about the possible risks of long-term neuroleptic medication, especially tardive dyskinesia, and so resolved to work hard to try to control herself rather than relying exclusively on medication to do so. In the first stage of this work, she wrote a detailed account of her life history, starting from her earliest memories to the present, including all events that she considered important. The purpose of this narrative was to encourage her to use the first-person singular, the 'I', which established a sense of self important in dialogical work. From this account it emerged that her elderly parents were extremely strict and distant. They found it difficult to deal with feelings and emotional intimacy, and they never allowed her to forget that they had saved her by adoption. Peg was puzzled as to what it was they had saved her from, and she felt in debt to them, a debt she was unable to repay. Consequently, she felt that she had to 'behave' and be the perfect daughter in order to feel worthy of their love and affection. She always had to 'keep herself in check', that is to monitor her behaviour and to edit out impulses to do things that she thought would be unacceptable to her parents. She believed that in some way, the part of her self that she held in check was related to her biological mother. In adulthood she had traced her biological mother and discovered that she had to give up caring for Peg when she was having to look after her own mother who was dying of cancer.

The next stage involved a detailed description of the pragmatic features of her voices, using the semi-structured interview. From this, the following description of her two voices emerged:

Voice 1 – 'the Guardian Angel'
This voice came on when she was under stress. She once thought of it as her friend, but she had started to doubt this because of the things it told her to do. It had no gender features, but sounded 'adult'. Although she called it the 'Guardian Angel' (GA), it sounded like no one she knew, but as she spoke, she realised for the first time that it reminded her of her father. Like him, it had an opinion about everything. It directed her and instructed her what to do. It came on particularly in the company of old people who 'invaded' her space, especially if she felt obligated to help them. In a recent incident she heard the voice whilst visiting an elderly friend in hospital. It told her to smother the old lady who was very ill. Peg felt powerless to help, and she then went on to describe an incident from her childhood in which her mother's hands had become trapped in the rollers of a mangle. Her mother was in great pain and Peg had felt 'absolutely impotent to relieve her suffering'. She then

remembered that the first time she had ever heard voices was in 1966 following the Aberfan disaster,[6] when she was working with physically handicapped children. She recalled[7] '... seeing the suffering in their eyes, hearing their [the victims'] screams and being powerless to help ...'.

The GA first appeared when her elderly mother was seriously ill in a residential home ten years later. Again she had felt powerless to help, and the voice suggested that she should give her mother an overdose of pills to ease her suffering. It told her to do 'wicked' things which she found it impossible to resist. Other than tell the voice to go away, which was ineffective, she would not talk to it or question its instructions, and would act automatically on its instructions. More recently, however, she had tried to cope with it by avoiding situations which precipitated the voice.

Voice 2 – 'my Little Devil'
This voice sounded younger than the GA, although still adult. She called it 'my Little Devil' (LD) because she could see it sitting on her shoulder. It came on when she had 'destructive' thoughts, such as those which usually heralded the appearance of the GA. This voice was a friend which helped her, telling her to do things such as take the Host from the tabernacle in the local Catholic church. She would not question the voice, and would act 'automatically' in response. Her interpretation was that taking the Host enabled her to resist the GA's instructions.

Peg had frequent internal dialogues with herself, but these did not involve the voices. She had no form of interaction with either voice, and never commented back to them what she thought of their commands. Her response to both voices was unusual in that it was impulsive rather than mediated. However, when she discussed what the voices ordered her to do, she was horrified. The difficulty was that she was unable to use such mediation to modify her response to the commands, and she relied on other people to stop her from acting as the voices demanded. The strategy here was to introduce moral considerations to the voices' commands, and thus mediate between

---

6   On 21 October 1966, in Aberfan, Wales, a coal slag-heap shifted and sent an avalanche of debris down on to the school below, killing 116 children.

7   This, and following dialogues between Peg and her voices are taken verbatim from her own detailed, daily journal over the course of our work together.

her and the voices. This was achieved in the next stage, the purpose of which was to encourage her to engage with the voices dialogically, making it possible for her to comment explicitly on the instruction they gave her. The difficulty here was that the voices only came on at particular times, so she was asked to rehearse situations in which they appeared. This would enable her to write out typical sequences of statements made by the voices, into which she could write her own responses. The process was rather like writing the text of a play. The parts for two *dramatis personae* (the two voices) were present, but not the third (her own). She had to write her own part commenting on the voices' commands.

At this stage (immediately after the first interview) she felt under considerable stress and started to hear a new voice, which she had never heard before, telling her that the GA would not destroy her. She called it 'my Holy Angel', although she thought it was her own voice. The Holy Angel (HA) reassured her, saying that she would be all right and that she would come through her problems. The other voices would not destroy her. This new voice was '... like me speaking ...', and it reassured her with positive and encouraging comments. Over the next few days the voice became very prominent, and her own verbatim notes indicated that true dialogues took place between her and the HA:

> HA: 'There is no need to try me out. I am here for you.'
> Peg: 'You know me well.'
> HA: 'Yes I know you.'
> Peg: 'Will you stay with me always?'
> HA: 'Yes I'll stay with you.'

Its reassurance was spontaneous as well as in response to her questions. The HA also mediated between her and the other voices, commenting to her that what they told her to do was wrong. These dialogues were rich and complex in nature, and indicated that the HA made moral judgements about the other voices' imperatives. These dialogues were initiated by either participant. One set of dialogues concerned her biological mother and adoptive parents. The HA answered Peg's quest for reassurance that her biological mother had loved her, despite the fact that she had given her daughter up for adoption. The voice commented that she should not 'punish' or deny that part of herself that represented her biological mother. This was the part of her that needed love and acceptance, and it was important that she was able to do this for herself. Throughout this period, she kept a detailed diary describing her progress. In the weeks following the appearance of the HA her confidence increased and she drove the car for the first time in two years. Four weeks later the dose of her depixol was reduced at her request. She had heard neither the GA nor the LD, and was hearing the HA less frequently, about once a week. Six weeks later, at Christmas, she experienced a number of difficult situations. First, they had to visit Sheila's ageing mother who was ill in hospital. During the visit she heard the GA, which suggested that it would be easy for her to ease the old lady's suffering, but the HA appeared telling the other voice to go away, which it did. This was immensely reassuring because she was certain that had the new voice not intervened, she would have acted on the GA's suggestion. On Christmas Day she accepted the role of sacristan at church, which meant having access to the Host. This passed without difficulty and without the appearance of the LD.

Then, on 13 March 1996, fifteen children and a teacher were shot dead in the Dunblane massacre in Scotland. At some point during the day Peg started to hear the children's voices crying out in their distress, in her head. She was also disturbed by vivid visual images of the carnage in the gymnasium. 'It was like Aberfan again.' The children's voices took over, despite her attempts to distract herself by knitting and watching the television. She decided to talk through her response with the HA (she had heard no voices for three weeks before Dunblane) and the new voice comforted her above the cries. It told her that although the tragedy was terrible, the children were no longer suffering, because they were out of this world so there was no more pain for them. As the HA continued to reassure her, the cries abated and at some stage she fell asleep. Over the next few days the children's cries recurred in response to reminders of the tragedy, such as media coverage of the funerals, but on each occasion the HA returned to reassure her. She remained free of voices for over three months, until a further deterioration in the health of Sheila's elderly mother. This necessitated frequent journeys to the Midlands to monitor the situation, but each time the frail, elderly lady was discharged home from hospital, the situation broke down again. Peg felt powerless to help, and recognised that she was in a vulnerable situation, but she wanted to be with her friend to offer her help and support. On two or three occasions she was left alone with Sheila's mother, and on each occasion she appealed inwardly to the HA which reassured her. The voice told her what to do, instructing her to make the old lady a cup of tea, offer her a cake, go and pack her case, and so on. With the new voice's help she said she was able to keep going.

Two weeks later the situation deteriorated again, and the old lady had to be readmitted to hospital. When Peg heard this she started to hear the GA again, almost immediately. She felt the situation with Sheila's mother was starting to threaten the stability of the life which she and Sheila had worked hard to establish over the last twenty years. The day before they were due to return to the Midlands, the GA told Peg that she could give the old lady some temazepam in her tea, just as she had done with her own elderly mother twenty years before. She even rehearsed the GA's instructions by dissolving some temazepam in a cup of tea, to show that it would work. The voice told her: 'Go prepared next time.' As soon as she had done this she heard the voice of the HA telling her that what she was planning to do was wicked, that she would be found out, and everything that she had ever achieved would be in ruins. It told her: 'You cannot, you will not do it.' She then wrote the following in her journal:

> I need help. *I am torn two ways ...* decided not to tell Sheila and Dr Thomas about the reoccurrence of my GA. *They will only want me on more medication. I will see if it reoccurs.*
> [the next day ...]
> *Confided in Sheila, showed her my notes.* Sheila now has all my temazepam tablets and will give me them when required.
> (emphasis added)

This was an important step forward for Peg. There is no doubt that the situation she was in shared many features in common with that she experienced over twenty years earlier with her own mother, and which resulted in her acting in a dangerous manner in response to imperative VHs. But for the first time ever she had been able to reflect on her predicament and act independently of the voices. This is set out clearly in the notes from her journal above. She recognised that she was in a dilemma and needed help. She was in conflict over the instructions she was under from the two voices. Initially she decided not to confide in Sheila and her therapist because she feared the response would be to increase her medication. But then she changed her mind and confided in them. This was the first time that she had ever managed to do this, for previously she had always *acted automatically and without reflection* whenever she heard the GA or LD. On this occasion, Peg had mediated her own behaviour in relation to the GA's commands.

WHOSE VOICE COUNTS?

The development and changes in Peg's voices may be linked to the socio-cultural model of mind described above. We may, if we so choose, discern the shadow of Bakhtinian thought in the account. The utterance of one of her voices (GA) had echoes of her father's utterance (like him, it had an opinion about everything). She made this link for herself immediately before the appearance of the new voice (HA). Indeed, the new voice was unlike any voice she had heard before, although she partly identified it with her own voice as well as those of her close friend and her therapist. Like them, it was a voice which spoke to her positively. Perhaps the most interesting Bakhtinian feature of Peg's voices was the fact that some of them (the crying of the children) were clearly related to the culture and time in which Peg lived. These voices came on after the Aberfan disaster and Dunblane massacre, both events which reverberated through our shared cultural lives, posing deep questions about the nature of our society, our values and our common future. Peg's response to these events is symbolised through her reliving the suffering of the innocents, her own deep identification with their pain.

We may also see, for example, how Mead's notion of 'I' and 'me' establish a reflexive structure of self, in which inner speech performs a mediating role. Peg had never engaged in dialogue with her voices, nor had she ever commented to herself, internally, on their content. The voices took over and she would act automatically on their content without pausing to reflect on the nature of their commands and the implications of these. This inability to comment on these aspects of her voices led to serious problems and her coming into contact with psychiatry. Gradually, she became able to comment on the voices' commands. At first this happened through the agency of the new voice (HA) which acted as an intermediary between Peg and the other two voices. The HA appeared to have two functions. It reassured, consoled and supported her, and valued her as a person. Indeed, it became a powerful support and source of self-esteem for her. On the other hand, it responded to and dealt with the other voices on her behalf. It kept them at bay whilst helping Peg to become aware that there were moral concerns in respect of these voices' instructions. In a way, it acted as a conscience, mediating her behaviour in accordance with moral principles. Normally, Peg had a very highly developed sense of right and wrong, but in the face of the onslaught of her two voices she lost her sense of autonomy and agency. In the end she was able to regain this without the intercession of the new voice, when she confided in Sheila and her therapist her plans to dissolve the temazepam in a cup of tea. The final extract from her journal above, following the HA's exhortation 'not [to] do it', is followed by a self-reflective inner dialogue in which she assumes the position of Sheila and her therapist ('*They* will only want *me* on more medication'). The next day she confided her intentions to Sheila. This was the first time this had happened.

This is all well and good. We may be able to establish links between the experience of a person and a set of concepts and ideas which assist in the understanding of that experience. But we must never be complacent or comfortable about this, for there is still an act of interpretation here. My own preoccupation with the nature of self and the importance of its experience, placing all that in the centre of my stage in my emphasis on what I believe to be the importance of self-awareness in coping with psychosis, is no different from any of the professional languages that I presented earlier in this book. Perhaps all I have managed to achieve here is yet another technology of self, or psyche, to be juxtaposed oppressively against the experience of another. Here we have yet another conflict unfolding. It is, therefore, clear that what I have just presented here is *not* truly a phenomenological approach, because I have failed to take into account my own position as an observer, my own subjectivity. This leads us to consider the one thing that I have avoided contemplating throughout this book: the person of the doctor.

10 Alienation or Integration?

It made me think. I have to say it really made me think. At first, I thought, 'Oh God, another one of these wearing-your-heart-on-your-sleeve jobs', but there was much more to it than that. That psychiatrist felt just how I feel now. You see I've just started my training – about three months ago, and the problem is nobody prepares you for what you've really got to deal with. I know it's not the done thing to admit to it, but I still feel completely lost. To be honest I don't know what the fuck I'm supposed to be doing. Their lives are so full of misery that the only thing that I think I can do is listen to them and try to be as sympathetic as I can. But I don't have time to do that. Always under pressure, so much bloody pressure to see more and more patients who've been coming up to the clinic for years and I'm the only chance they have to be listened to. Like the other day, this man comes into the clinic. He's heard voices for twenty years. They keep telling him to kill himself. He's tried five times already and he'll do it one day, I know he will. It said in his notes, somewhere right at the beginning, that his voices started after his twin brother was killed in a motor-cycle accident. Then his voices became much worse recently after his mother died. He was beside himself, really distressed. All I could do was put my arm around him, but it mattered, it felt right. But we're taught not to do that. You're not supposed to do that if you're a doctor, a psychiatrist. My consultant told me. She said it was important to observe strict boundaries with our patients. It was that sense of distance, I don't know, impartiality, that was part of the process of helping them psychologically. That can't be right. It just doesn't seem right to me. But then, who am I to stir it? I've got to keep on the right side of her because I need a reference for my next job, and to be able to sit the membership, and if I put a foot wrong she'll have my balls and that's that. Bang goes my career! Jesus! You know ... it really reminds me of the way I felt the day after I started in my first house job, just after qualifying. It's strange, but I've never talked about this before, not to anyone, not even my partner. Anyway, the first thing that happened was that this guy in my year killed himself. The day after he got his results, he just locked himself up in his room and threw away the key. They found him two days later – he took a massive overdose. Six weeks later I understood why he did it. That guy knew what was coming. He really could see what we were up against. Perhaps he had too vivid an imagination, I don't know, but it didn't hit me until my second day as a houseman. The first time that I had to tell the parents of a three-year-old girl that their daughter had died and we hadn't been able to save her life. I know this sounds incredibly selfish but I was really sobbing for myself, not for them, that night when I got home. I couldn't believe that there would be times when I would fail. You know medical school fills your head with all sorts of macho bullshit. It's an all-boys' club, medicine, and you daren't upset the apple cart. You come to think of yourself as some sort of medical techno-warrior, like something from a Schwarzenegger film. Walled up behind your white coat, armed with your BNF you think you are impervious to disease, suffering, misery. Yeah! Even some of the terminology plays into that – you know – magic bullets, laser treatment, atomic scans, all the high-tech stuff. You end up thinking that you're superhuman, invincible, above the concerns and feelings of ordinary people. But you're not. I cried that night because I realised for the first time that that was the way it was going to be for the rest of my days as a doctor, and that I would never really be allowed to have feelings about things that happened, let alone show them to anyone. I don't know why I'm saying this now ... it must be that bloody play! It made me think. It made me realise that I have to learn to be with unbearable situations – that I don't always have to come up with the answer. I suppose that we are trained to wear a mask for good reasons ... patients wouldn't take us seriously if we dropped our barriers. I don't know. But there has to be some sort of middle way. Doctors are people. The play helped me to remember the person within the doctor.

This monologue, although an invention, is distilled out of several contributions made by postgraduate psychiatrists in discussions following performances of a play called *On the Edge of a Dilemma*, written by Sharon Lefevre and performed by Sharon and myself. The play deals with some difficult issues about the nature of doctor–patient relationships in general, and in psychiatry in particular. It provides a rare opportunity for doctors to talk openly about the way they see themselves as doctors and as people. So far, we have looked dispassionately at the language of psychiatry and the assumptions which underlie it. But there is an important perspective missing, without which my attempt to move forward will flounder. The one thing we have not commented on is the speaker of the language, the psychiatrist. Psychiatrists are, of course, medically qualified, and this provides an important context in which to place the nature of psychiatric discourse. We cannot hope to understand the implications of the account that I have provided of the nature of psychiatric languages without considering the nature of medicine as a profession and institution. Speaker and language are so closely engaged that in order to understand one, we have to consider the other. This is important because much of what has been said earlier in this book has implications for the practice and training of psychiatrists, so it is important that we locate the profession's interests in relation to these issues. Unless everyone is clear about these interests we have no hope of dealing with what I call the *iatrocentric* tendency, that is the propensity of the medical profession to use what it calls 'patients' interests' as a means of disguise for its own interests. We shall see that the medical profession has certain social and demographic features that must be understood in relation to the social and demographic features of the majority of psychiatric patients, especially those suffering from schizophrenia. These features result in a strengthening of the barriers which already exist between the psychiatrist and his or her patient by virtue of the nature of psychiatric language. These characteristics of medicine also have important implications for the manner in which the profession acquires and passes on knowledge, and thus power. There are two features of the medical profession that are important here. The first concerns medical ethics. Since the time of Hippocrates the practice of medicine has been governed by a set of principles that have changed little to the present day. These principles are important in shaping the way doctors think about themselves in relation to their patients. If we examine the salient features of medical ethics we discover a conflict at the core of medicine which helps us to recast the dissatisfaction of service users. It opens a new window on this conflict to be taken up elsewhere. The second feature concerns the social inequalities which characterise the medical profession, which tends to be drawn from the more privileged classes of society. This has a powerful effect on those who have to come into contact with psychiatric services. There is little point in changing the language used by psychiatrists if we fail to challenge the nature of their training, and, more particularly, who is involved in their training.

HIPPOCRATES AND THE MEDICAL OATH

We may understand more clearly the points I am trying to make here if we consider the origins of medicine as we know it today. As with so many other aspects of our culture we can trace this to the Greece of the Classical period. In the fifth century BC the first medical schools were established in the Ionian cities of Cos and Cnidus. Each had its own corpus of knowledge, and it is worth noting that these were closely associated with the development of associated schools of philosophy (Boardman *et al.*, 1986). The most famous of the schools was that attributed to Hippocrates of Cos, and the *Hippocratic Corpus* consists of a collection of treatises on anatomy, physiology, gynaecology, pathology, epidemiology and surgery. It represents one of the first attempts by physicians to carve out an area of knowledge distinct from philosophy and so-called 'irrational' medicine (magicians, seers and quacks). Through the Hippocratic Oath the values of these early physicians persist to this day, influencing the ethical and moral basis for the practice of medicine. Most modern codes of medical conduct, including the World Medical Association's declarations, the Helsinki and Geneva Conventions, all stem from the Hippocratic Oath (Gillon, 1985). The Oath is worth reproducing in full:

> I swear by Apollo the physician and Asclepius and all the gods and goddesses, that, according to my ability and judgement, I will keep this oath and its stipulation. I reckon him who taught me this art equally dear to me as my parents, to share my substance with him and relieve his necessities if required. To look upon his offspring in the same footing as my own brothers, and to teach them this art, if they shall wish to learn it, without fee or stipulation. And by precept, lecture and every other mode of instruction, I will impart a knowledge of the art to my own sons, and those of my teachers, and to disciples bound by a stipulation and oath according to the law of medicine, but to none others. I will follow that system or regimen which, according to my ability and judgement, I consider for the benefit of my patients, and abstain from whatever is deleterious and mischievous. I will give no deadly medicine to anyone if asked, nor suggest any such counsel, and, in like-manner, I will not give to a woman a pessary to produce abortion. With purity and holiness I will pass my life and practise my art. I will not cut persons labouring under the stone, but will leave this to be done

by men who are practitioners of this work. Into whatever houses I enter, I will go on into them for the benefit of the sick, and will abstain from every voluntary act of mischief and corruption, and further, from the seduction of females or males, of freemen and slaves. Whatever, in connection with my professional practice or not in connection with it, I see or hear in the life of men, which ought not to be spoken of abroad, I will not divulge, as reckoning that all such should be kept secret. While I continue to keep this oath unviolated, may it be granted to me to enjoy life and the practice of the art, respected by men in all times. But should I trespass and violate this oath, may the reverse be my lot.

There are two things that I want to draw attention to here. The first concerns the code of ethics which the Oath lays down. The second concerns special dispensations which determine who is, or is not, likely to acquire the art and skills of physician.

In Britain, the medical profession is regulated by the General Medical Council (GMC), which is responsible for the standards of care, competence and conduct maintained by all registered medical practitioners. It is an extremely powerful body. If a practitioner is found guilty of a serious breach of professional misconduct, the GMC may remove that doctor's name from the list of registered medical practitioners, which means that he or she loses his or her livelihood. Although doctors no longer take the Hippocratic Oath on qualification, the code of conduct by which all doctors' behaviour is judged is heavily influenced by the Oath. This is seen in a list of duties of doctors registered with the GMC, taken from a booklet called *Good Medical Practice* (GMC, 1996).

- make the care of your patient your first concern
- treat every patient politely and considerately
- respect patients' dignity and privacy
- listen to patients and respect their views
- give patients information in a way they can understand
- respect the rights of patients to be fully involved in decisions about care
- keep your professional skills and knowledge up to date
- recognise the limits of your professional competence
- be honest and trustworthy
- respect and protect confidential information
- make sure that your personal beliefs do not prejudice your patients' care

- act quickly to protect patients from risk if you have good reason to believe that you or a colleague may not be fit to practise
- avoid abusing your position as a doctor
- work with colleagues in the ways that best serve patients' interests

In all these matters you must never discriminate unfairly against your patients or colleagues.

This code of ethics for doctors is of great importance. Ill people are vulnerable. Doctors exercise great power over their patients. There has to be a code which sets out clear principles by which doctors practise medicine, which safeguards the interests of the sick and vulnerable. The existence of the code over many centuries, and the fact that the great majority of doctors have followed the code scrupulously, has been one of the reasons for the esteem and trust which the medical profession has enjoyed, at least until recently. But there is more to these codes than simply telling doctors not to make love to their patients. They reveal some important assumptions about the nature of the relationship between doctor and patient, and particularly, the distribution of power within that relationship. Here, I am concerned with the concepts of paternalism, beneficence, non-maleficence and autonomy. The first three are enshrined within the Hippocratic Oath and lie in conflict with the fourth. Let us examine each of these and how they influence the doctor–patient relationship. The following is based on Gillon's (1985) account of philosophical medical ethics.

Paternalism

This is summed up succinctly as 'Doctor knows best'. To act paternalistically means that you act in what you consider to be the person's best interests, whether or not the person happens to agree with you. Situations arise in medicine where it is clearly appropriate that physicians act in what they consider to be their patients' best interests. If a patient's heart has stopped beating following a heart attack, the doctor is in no position to stop, outline a treatment plan and ask the patient what he or she thinks about it. In situations of life and death, or pressing urgency, doctors have to respond according to their knowledge and experience, and act in what they consider to be the patient's best interests. No one would expect, or want, a doctor to act any differently under such circumstances. Paternalism is represented in the following extract from the Hippocratic Oath: 'I will follow that system or regimen which, according to my ability and judgement, I consider for the benefit of my patients'. The problem is that uncritical adherence to paternalism leads to the assumption that patients themselves are incapable of making decisions about their treatment, because they do not have their doctors' knowledge, experience and understanding. Under these circumstances, doctors may believe that patients are likely to make inappropriate decisions about their care. The problem with this argument is that it assumes that the only basis on which decisions about treatment should be made are medical ones. This disregards the particular circumstances of the individual patient. The side-effects, or potential adverse effects or complications of a therapeutic intervention, may have quite devastating implications for one patient's quality of life, whereas another patient may find the same set of complications quite acceptable. Doctors have to inform patients about the risks of treatment, they may even advise patients about a particular course of action, but it is presumptuous to assume that they necessarily know what is best for a particular patient. Another justification for paternalism is that patients should not be given bad news about their conditions. Patients in severe pain secondary to cancer are already very distressed, so what is the point in adding to this by telling them that there is no treatment for their condition? The problem here is that in order to avoid telling them the truth, downright deceit has to be used, especially when other family members may know what is going on. This can place an intolerable strain on the family when this is the last thing they need. And what happens if the patient discovers the true nature of the condition and that his or her family have been complicit in the deceit? In any case, it is arguable that patients have a right to be distressed about their circumstances. Medical paternalism may mean well, but there is little justification for it.

Beneficence

This is encapsulated by the expression 'Doing good for others'. It provides the stock answer for applicants to medical school when asked, 'Why do you want to become a doctor?' Indeed, the medical profession regards itself, and is widely regarded by society, as having a duty to do good for the sick in general. The problem here is, as Gillon points out, that the extent to which we have a moral obligation to do good for other people is contested by moral theorists. Whilst it is generally accepted that we all have a moral duty to do no harm to each other, some argue that there is no such thing as a moral duty to do good, although everybody agrees that it is desirable, and the idea that doctors should go around doing good for suffering humanity is appealing. Indeed, there are limits on the extent to which a doctor's actions should be guided by beneficence, especially if the act of doing good stands in the way of the patient's autonomy, or occurs at too high a price, or gets in the way of the rights of other people. Indeed, paternalism and beneficence bring serious problems for autonomy, and may be associated with the problem of doing harm.

Autonomy

Gillon defines autonomy (or self-rule) as the capacity to think, decide and act independently and free of any constraint. Autonomy is an important feature of Western philosophy. Both Aristotle and Kant considered it to be a feature of rationality, one of man's specific attributes. There are three types of autonomy. Autonomy of thought is equivalent to thinking for ourselves, and includes decision making, having beliefs, making moral assessments and having aesthetic preferences. Autonomy of will is the freedom to make a decision to do something on the basis of our thought. Gillon suggests that it is this capacity which is often adversely affected by illness or disease. Autonomy should be distinguished from the principle of respect for autonomy, or the moral requirement to respect other people's autonomy. We all believe that we should be free as individuals to think decide and act for ourselves, so we have a moral duty to recognise that other people have the same right.

The problem here is that medical paternalism and beneficence are potentially in conflict with the principle of respect for the autonomy of others. Let us consider beneficence. If a doctor really wants to do good for a patient, she has to find out what it is that the patient wants. The difficulty is that even in the most simple of situations, patients may want quite different things from their doctor. Consider the experience of hearing voices. One patient may want admission to hospital. Another may want neuroleptic medication. Yet another may not want to see a psychiatrist because past experience has told her that this will result in compulsory admission to hospital. A fourth patient may simply want to talk about the experience to try to make

some sense out of it. In each case, the psychiatrist's duty of beneficence means that it is essential that they try to establish exactly what
it is that patients want, what the implications of such courses of
action would be, and what alternatives there might be. Doctors are
more likely to act with beneficence if they take into account their
patients' preferences. There are, however, many situations where it
may be difficult for psychiatrists to respect patients' autonomy (see
Gillon, 1985, pp. 75–6 for a full discussion of this). The most important psychiatric example is where respecting patients' autonomy
means that a third party's autonomy may be compromised. For example, if the patient who is hearing voices tries to kill his or her
neighbour because the patient thinks that the neighbour is responsible for the voices, or because the voices instruct the patient to kill the
neighbour, then this has major implications for the autonomy of the
neighbour. Psychiatrists are frequently placed in situations where
their duty of respect for their patients' autonomy may conflict with
the interests of the autonomy of a third party.

Non-maleficence

Another important principle jeopardised by modern medicine is the
doctor's duty to do no harm, the duty of non-maleficence. Here,
paternalism and beneficence on the part of the doctor may conspire
together with the result that the harmful effects of an intervention
may outweigh any potential benefits. Again, the problem here is that
each individual's notion of what is harmful or beneficial is extremely
personal, which means that no doctor may assume that he or she
knows best for a particular combination of patient, illness and treatment options. If doctors think and act paternalistically and benefi-
cently, then they may mistakenly believe that they know what is best
for the patient and push the patient into accepting the treatment
option the doctor considers to be best, without a thorough discussion
of the advantages and disadvantages of the available choices.[1] Under
these circumstance the patient's best interests are not necessarily

---

1   Of course, some would regard this as a rather lenient view, because it
    could be argued that the reason that doctors do not enter into thorough
    discussions of the advantages and disadvantages of treatment is because
    this is a lengthy time-consuming process. Indeed, it is not unknown for
    doctors to push a particular treatment option because they have an
    interest in doing so, such as has been known to occur in drug trials.

being served, with the result that the intervention may have, from the patient's perspective, harmful effects. The only way this can be avoided is through detailed and sympathetic discussion of all the risks and benefits.

The point that I want to bring out is that doctors are in a position of great power over their patients. They can do great good, but they can also do great harm. They believe that they should be doing good, and so does society as a whole. They are therefore expected to do good. The problem is that this may lead them to believe that they know what is best for their patients, and that patients are incapable of fully understanding the complexities of illness and treatment in the way that they do. Of course, this is because they possess expert knowledge and experience which gives them a highly influential perspective on an individual's situation, but theirs is not the only perspective. The patient's perspective must be acknowledged, as must that of close family or friends. This requires a complex process of negotiation if the correct balance is to be achieved. But there is a huge obstacle here, rooted in the social and cultural characteristics of the medical profession. This constitutes a barrier to the process of negotiation.

HIPPOCRATES AND THE MEDICAL TRIBE

The Hippocratic Oath accomplishes much more than simply ordaining a code of conduct for the behaviour of medical practitioners towards patients. It also determines who has precedence in acquiring the art of medicine. Consider the following extract from the Oath:

> I reckon him who taught me this art equally dear to me as my parents, to share my substance with him and relieve his necessities if required. To look upon his offspring in the same footing as my own brothers, *and to teach them this art, if they shall wish to learn it, without fee or stipulation.* And by precept, lecture and every other mode of instruction, *I will impart a knowledge of the art to my own sons, and those of my teachers, and to disciples bound by a stipulation and oath according to the law of medicine, but to none others.* (emphasis added)

This shows that the Hippocratic Oath is much more than just a code of ethics. It specifies who should and should not practise the art of medicine. First, it establishes an authoritarian relationship between senior and junior members of the profession. It elevates the status of those who teach a doctor to the same level as her parents, and she is thus expected to respect her teachers in the same way. This means that her teachers carry the same authority as her parents, and must therefore be deferred to in the same way. This has implications for the way the profession handles knowledge. The tradition of medicine is such that it attaches great weight to established knowledge and practice, particularly when these are enshrined in the work of older and wiser peers. This makes it very difficult to challenge the wisdom and authority of these accounts, and results in medicine being a very conservative profession. In some ways this is a good thing. Medicine deals with human life, and its practice has evolved slowly over the centuries, painful lessons hard-learned through human suffering and tragedy. In a sense, medicine has learned through its mistakes, so it has to think very seriously indeed about claims made by new knowledge. It takes a great deal of persuading before its practice changes. But the other side of this inherent conservatism is a reluctance to adapt to change or to challenge the established way of doing things. The main priority for the medical profession is the preservation of the status quo. This applies not only to the practice of medicine, but also to the preservation of essential characteristics of the profession, the practitioners themselves, for the Oath specifies that relationships between medical practitioners take the form of kinship relationships. The doctor is expected to regard the offspring of her teachers as her own sisters, and to grant them special privileges if they choose to become doctors themselves. However, my account here is inaccurate, because the Oath uses only male pronouns, the assumption being that women never become doctors. Indeed, exclusivity is built into the Oath for knowledge of the art of medicine is to be imparted only to the physician's own sons, and those of his teachers, and to those other disciples who follow an approved path, but to no others. Given these tenets, it is not surprising that, for centuries, medicine has been regarded as a closed profession into which it is difficult to penetrate, unless you have a male relative who is a member of the profession. In anthropological terms, we may regard the medical profession as a 'tribe'.

Of course, many will say that this is a spurious argument. This deconstruction of the Hippocratic Oath is irrelevant today because the Oath itself guided the practice of medicine 2500 years ago. This is a fair comment, were it not for Gillon's point about the contemporary influence of the Oath. Indeed, there is evidence to suggest that this aspect of the Oath, and its tribalism, still shapes the way the profession thinks and acts in relation to other social groups. Whilst it may be true that we think less in terms of medical 'tribalism', there are still powerful influences which seek the exclusion of the 'other', predicated upon notions of difference such as skin colour, race, social class and gender. For example, it has long been known that going to medical school is familial. Doctors are more likely to come from medical than non-medical families. Huckle and McGuffin (1991) were interested to find out whether more modern procedures for the selection of medical students had changed this. They gave all first- and second-year students at the University of Wales College of Medicine, and first-year zoology students, a questionnaire designed to establish what proportion of their close relatives had gone to medical school themselves. For the medical students, 13% of their first-degree relatives had attended medical school, compared with 0.22% of the general population. Over 20% of the medical students' siblings were at medical school themselves, compared with 4% of the zoology students' siblings. The authors concluded that going to medical school is a highly familial characteristic mediated by cultural and social factors. This conclusion is all the more striking given that one of the authors, Peter McGuffin, is a leading authority on genetics and psychiatric disorders. The point of this study is that it was undertaken to see whether or not more modern selection criteria have changed this familial tendency. Clearly they have not, and medical students are still much more likely (over sixty times more likely than the general population) to come from medical families themselves. Advantage breeds advantage.

We can see this even more clearly in the overwhelming evidence that working-class people and those from ethnic minority groups are discriminated against as far as entry into medicine and career progression are concerned. The reasons for this are complex, but they all suggest that discrimination operates prior to application for medical school, during the processes of selection, and on qualification in the early stages of higher professional training. A series of studies over the last ten years demonstrate inequality and bias in the selection of medical students, which actively excludes those from less privileged backgrounds, especially those from lower social classes and ethnic groups. McManus (1982) examined possible explanations for the over-representation of social classes I and II in medical students compared with the general population. He concluded that this could not be explained satisfactorily in terms of social class differences in intellectual ability, or the fact that medical students were more likely to come from medical families. His study raised the possibility that children from lower social classes may be discouraged from applying for medicine, either by their parents or by their schools. McManus and Richards (1984) audited all acceptances and rejections for medicine to St Mary's Hospital Medical School, one of London's principal teaching hospitals. They looked at the outcome of over 1300 students, which constituted over 12% of all applicants to British medical schools in 1980. They were able to look not only at those accepted by St Mary's, but through the Universities Central Council on Admissions (UCCA), they were also able to establish what happened to those unsuccessful St Mary's applicants who applied elsewhere. The social class structure of applicants was very similar to that of the medical profession as a whole, with an over-representation of the higher social classes: 48.1%, 35.2%, 12.9%, 2.0% and 1.7% were from the Registrar General's social classes I to V respectively. It will come as no surprise, therefore, that the acceptances came from the higher social classes (54.3%, 32.6% and 11.1% from social classes I to III respectively). This study, like Huckle and McGuffin's, indicates that there are factors influencing who gets to medical school, long before potential students actually apply. But there is more to it than this, for there are more subtle, more baleful influences at work than the cosy picture of an 'old boys' club that has emerged so far. In a subsequent paper, McManus et al (1989) looked at the extent to which the ethnic origin of applicants to medical school affected their chances of acceptance. The method they used was similar to that of their first study, only this time they asked candidates to describe their own ethnic origin.[2] In addition, they classified the surnames of all applicants as European or non-European. Over one-fifth of the UK applicants either described themselves as coming from an ethnic minority, or had non-European surnames. These students had lower rates of offers and acceptances for all medical schools, quite independently of A-level results, and there was a 'conspicuous deficit' of applicants from Afro-Caribbean backgrounds.

The most worrying evidence of selection bias in admission policy to medical school came from a report by the Commission for Racial Equality (CRE), who, in 1988, found St George's Hospital Medical School guilty of practising racial and sexual discrimina-

---

2   This is important because many people from Afro-Caribbean backgrounds have British-sounding surnames, which were given originally by their slave-masters to their forebears after leaving Africa.

tion. In 1986 the CRE was notified by two senior lecturers at St George's that a computer programme used to screen applicants for places at the medical school, discriminated against people with non-European names, and women. These candidates had a reduced chance of being interviewed with a view to admission, independently of how good their academic qualifications were. Approximately sixty candidates a year (out of 2000 applicants) were denied interviews simply on the grounds of their sex or ethnic origin. The programme had originally been devised in the 1970s with the purpose of simplifying the selection process by eliminating inconsistencies in the way the admissions staff performed their duties. In its final version the programme provided over 90% agreement with the selection panel. This is important because the programme was simply reflecting the discrimination already present in the system, and was not introducing a new source of bias (Lowry and Macpherson, 1988). This discrimination was therefore deeply engrained in the institutional practices of the school. Even more worrying was the fact that St George's had a more enlightened attitude to ethnic affairs, having a higher proportion of students with non-European surnames (12%) than, for example, the Westminster Medical School (5%). St George's was guilty only by virtue of the fact that it had been found out. There is little reason to believe that other medical schools are any better.

If discrimination occurs before and at selection, then there can be no doubt that it continues during the course of a career in medicine. McKeigue *et al.* (1990) followed the early careers of over 1500 doctors who graduated from five British medical schools over a period from 1981 to 1985. Graduates from ethnic minorities were almost twice as likely to report difficulties finding pre-registration jobs[3] (14% versus 8%) and had a substantially higher number of unsuccessful job applications at all training-post levels than native European graduates. They were also three times more likely to have accumulated more than three months' unemployment. Psychiatrists are no exception. A study of doctors who had gained the membership of the Royal College of Psychiatrists (the most important higher professional qualification in psychiatry, without which it is not possible to be appointed as a consultant psychiatrist) in 1981 and 1982 found that

---

3   These are the posts that all graduates have to complete for the first year following qualification. It is not possible to proceed to full registration as a medical practitioner with the GMC unless you have spent twelve months in approved pre-registration posts.

overseas graduates were four times more likely to remain in registrar grades than British graduates three years later (Bhate, 1987). By this time a registrar would expect to be in a senior registrar post. A survey undertaken by Toone et al. (1979) found that the majority of the seventy-nine doctors surveyed at the Maudsley Hospital – England's most prestigious training hospital – were from the higher social classes. We have to conclude that this discrimination, which favours the privileged for a career in medicine and psychiatry, is a prominent feature of the medical profession, repeated over and over again in countless interactions between psychiatrists and their patients. What are the consequence of this?

It is impossible to resist the conclusion that a gulf exists between the majority of doctors and their patients, and we may describe the implications of this for individual doctor–patient dyads in a number of ways. First, there is a lack of understanding on the doctor's part of the exigencies of the patient's situation. Second, the demographic differences between doctor and patient have implications for the type of explanatory model used by the doctor, and how he or she uses (or imposes) this on the patient. Discrepancies in social class and ethnicity mean that doctors may have little or no comprehension of the effects of deprivation and disadvantage on the health of their patients. It seems that the underclass and the medical profession are immiscible. Perhaps more important here is the extent to which doctors' middle-class values influence their opinions about their role in responding to deprivation and disadvantage. These problems emerged in a survey of medical students' experience and opinions about inner-city deprivation and health (Yiangou et al., 1988). This study was interesting because it was undertaken by a group of medical students at St Mary's hospital, of a group of over 300 of their colleagues. Over 75% of the respondents had no direct experience of the living conditions in the inner city prior to coming to medical school, and they remained isolated from these conditions until well into the later, clinical parts of their training.[4] Perhaps the most revealing part of the study con-

---

4   Medical training, which lasts five years, takes place in two parts. The first two years are pre-clinical, in which the students are not exposed to patients and acquire the basic sciences necessary to understand diseases. The final three years are spent clinically, acquiring the clinical skills necessary for the practice of medicine. Here, they learn by precept (remember the Hippocratic Oath) predominantly at the hands of influential, charismatic, male, middle-class, white European consultants.

cerned changes in students' attitudes as their training progressed. The majority of pre-clinical students wanted greater contact with the community early on in their course. By the time students had progressed to clinical work, less than one-third thought that this would be useful. It appears that the lure of clinical medicine, the power and authority of the expert, and the demands of high-tech medicine, simply becomes too great. This is yet another manifestation of the great divide between doctors' and patients' explanatory systems which we examined in Chapters 7 and 8.

At the end of Chapter 8 we briefly examined the influence of Jaspers' phenomenology on modern psychiatry. It is worth reconsidering the techniques of phenomenology described by Sims (1988) in the light of the differences between doctor and patient described here. Unlike general medicine, where it is possible physically to examine the patient's body in order to detect signs of illness, it is not possible to examine, say, a patient's hallucination. In order to overcome this, the psychiatrist has to use empathy as a way of trying to understand exactly what the patient must be experiencing:

> Empathy is the ability to feel oneself into the situation of the other person. It consists of asking appropriate, persistent, insightful questions; rephrasing and reiterating where necessary until being sure that one understands what he is describing.
>
> (Sims, 1988, p. 7)

The point I want to bring out here is that our ability to feel ourselves into another person's situation is dependent upon our closeness to that person. Closeness here may be defined in a number of ways. It may represent the interpersonal intimacy that we experience with our partners. This, of course, is not a characteristic of the relationship between psychiatrist and patient. On the other hand, it may be defined in terms of socio-demographic characteristics, such as social class, gender, ethnic origin, first language, age and so on. These most certainly are relevant to the relationship between psychiatrist and patient. The socio-demographic differences that exist between doctors and their patients pose a major problem for the process of empathy which many psychiatrists consider to be an important process in understanding their patients. How close is a white, middle-aged, middle-class doctor, in employment, living in a pleasant four-bedroom detached house in the suburbs, to a black, young, unemployed person who lives in a damp, delapidated flat in the inner city? What possibilities are there here for psychiatrists to feel themselves into their patients' experiences?

The popular view of doctors – indeed, a romanticised and ideal-ised view that many of my colleagues hold of themselves – is that they are hard-headed men and women of science whose knowledge is unsullied by the messy world of social inequality and injustice. In Chapter 7 I argued that there was a connection between the demise of the state and the rise of individualism, on one hand, and the ascendancy of neuroscience in psychiatry, on the other. As far as individual psychiatrists are concerned, there has been much interest in how personal beliefs and characteristics influence the type of explanatory models they favour. For example, Pallis and Stoffelmeyer (1973) found a significant positive correlation between a preference for physical methods of treatment and measures of conservatism in a group of psychiatrists. In fairness, it should be pointed out that these measures do not reflect support for a par-ticular political party, more a set of attitudes. In general, though, there is considerable variation in the results of studies examining personal features of doctors and their explanatory models. Toone *et al.* (1979) found that sex, social class and political allegiance pro-vided little insight into the orientation of psychiatrists in training at the Maudsley Hospital. But the most interesting finding from this study was that as trainees became more experienced, their interest in psychoanalytic and social models of mental illness waned at the expense of biological models. At this point it is worth recalling the responses of the young psychiatrists with which I started the chapter. It may be that their rawness in the face of their patients' suffering, and the fact that their training in medicine has not equipped them to handle this, will force them as time passes by, to adopt the detached and objective approach of neuro-science. This offers a comfortable means by which to relate them-selves and their powerlessness to their patients' suffering. But at what cost to patients?

The situation is a mess. Psychiatrists, embedded within a pro-fession whose values are dominated by middle-class, white values in which paternalism and deference to authority predominate, minister to psychiatric patients, the majority of whom come from the functional underclass. As McKenzie (1995) comments, equity for our patients is unlikely if doctors are not treated fairly. An-other way of looking at this is to say that patients might feel that they are being understood if their doctors are closer to them in terms of social class, gender and especially ethnicity. Medical schools have an important responsibility to ensure that doctors are not discriminated against on any grounds, but interventions made by the universities, whilst welcome, are only likely to make a significant contribution to change in the longer term. This raises the difficult question of what we should be doing now to tackle the imbalance of power and different perspectives on the experiences of service users. Can we accept their otherness, differences which, as Kristeva (1991, p. 185) comments, '... [worry] us the more as we dimly sense them in ourselves'? At least it should be possible to help psychiatrists (and other mental health professionals) to become more aware of the power that they possess over their patients' lives, and to help them become more sensitive to their patients' perspectives in ways which acknowledge and accept this difference. Some argue that working in partnership with users is one way of doing this, but I am suspicious of the notion of partnership. The word implies that the participants are involved in an equal relationship, yet the main feature of the relationship between doctor and patient, between psychiatrist and psychiatric patient, is that it is founded on inequality. From the patients' perspective, nothing useful is to be gained by an approach which denies the reality of this imbalance of power. Similar problems are present in the notion of 'consumerism' applied to mental health care. Many believed that recent government reforms of the NHS, such as the introduction of the purchaser–provider split, would bring the heady breeze of consumerism into the arena of mental health. But if we are to be consumers we have to be offered choice. The idea that I am a consumer is only meaningful if I have choice, and if I am free to exercise that choice. The experience of service users suggests that this is not so. I also suspect that the interests of the medical profession are not served by consumerism, which is one reason why the profession reacted strongly against (and still does) the internal market in health. The use of the words 'partnership' and 'consumerism' allow professionals to walk away, misty-eyed with idealism, and turn their backs on the reality of patients' lives. A more realistic way of describing the type of relationship required to challenge the power of professionals, and which enables service users and mental health professionals to work together to achieve this, is *alliance*. Alliance implies the sharing of a set of qualities or ideals, but it brings no presuppositions about the power or status of the participants. Alliances may be forged between the large and the small, the powerful and the disempowered, the strong and the weak. It is the recognition of these differences in power and the injustices which thus arise that makes alliances valuable. Alliances acknowledge the existence of differences between participants. It is these differences which give alliances their strength. Participants in alliances maintain their different perspectives, values and languages, and, in acknowledging the existence of these differences, they are able to work together for a common purpose. I want to end this chapter by considering some examples of alliances between service users and professionals, and how these are particularly valuable in the training of professionals, as well as their work.

WORKING WITH USERS: ALLIANCES FOR CHANGE

Perhaps the most important way to try to deal with the problems raised by this chapter concerns who should be involved in training psychiatrists. In Chapter 8 we saw that the traditional interpretation of phenomenology in the training of psychiatrists has resulted in second-hand accounts of psychiatric symptoms. These experiences lose their meaning and immediacy when taken away from those to whom they rightly belong. Those responsible for the training of psychiatrists must recognise that users themselves have the principal role to play in rectifying this form of alienation. Of course, attempts to understand hallucinations from a scientific perspective are important, but these must be complemented by users' accounts. This is essential if we are to be helped to understand the nature of the personal significance and meaning which underlies these experiences. Even this is no guarantee that alienation will not occur, for the psychiatrist will remain the expert. In Holland service users are increasingly referred to as *Ervakingsdeslunbige*. It is interesting to note that the word defies exact translation into English but, roughly translated, it means that they are professionals by virtue of their own experience. The message here is that psychiatrists have as much to learn from their patients' accounts of their experiences as they have from their learned professors. Once they appreciate that patients are people who have expertise and skills in their own rights, it may be possible to move into a position where an alliance is possible. The situation is starting to change, and over the last three years I have participated in two different forms of training in alliance with service users.

Whose voice is it, really?

I first met Ron Coleman about four years ago, after a project worker at the Hearing Voices Network in Manchester had contacted me suggesting that it would be useful if we met. I found my way to the Network office, but Ron wasn't there. I was whisked two blocks away to a small, dingy café at the back of Piccadilly, where we were to wait. I was bemused. The day was turning out to have overtones of espionage. After ten minutes or so Ron arrived. He looked about nervously, but was reassured by his friends who had accompanied me to the café. One of them told me that the reason for the security precautions was that Ron was on a Section 3 of the Mental Health Act and had run away from hospital. Ron himself added that he had stopped taking his clozaril six weeks earlier. The drug had helped damp his voices down, but it made him feel ill, and he was not prepared to go on putting up with that. He had already had a narrow escape a couple of days earlier, when the police came round to his flat looking for him. 'Does Ron Coleman live here?' the officer asked. 'Aye, but he's not been around for a few days. I'll let you know if he comes back,' replied Ron. 'And if they turn up now looking for Ron Coleman, we'll tell them that you're Ron,' he said, pointing at me. Perhaps my opportunity unintentionally to repeat Rosenhan's famous study was closer than I thought.

Over the next few months, Ron and I met regularly and we became good friends, and as he began to trust me he revealed more of his experiences at the hands of psychiatrists. Ever since he started to hear voices over ten years earlier, he had had a lot of contact with psychiatrists and had been treated with ECT, neuroleptics, lithium and antidepressants, none of which had made any difference to the experiences. His voices continued largely unabated, and now, because he had told his psychiatrist that he had stopped the clozaril, they had put him on a Section 3 so they could treat him against his wishes. He was determined to come off medication and accept the fact that he heard voices, even though some of the voices were distressing and told him to take his own life. Ron was angry. He was angry and bitter that a system which was supposed to help him, had imprisoned him, forced him to take treatment against his wishes, and had provided him with scant opportunity to understand the nature of his experiences. He himself was only too well aware of the reason why he heard voices. He knew and understood where his voices were coming from, and his friends, supporters and advocates in the Hearing Voices Network understood that – but not the psychiatrists, the people who had the power to deny him his freedom. He was implacably opposed to this system and wanted to make his disaffection known for the benefit of others.

Ron's passion in the face of his adversity, his deep sense of injustice at the way he, and thousands of others like him, had been treated, became the driving force behind his work, first with the Hearing Voices Network, and more recently during the course of his training work, in which on occasions, I have been fortunate to partner him. Ron is at his most effective when he is in the devil's lair, talking to psychiatrists. Over the last two years we have contributed a workshop on the experience of hearing voices for postgraduate psychiatrists in training at the University of Birmingham. This starts with Ron's own deconstruction of the psychiatric view of voice-hearing experiences, as a First Rank Symptom. He argues that such a view of the experience would have had Christ, the prophet Mohammed, Joan of Arc and a host of other religious figures incarcerated on the grounds that they were suffering from schizophrenia. The most telling feature of his contribution comes when he presents his own moving account of his life story, his narrative. Through this his voices become understandable in the context of a bereavement and a series of events which took place earlier in his life. The humanity of this account is then set in stark contrast to my contribution, which considers a variety of ways of talking about the experience. This contrast provides the students with food for thought. It is a clear demonstration of the conflicts between objective and subjective accounts of human experience. Ron challenges the orthodox psychiatric account of his experience, but does so by putting over his own account. He does not need to shout at them to do this. His account of his struggle to understand and accept his voices stands in place of everything else. He maintains a dialectical position, in which these different accounts of his experience are valid, struggling with each other. Indeed, he joins the struggle himself, revisiting it in the workshop so that the participants can understand more fully the complexity of the issues they are dealing with. Ron's anger becomes apparent only when he has to deal with the inequalities and injustice that are a feature of the blind application of psychiatric knowledge, the exercise of power for power's sake, the failure to see one man as a person. That is not to say that there is anything wrong with the way psychiatrists talk about voices. The problem arises when they apply that model uncritically. Knowing when and how to apply it is so important.

Ron's is an important message, which he has taken across Europe and the US. It challenges the languages used by psychiatrists to talk about his experiences, and he needs no input from me to deliver it. But there is a significance in the fact that we stand together, sharing a platform in the training of psychiatrists. In one sense this presents a contrast to the way that we, as doctors, are encouraged to think about ourselves as a profession and our relationship with our patients. We believe that we can learn only from older and more experienced members of our profession. All we expect our patients to do is to suffer dutifully in silence, passively displaying signs and symptoms so that we may exercise our skills in diagnosing and treating them. But then we will have nothing to learn from them. I hope that one of the things that my work with Ron has achieved is that it encourages the trainee psychiatrists present to open their minds to the possibility that they have as much if not more to learn from their patients as they have from people like me.

On the Edge of a Dilemma

If Ron deals with the languages used by psychiatrists about their patients, then my work with Sharon Lefevre deals with the relationship between doctors and patients. My first meeting with Sharon left quite an impression. Her GP had contacted me asking me to see her urgently. He was very concerned about her and had admitted her to the local cottage hospital after she had cut her arms very badly. I arrived at the hospital to find that she was being 'guarded' by three nurses in a single room, just in case she tried to harm herself again. My heart sank, because I had had little experience of helping people who self-harmed, and I really did not know what I was going to do to help her. She had a year's psychotherapy with one of my colleagues, but somehow Sharon and I knew that that was not the answer. At the end of this she had achieved a fair degree of intellectual 'insight', but that had not made a great deal of difference to the way she felt about herself. She was left understanding why it was she had such intensely negative feelings about herself, which, on occasions, became so overwhelmingly powerful that they still led her to inflict deep lacerations on her forearms, but she was unable to change the way she felt. I saw her in an out-patient clinic where we spent much time talking about her problems and my response to them as a doctor. Then, one day, towards the end of one of our sessions, she said something which intrigued me. First, she told me that she wanted me to listen to what she was about to say and to hear her through without making any comments, no matter how odd or bizarre I considered it. If I did not agree with what she was about to propose, then it would be left at that, and the matter would be forgotten. She then went on to say that she wanted to write a short play about an encounter between a patient and a psychiatrist who had admitted himself to a psychiatric ward in a crisis. She wanted me to play the part of the psychiatrist and she would be the patient. She said that if we could do this it might make it easier for other people to understand the way that she felt. Sharon was well-qualified to write such a play. At the time she was in her second year as a mature student of drama and theatre studies at a local university. Besides, there was something about the idea which struck me intuitively as being correct. Much to her surprise I agreed, but made it clear that if I was to work with her in this way it would mean that our relationship would change in such a way as to make it impossible for me to continue being her psychiatrist or therapist. Over the next three or four months we spent more time discussing my response to her as a doctor and psychiatrist, as well as the responses she herself had experienced from professionals, many of them highly negative, as a result of her problems. In August 1995 she had written the play, *On the Edge of a Dilemma*, which we first performed at an international conference in Maastricht organised by Sandra Escher and Marius Romme.

The play is set in the kitchen of an acute admission ward of a psychiatric unit. It starts with a lengthy monologue in which the female patient reveals her preoccupations with the state of the world. She is interrupted by a stranger who turns out to be the psychiatrist. He reveals that he has become disillusioned with his work and has admitted himself to hospital, partly because he is going through a personal crisis, and partly because he thinks it is an ideal way to experience what his patients have to experience. Not surprisingly the woman attacks him for his shallow approach to complex issues, and following this, the attention switches to her. In response to his questions she tells him that she is in hospital because she cuts herself, revealing her scars to the psychiatrist. He feels exasperated with her because this is a problem that he has never been able to understand. Furthermore, her problem confronts professionals with their powerlessness to help. People who cut themselves take the law into their own hands, and deny the professionals, who are trained to heal, any chance to 'cure'. Despite his frustrations she offers to help him try to understand why she behaves in the way she does, and in doing so she becomes very distressed. She is on the verge of cutting herself when he grabs the razor blade in the belief that, knowing what she knows and experiencing what she is experiencing, he can cut himself. But he cannot because he does not have the destructive inner voice that leads her to cut herself. Now he becomes the focus of attention, as he reveals more of his own predicament, talking about his unsatisfactory relationship with his father. But the barriers return as soon as he senses that he is close to revealing something important about himself. She points this out, and the play ends with the antagonists left questioning whether they can really trust each other.

The tension arising from the unsatisfactory resolution of the drama provides an ideal opportunity to engage the audience in discussion. Indeed, the monologue which started this chapter was drawn from comments made by the forty or so trainee psychiatrists in Birmingham who have seen the play over the last two years. The play raises a number of interesting points. It deals, of course, with the poorly understood phenomenon of self-harm. It also deals with the barriers which exist between all mental health professionals and their patients or clients. We may now begin to understand that these barriers arise as a consequence of the medical drive to control, to exercise knowledge and power. Psychiatrists often talk about the importance of boundaries in their relationships with their patients. Boundaries and barriers are closely related. Whether you regard a boundary as a barrier depends upon who is in control, and on which side you are situated. Barriers and boundaries are an integral feature of the practice of psychiatry, so it is important that the profession is aware of the consequences. To achieve this we must become aware of their extent and nature, how they impinge upon our daily work and affect our patients. We can best do this by stepping outside them. If I look at a barrier from one side, I do not obtain a clear view of its extent. My horizon is constrained and I cannot see what is on the other side. We can only understand the significance of barriers if we are prepared to step outside their confines and look at them from different perspectives: from the patients', from the doctors', from above and beyond. From the psychiatric patient's point of view, the doctors' need to isolate themselves behind professional role and language, their self-protective need to don the mask and robes of 'expert', constitutes the single most important obstacle to understanding. It is at this point that we really start to come to terms with the problem of the great panoply of professional and specialist interventions – physical, pharmacological, psychotherapeutic, behavioural, cognitive, dialogical or whatever – that are directed with steely intent against the experience of the schizophrenic subject. On the Edge of a Dilemma tries to deal with these issues. It acknowledges the shortcomings of psychiatry as far as the experiences of psychiatric patients are concerned, and it asks if it is possible for psychiatrists to feel what their patients feel, to experience what they experience. In the play, the woman asks the psychiatrist if he believes that simply admitting himself to the ward really does help him to understand how she feels. Simply putting yourself into the position of the other, whether socially or experientially, is not enough. The psychiatrist is like a voyeur. He cannot escape the need to observe. His position as a detached observer of her as object, means that it is impossible for him to understand her as a subject. This constitutes the most serious barrier to the possibility that they may understand each other. Through this he keeps himself apart and is not fully engaged with her as a person. This detachment contrasts with the engagement that the audience experience as they witness the drama unfold. They bring their own experience to bear, as psychiatric patients and psychiatrists, as they engage with the drama. Through the play, members of the audience may enter the inner worlds of the two characters. The psychiatrists in the audience are presented with this conflict between objectivity and subjectivity, and are invited to consider its implications for their work outside. This has important implications for the training of psychiatrists.

The play is also an example of a recent growth of interest in the role of the humanities in the training and work of doctors. Over the last twenty years, a number of critics have commented on the growing influence of science and technology in medicine (see, for example, Ian Kennedy's 1980 Reith Lectures, published in 1981). This has led some, such as McManus (1995), to suggest that the humanities basic to medicine, which include literature, philosophy, history, art, music, cinema, theatre, law, economics, politics, theology and anthropology, may play an important part in helping doctors maintain their humanity. McManus argues that the notion of the humane physician rooted in the humanities, is as important now as it has ever been. An interesting example of the integration of the humanities and clinical medicine has been described by an American physician, Horowitz (1996). As an experiment, he introduced a twenty-minute slot at the start of each ward round, in which the clinical team read and discussed a poem chosen by a team member. After some initial resistance, the junior doctors involved warmed to the idea, and the discussion blossomed, and the majority considered the idea enjoyable and worthwhile. Some of the points raised in Horowitz's discussion are pertinent to the hierarchical and authoritarian nature of professional relationships in medicine, in that participants discussed their emotional and intellectual responses to poems on an equal footing. Humanism is best experienced, not taught. In a recent paper, Holmes (1996) has argued the value of poetry in psychiatry. We need, he says, value-based medicine just as much as we need evidence-based medicine.

These are just a few examples which demonstrate the importance of the humanities in medicine and psychiatry. It remains to be seen how effective they will be in changing the way psychiatrists think and work with their patients. Medicine changes slowly. It has guarded its ways and secrets warily for 2500 years. But ritual remains an integral part of medicine, just as it was when the Cult of Asclepius brought thousands of pilgrims from all over Greece to Epidaurus. The act of ritual required that the participants cover themselves up, that they hide themselves beneath masks and adornments. The masks, adornments and rituals may have changed, but they remain as barriers. Psychiatrists continue to practise in ways that are out of touch with the help their patients want. Medicine only works as long as both patient and doctor believe in what is taking place. This means that the relationship must be based on mutual trust and respect. Many patients no longer believe that the traditional power and authority invested in the doctor is an appropriate basis from which to offer help to people experiencing mental health problems. Society has moved on, but the profession still hides behind its mask of mystery and power. Perhaps it is too frightened to face the world without. Perhaps it is too frightened to contemplate the implications of this.

Conclusions

In some ways there is nothing new about the conflicts that I have presented in this book. They have been around a long time, although recently there appears to have been an upsurge of interest in them. Indeed, a number of senior academic psychiatrists have acknowledged the limitations of a psychiatry which restricts itself to science at the expense of the humanities. This view has been expressed cogently by Cawley (1993), who has suggested that advances in the scientific basis of psychiatry have rendered us inarticulate about those areas which do not fall within the boundaries of science. According to Cawley, it is the psychiatrist–patient relationship that lies at the heart of psychiatry. It is its single most important feature. But, like all other human relationships, this is something which lies beyond the explanatory power of science. He argues that the key features of what he calls these *non-science* aspects of psychiatry can be derived from six axioms, self-evident truths which are independent of science:

(a) both idiographic and nomothetic viewpoints must always be recognised;
(b) each person has direct experience of his/her unique self and identity with past, present and future in continuity (that is, has self-awareness);
(c) subjective experiences (intrapersonal processes) are of central importance as aspects of the unique self;
(d) transactions between people (interpersonal processes) constitute a major set of life experiences, as do interactions with other environmental influences;
(e) empathy is ever-present, and an essential tool;
(f) communication is a complex variable which is at the heart of the matter.

(Cawley, 1993, pp. 155–6)

These axioms share much in common with several points that I have made in Parts II and III of this book. Cawley points out that they fall within the boundaries of the humanities, which stress the importance of human experience as the starting point for man's understanding of himself and others. Psychiatrists would do well, he argues, to be acquainted with literature, philosophy, biography, history and theology. Whilst I agree broadly with the point he makes, there are problems with some of the claims that he goes on to make for his axioms. In particular he states that they are ethically neutral and formally independent of culture. Concepts such as idiographic and nomothetic can only be understood in terms of a culture in which the concept of the individual emerges in contrast with that of a society which is made up out of other groups. Indeed, the single most striking feature of modern Western culture is the extent to which it raises the notion of the individual to a position of unparalleled importance. Consider for a moment the great richness and diversity of experiences of self to be found in the work of the African novelist, Ben Okri. In his novel *The Famished Road* (Okri, 1992), he provides us with a glimpse into a world of spiritual experience which is all the more significant for Western readers because of the extent to which a spiritual dimension is missing in our lives. The experience of self to emerge from this work is a magical spirit world in which the individual is seen only in relation to ties with family members, mother, brothers and sisters. Whilst Cawley is correct, in my view, for attaching the importance he does to subjective experiences and self-awareness, it is not true to say that this is culture free. At all times we must be aware of the dangers in attaching too much significance to the notion of selfhood and the individual, at the expense of our common, social world. This message was at the heart of Chapter 7.

Professor Andrew Sims has taken a rather different line in pointing out the perils of brainless or mindless psychiatry. Earlier I referred briefly to his approach to phenomenology as an example of the uncritical application of Jaspers' ideas to the problems of understanding another's experience in psychiatry. In a recent paper, Sims (1994) has referred to this problem himself. He acknowledges the problem of (Jaspersian) phenomenology in psychiatry, as the study of the subjective experience of another person. In a remarkable shift of frames, he goes on to argue for the immense significance that the patient's religious beliefs must have in understanding his or her experience. Psychiatrists may routinely ask patients about their religious beliefs, but only in a very cursory manner. There is rarely any attempt to examine the significance of the spiritual aspects of their lives. His notion of spirituality includes our aims and goals, our human solidarity, the wholeness of the person, moral aspects and awareness of God. He points out that religion is not a word to be found in the index of most psychiatric textbooks, yet these aspects of spirituality are an important feature of our lives which concern psychiatry. At the same time, Sims is aware that psychiatry touches on areas of deep complexity. He points out that there is no such thing as 'valueless' psychiatry:

> ... all of us, as we practise, carry our values, standards, aims and goals from the rest of life into psychiatry, and, much more to the point, so do our patients ... We do not try to impose our values on our patients.
>
> (Sims, 1994, p. 443)

This is an important point. In Chapter 10 we considered an important conflict that arose out of the doctor's mask, behind which the person remained hidden, cloaked and out of view. That person is just as much a member of society as the patient, and Sims is correct to point out the difficulty of keeping person and doctor apart. The problem is that I am not convinced that we are successful in our attempts not to impose our values on our patients. The inexorable drive towards science and technology in medicine, and psychiatry in particular, can easily seduce us into believing that what we do to our patients is *de facto* right and good. But the belief that science is value-free is a dangerous one; anyone who doubts this has only to consider the application of eugenic or atomic theory in the Second World War. Scientific theories are value-free only in so far as scientific languages enable us to ask scientific questions. These are quite unrelated to the questions asked by moral and ethical languages, which concern the issue, for example, of what is right and what is wrong. As soon as fractured humanity moves to apply scientific knowledge, we are obliged to consider the moral and ethical dimensions of this. The increasing preoccupation of medicine with science and technology leaves little room for anything, least of all the opportunity for the doctor to reflect on what he or she is doing, and whether this is right or wrong. In my view it is impossible for us to avoid imposing our values on our patients, and thus judging them, unless we are encouraged to become aware of ourselves as subjects and our patients as subjects. We must face our own values, beliefs and intentions in every encounter with every patient, so that we may become aware of how these conflict with our patient's values, beliefs and intentions.

A similar line of argument has been developed by HRH The Prince of Wales (1991) in a lecture to the Royal College of Psychiatrists on the occasion of its 150th Anniversary. No one denies the benefits of neuroscience, but he cautioned that psychiatrists must not forget the value of growth and healing that are to be found in suffering. He, too, argued that we must consider carefully the links between society and the 'scientific materialism' which dominates psychiatry:

> Should we not be asking ourselves pretty carefully where scientific materialism has been leading us – and, indeed, what kind of society it has been creating? Is there not an imbalance that needs correcting; an abandoned element that requires rehabilitation?
>
> (HRH The Prince of Wales, 1991, p. 765)

This 'abandoned element' is the spiritual dimension of our lives, without which there is no hope of Western man being able to find any hope or meaning in existence. Psychiatry must recognise the importance of this spiritual dimension, for it reflects the way in which we are interdependent and interconnected. His argument has important implications for the training of psychiatrists, which, he claims, places too much emphasis on the medical approach. Indeed, it is worth considering the following extract from his speech in relation to On the Edge of a Dilemma:

> I believe there is a need for training which emphasises to psychiatrists that there *will* be times when they will feel overwhelmed when faced with people who have suffered greatly; that there *will* be times when it is important to remain with, and comfort such a person in their suffering.
>
> (HRH The Prince of Wales, 1991, p. 765; emphasis in the original)

Of course, some may recognise HRH The Prince of Wales as the scourge of the expert. In May 1984 he made a speech at the Royal Institute of British Architects in which he criticised the profession for designing buildings which placed modernist style and theory before the needs of the public. Indeed, it was this model of the relationship between the architect as professional and the general public which led to the construction of concrete tower blocks which had such a negative effect on the quality of urban life thirty or forty years ago. This places the conflict between modernism and post-modernism firmly in the conclusions of my argument. Post-modernism is notoriously difficult to define, and I shall not attempt to do so. In the arts and literature, we may regard post-modernism as a reaction against the various modernist movements which have dominated Western thought since the beginning of the twentieth century. In the context of the arguments developed in this book, it can be seen as a reaction against the expert languages and technologies that have dominated psychiatry. This has been accompanied by the elevation of the status of 'expert' in society, and a corresponding relegation in the value of lay beliefs and opinion. A recent editorial in the *British Medical Journal* (Hodgkin, 1996) has commented on the significance of post-modernism for medicine. Modernism in medicine is represented by the belief that there is an external reality and objective truths to be explored by its expert languages. In contrast, post-modernism denies such a reality. Truth is intangible, uncertain, to be glimpsed fleetingly and understood only in terms of contexts and power. Medicine's response to this uncertainty can be seen in the rise of 'evidence-based medicine', which represents a retreat into what medical truths there are. Hodgkin argues that it is difficult for medicine to escape post-modern critique. Doctors are increasingly expected to be comfortable with multiple and conflicting interpretations of reality – those of their patients, relatives, managers and so on; an idea that has formed a central part of my own argument. Multiple interpretations of reality and multiple truths lead us perilously into a world where everything is relative, and there are no absolute values or beliefs. Where does this lead us?

The death of certainty presents a great challenge to psychiatry. We must consider the implications of this for three areas of our thought and work. First, relativism threatens the long-established system of ethics upon which medicine was constructed. My colleague Pat Bracken (personal communication) argues that one of the most important tasks facing psychiatry, indeed the whole of medicine, is that facing up to the loss of certainty means that it must redefine ethics. To this, I would add that psychiatry needs an ethics of intersubjectivity. This is because psychiatrists must recognise their own perspective and the way this affects and colours their relationships with their patients. Only then can the conflict between professional and personal languages be made explicit. Second, there is a need to replace the Jaspersian concept of phenomenology with a phenomenology of intersubjectivity. This is because of the importance of giving up the belief that the psychiatrist is capable of functioning as a detached observer of the other's experience. We must recognise the influence that our position, power and influence have upon the processes in which we engage with our patients. We can never understand our patients' experiences unless we are aware of the effect that we ourselves bring to this experience. Third, there is the issue of training. I have already made the case for the greater involvement of service users in the training of psychiatrists. These concluding points strengthen that argument. An inescapable feature our culture is our predilection for pitting idea against idea in gladiatorial contests. Everywhere we are forced to think in terms of opposites, one of which must be right, correct, the truth, at the expense of the other. Professional or user, male or female, young or old, black or white, middle class or underclass, sane or insane, psychiatrist or user, nature or nurture, neuroscience or social science, the list of polar opposites vying for dominance goes on and on. The Other. This expression, normally submerged deep in our minds, an unconscious auto-pilot which determines the way we explore ourselves and the world we share, steps into the foreground once again. The Other: the unseen, unheard, unknown opposite to that which *we* see, hear and know. To take the position of one, automatically places you in opposition to another, blinding us to the possibility of an encounter with understanding. But, as Kristeva (1991) points out, the Other is within us:

> In the fascinated rejection that the foreigner arouses in us, there is a share of uncanny strangeness in the sense of the depersonalisation that Freud discovered in it, and which takes up again our infantile desires and fears of the other – the other of death, the other of woman, the other of uncontrollable drive. The foreigner is within us. And when we flee from or struggle against the foreigner, we are fighting our unconscious – that 'improper' facet of our impossible 'own and proper'.
>
> (Kristeva, 1991, p. 191)

We must allow ourselves to be moved by others. Psychiatry has lost touch with this ability, indeed it is questionable whether it ever possessed it in the first place. Each step into the spurious certainty of neuroscience is a step away from matters of human concern. If we are to deal with the loss of certainty implicit in post-modern thought, we must be truthful with ourselves and others. We must allow ourselves to be ourselves with others.

References

Alanen, Y. (1975) 'The psychotherapeutic care of schizophrenic patients in a community psychiatric setting', in M.H. Lader (ed.), *Studies of Schizophrenia*. London: The Royal College of Psychiatrists, pp. 86–93.

American Psychiatric Association (1980) *Diagnostic and Statistical Manual of Mental Disorders* (3rd edn) Washington D.C.: A.P.A.

Andreasen, N.C. (1979a) 'Thought, language and communication disorders: I Clinical assessment, definition of terms, and evaluation of their reliability', *Archives of General Psychiatry* 35: 1315–21.

Andreasen, N.C. (1979b) 'Thought, language and communication disorders: II Diagnostic significance', *Archives of General Psychiatry* 36: 1325-30.

Andreasen, N.C. (1980) *Scale for the Assessment of Thought Language and Communication Disorders*. Iowa City: University of Iowa.

Andreasen, N.C. (1982a) 'Negative symptoms in schizophrenia: Definition and reliability', *Archives of General Psychiatry* 39: 784–8.

Andreasen, N.C. (1982b) 'Negative vs positive schizophrenia: Definition and validation', *Archives of General Psychiatry* 39: 789–94.

Andreasen, N.C. (1985) 'Positive vs negative schizophrenia: A critical evaluation', *Schizophrenia Bulletin* 11: 380–9.

Andreasen, N.C. and Flaum, M. (1991) 'Schizophrenia: The characteristic symptoms', *Schizophrenia Bulletin* 17: 27–49.

Bakhtin, M.M. (1986) *Speech Genres and Other Late Essays* (trans. V.W. McGee). Texas: University of Texas Press.

Baldessarini, R.J. and Viguera, A.C. (1995) 'Neuroleptic withdrawal in schizophrenic patients'. Commentary in *Archives of General Psychiatry* 52: 189–92.

Banks, M.H. and Jackson, P.R. (1982) 'Unemployment and the risk of minor psychiatric disorder in young people: cross-sectional and longitudinal evidence', *Psychological Medicine* 12: 789–98.

Barnes, T.R.E. and Bridges, P.K. (1980) 'Disturbed behaviour induced with high dose antipsychotic drugs', *British Medical Journal* 281: 274–5.

Barton, R. (1959) *Institutional Neurosis*. Bristol: Wright.

Beck, A.T. (1952) 'Successful outpatient psychotherapy of a chronic schizophrenic with a delusion based on borrowed guilt', *Psychiatry* 15: 305–12.

Bentall, R.P. (1990) (ed.) *Reconstructing Schizophrenia*. London: Methuen.

Bentall, R.P., Haddock, G. and Slade, P.D. (1994) 'Cognitive behaviour therapy for persistent auditory hallucinations', *Behaviour Therapy* 25: 51–66.

Bernard, C. (1865) *Introduction à L'Étude de la Médicine Expérimentale*. Paris: Garnier-Flammarion.

Bernard, C. (1957) *An Introduction to the Study of Experimental Medicine* (trans. H.C. Greene). New York: Dover Books.

Berrios, G.E. (1984) 'Descriptive psychopathology: conceptual and historical aspects', *Psychological Medicine* 14: 303–13.

Berrios, G.E. (1985) 'Positive and negative symptoms and Jackson: A conceptual history', *Archives of General Psychiatry* 42: 95–7.

Berrios, G.E. (1989) 'What is phenomenology? A review', *Journal of the Royal Society of Medicine* 82: 425–8.

Berrios, G.E. (1991) 'British psychopathology since the early twentieth century', in G.E. Berrios and H. Freeman (eds), *150 Years of British Psychiatry: 1841–1991*. London: Gaskell.

Bhate, S. (1987) 'Prejudice against doctors and students from ethnic minorities', *British Medical Journal* 294: 838.

Bhatti, N., Law, M.R., Morris, J.K., Halliday, R. and Moore-Gillon, J. (1995) 'Increasing incidence of tuberculosis in England and Wales: a study of the likely causes', *British Medical Journal* 310: 967–9.

Black, D. (1981) 'Inequalities in Health Care', *British Medical Journal* 282: 1468.

Black, D., Morris, J.N., Smith, C. and Townsend, P. (1982) *Inequalities in Health: The Black Report*. Harmondsworth: Penguin.

Bleuler, E. (1911) *Dementia Praecox or the Group of Schizophrenias* (trans. J. Zinkin, International Universities Press, New York, 1950). Leipzig: Deuticke.

Bleuler, M. (1978) *Die schizophrenen geistesstorungen im lichte langjahriger kranken und familien geschichten*. Stuttgart: Thieme, 1972. *Schizophrenic disorders: long-term patient and family studies* (trans. S.M. Clemens). New Haven and London: Yale University Press.

Boardman, J., Griffin, J. and Murray, O. (1986) *The Oxford History of the Classical World*. Oxford: Oxford University Press.

Bogerts, B., Ashtari, M., Degreef, G. *et al.* (1990) 'Reduced temporal limbic structure volumes on magnetic resonance images in first episode schizophrenia', *Psychiatry Research, Neuroimaging* 35: 1–13.

Boyle, M. (1993) *Schizophrenia: a scientific delusion?* London: Routledge.

Bracken, P. (1995) 'Beyond Liberation: Michel Foucault and the Notion of a Critical Psychiatry', *Philosophy, Psychology and Psychiatry* 2: 1–13.

Brain, Lord (1960) 'Space and sense-data', *British Journal for the Philosophy of Science* 11: 177–91.

Braude, W.M., Barnes, T.R.E. and Gore, S.M. (1983) 'Clinical characteristics of akathesia: a systematic investigation of acute psychiatric inpatient admissions', *British Journal of Psychiatry* 143: 139–50.

Brown, G.W. and Birley, J.L.T. (1968) 'Crises and life changes and the onset of schizophrenia', *Journal of Health and Social Behaviour* 9: 203–14.

Brown, G.W., Birley, J.L.T. and Wing, J.K. (1972) 'The influence of family life on the course of schizophrenic disorders: a replication', *British Journal of Psychiatry* 121: 241–58.

Brown, G.W. and Wing, J.K. (1962) 'A comparative clinical and social survey of three mental hospitals', The Sociological Review Monographs no. 5. (ed. P. Halmos). *Sociology and Medicine: studies within the framework of the British National Health Service.*

Brown, R., Colter, N., Corsellis, J.A.N. *et al.* (1986) 'Post-mortem evidence of striatal brain changes in schizophrenia', *Archives of General Psychiatry* 43: 36–42.

Bruce, M.L., Takeuchi, D.T. and Leaf, P.J. (1991) 'Poverty and psychiatric status', *Archives of General Psychiatry* 48: 470–4.

Bruton, C.J., Crow, T., Frith, C.D. *et al.* (1990) 'Schizophrenia and the brain', *Psychological Medicine* 20: 285–304.

Bunge, M. (1977) 'Emergence and the mind', *Neuroscience* 2: 501–9.

Butler, T. (1993) *Changing Mental Health Services: The politics and policy.* London: Chapman and Hall.

Campbell, P. (1993) 'Mental health services – the user's view', *British Medical Journal* 306: 848–50.

Cannon, T.D. and Marco, E. (1994) 'Structural brain abnormalities as indicators of vulnerability to schizophrenia', *Schizophrenia Bulletin* 20: 89–101.

Carlsson, A. (1990) 'Early psychopharmacology and the rise of modern brain research', *Journal of Psychopharmacology* 4: 120–6.

Carpenter, W.T., Bartko, J.J. and Strauss, J.S. (1978) 'Signs and Symptoms as predictors of outcome: A report from the International Pilot Study of schizophrenia', *American Journal of Psychiatry* 35: 940–5.

Caton, C.L.M., Shrout, P.E., Eagle, P.F., Opler, A. and Felix, A. (1994) 'Correlates of codisorders in homeless and never homeless indigent schizophrenic men', *Psychological Medicine* 24: 681–8.

Cawley, R.H. (1993) 'Psychiatry is more than a science', *British Journal of Psychiatry* 162: 154–60.

Chadwick, E. (1842) 'Report on the Sanitary Conditions of the Labouring Population' Parliamentary Papers for 1842, in A. Clayre (ed.) *Nature and Industrialisation* (1977). Oxford: Oxford University Press.

Chadwick, P. and Birchwood, M. (1994) 'The omnipotence of voices: a cognitive approach to auditory hallucinations', *British Journal of Psychiatry* 164: 190–201.

Chaika, E., (1974) 'A linguist looks at "schizophrenic" language', *Brain and Language* 1: 257–76.

Chouinard, G. and Jones, B.D. (1980) 'Neuroleptic-induced supersensitivity psychosis: clinical and pharmacological characteristics', *American Journal of Psychiatry* 137: 16–21.

Churchland, P.S. (1986) *Neurophilosophy.* Cambridge, Mass.: MIT Press.

Ciompi, L. (1980) 'The natural history of schizophrenia in the long term', *British Journal of Psychiatry* 136: 413–20.

Claridge, G. (1985) *Origins of Mental Illness.* Oxford: Blackwell.

Clow, A., Theodorou, A., Jenner, P. and Marsden, C.D. (1980) 'Changes in rat striatal dopamine turnover and receptors activity during one year's neuroleptic administration', *European Journal of Pharmacology* 63: 135–44.

Cohen, J.D. and Servan-Schreiber, D. (1992) 'Context, cortex and dopamine: a connectionist approach to behaviour and biology in schizophrenia', *Psychological Review* 99: 45–77.

Cohen, J.D. and Servan-Schreiber, D. (1993) 'A theory of dopamine function and its role in cognitive deficits in schizophrenia', *Schizophrenia Bulletin* 19: 85–104.

Committee on the Safety of Medicines (1990) 'Cardiotoxic effects of pimozide', *Current Problems* 29.

Cooper, B. (1995) 'Do we still need social psychiatry?', *Psychiatra Fennica* 26: 9–20.

Cooper, J.E. and Sartorius, N. (1977) 'Cultural and temporal variations in schizophrenia: a speculation on the importance of industrialisation', *British Journal of Psychiatry* 130: 50–5.

Cornblatt, B.A. and Keilp, J.G. (1994) 'Impaired attention, genetics and the pathophysiology of schizophrenia', *Schizophrenia Bulletin* 20: 31–43.

Crane, G.E. (1968) 'Tardive Dyskinesia in patients treated with neuroleptics: a review of the literature', *American Journal of Psychiatry* (supplement) 124: 40–8.

Crow, T.J. (1993a) 'The origins of psychosis and "The descent of man"', *British Journal of Psychiatry* 159 (supplement 14): 76–82.

Crow, T.J. (1993b) 'Origins of Psychosis and the evolution of human language and communication', in S. Langer, J. Mendlewicz and G. Racagni (eds), *International Academy for Biomedical and Drug Research*. Basel: S. Karger.

Crow, T.J. (1995) 'Constraints on concepts of pathogenesis: language and the speciation process as the key to the etiology of schizophrenia', *Archives of General Psychiatry* 52: 1011–14.

Crow, T.J., Done, D.J. and Sacker, A. (1994) 'Childhood precursors of psychosis as clues to its evolutionary origins', *European Archives of Psychiatry and Neurological Sciences*. In press.

Crow, T.J., MacMillan, J.F., Johnson, A.L. and Johnstone, E.C. (1986) 'The Northwick Park study of first episodes of schizophrenia: II. A randomised controlled trial of prophylactic medication', *British Journal of Psychiatry* 148: 120–7.

Crumpton, N. (1967) 'Maintaining patients in the community. The role of drugs', *British Journal of Geriatric Practice* 4: 186–92.

Curson, D., Patel, M., Liddle, P.F. and Barnes, T.R. (1988) 'Psychiatric Morbidity of a long-stay hospital population with chronic schizophrenia, and implications for future community care', *British Medical Journal* 297: 818–22.

Davies, L.M. and Drummond, M.F. (1994) 'Economics and Schizophrenia: The Real Cost', *British Journal of Psychiatry* 165 (supplement 25): 18–21.

Davis, J.M. and Casper, R. (1977) 'Antipsychotic drugs: clinical pharmacology and therapeutic use', *Drugs*, 14: 260–82.

Davis, J.M., Schaffer, C.B., Killian, G.A. *et al.* (1980) 'Important issues in the drug treatment of schizophrenia', *Schizophrenia Bulletin* 6: 70–87.

De Alarcon, R. and Carney, M.W.P. (1969) 'Severe depressive mood changes following slow release intramuscular fluphenazine injection', *British Medical Journal* iii: 564–7.

Delay, J. and Deniker, P. (1952) 'Trente-huit cas de psychoses traitees par la cure prolongee et continue de 4560 RP', *Le Congres des Al. et Neurol. de Langue Fr. In, Compte rendu du Congres.* Paris: Mason et Cie.

Dencker, S.J., Lepp, M. and Malm, U. (1980) 'Do schizophrenics well adapted in the community need neuroleptics? A depot neuroleptic withdrawal study', *Acta Psychiatrica Scandinavica* (supplement 279): 64–76.

Dennett, D.C. (1991) *Consciousness Explained.* London: Allen Lane.

Department of Health (1995) *Variations in Health: what can the Department of Health and the NHS do?* London: Department of Health.

Der, G., Gupta, S. and Murray, R. (1990) 'Is schizophrenia disappearing?' *Lancet* 335: 513–16.

Dimascio, A., Haven, L.L. and Klerman, G. (1963) 'The psychopathology of phenothiazine compounds: a comparative study of the effects of chlorpromazine, promethazine, trifluoperazine and perphenazine in normal males: II. Results and discussion', *Journal of Nervous and Mental Diseases* 136: 168–86.

Disraeli, B. (1845) *Sybil.* Oxford: Oxford University Press.

Done, D.J., Crow, T.J., Johnstone, E.C. and Sacker, A. (1994) 'Childhood antecedents of schizophrenia: social adjustment at ages 7 and 11', *British Medical Journal* 309: 699–703.

Drake, R.E. and Ehrlich, J. (1985) 'Suicide attempts associated with akathesia', *American Journal of Psychiatry* 142: 499–501.

Eagles, J. and Whalley, L. (1985) 'Decline in the diagnosis of schizophrenia among first admissions to Scottish mental hospitals from 1969–1978', *British Journal of Psychiatry* 146: 151–4.

Edwards, G. (1972) 'Diagnosis of schizophrenia: An Anglo-American comparison', *British Journal of Psychiatry* 120: 385–90.

Engel, G.L. (1977) 'The need for a new medical model: a challenge for biomedicine', *Science* 196: 129–36.

Engelhardt, D.M. and Freedman, N. (1969) 'Maintenance drug therapy: the schizophrenic patient in the community', in A. Kiev (ed.), *Social Psychiatry* vol. 1. London: Routledge and Kegan Paul, pp. 256–82.

Ensink, B. (1992) *Confusing Realities: A study on child sexual abuse and psychiatric symptoms.* Amsterdam: VU University Press.

Ensink, B. (1993) 'Trauma: A study of child abuse and hallucinations', in M. Romme and S. Escher (eds), *Accepting Voices.* London: MIND.

Falloon, I.R.H., Boyd, J.L., McGill, C.W., Williamson, M., Ranzani, J., Moss, H.B., Gilderman, A.M. and Simpson, G.M. (1985) 'Family management in the prevention of morbidity in schizophrenia: clinical outcome of a two year longitudinal study', *Archives of General Psychiatry* 42: 887–96.

Famuyiwa, O.O., Eccleston, D. and Donaldson, A.A. (1979) 'Tardive dyskinesia and dementia', *British Journal of Psychiatry* 135: 500–4.

Farde, L., Wiesel, F.-A., Hall, H., Halldin, C., Stonelander, S., Sedvall, G. (1987) 'No D_2 receptor increase in PET study of schizophrenia', *Archives of General Psychiatry* 44: 671–2.

Faris, R.E.L. and Dunham, H.W. (1939) *Mental Disorders in Urban Areas*. Chicago: University of Chicago Press.

Fish, B., Marcus, J., Hans, S.L. et al. (1992) 'Infants at risk for schizophrenia: sequelae of a genetic neurointegrative defect', *Archives of General Psychiatry* 49: 221–35.

Forrer, G.R. (1960) 'Benign auditory and visual hallucinations', *Archives of General Psychiatry* 3: 119–22.

Freeman, H.L. (1984) 'The scientific background', in H.L. Freeman (ed.), *Mental Health and the Environment*. London: Churchill Livingstone.

Freeman, H.L. (1994) 'Schizophrenia and city residence', *British Journal of Psychiatry* 164 (supplement 23): 39–50.

Freud, S. (1973) *New Introductory Lectures on Psychoanalysis* (trans. J. Strachey). London: Pelican.

Freud, S. and Brener, J. (1974) *Studies on Hysteria* (trans. J. Strachey). London: Pelican.

Frith, C., (1992) *The Cognitive Neuropsychology of Schizophrenia*. Hove, UK: Lawrence Earlbaum Associates.

Fromkin, V.A., (1975) 'A linguist looks at "a linguist looks at 'schizophrenic language'"' *Brain and Language* 2: 498–503.

Galbraith, J.K. (1992) *The Culture of Contentment*. London: Sinclair-Stevenson.

General Medical Council (1996) *Good Medical Practice: Guidance from the General Medical Council*. London: GMC.

Giggs, J.A. and Cooper, J.E. (1987) 'Ecological structure and the distribution of schizophrenia and affective psychoses in Nottingham', *British Journal of Psychiatry* 151: 627–33.

Gilbert, P.L., Harris, J., McAdams, L.A. and Jeste, D.V. (1995) 'Neuroleptic withdrawal in schizophrenic patients: a review of the literature', *Archives of General Psychiatry* 52: 173–88.

Gillon, R. (1985) *Philosophical Medical Ethics*. Chichester: Wiley.

Goffman, E. (1968) *Asylums: essays on the social situations of mental patients and other inmates*. Harmondsworth: Penguin.

Goldberg, E.M. and Morrison, S.L. (1963) 'Schizophrenia and Social Class', *British Journal of Psychiatry* 109: 785–802.

Goodwin, G. (1995) *Proposal for a Special Interest Group for Neuroscience in Psychiatry*. Discussion document. London: Royal College of Psychiatrists.

Gottesman, I., McGuffin, P. and Farmer, A. (1987) 'Genetics and Schizophrenia – Current State of Negotiations', in F. Vogel and K. Sperling (eds), *Human Genetics*. Berlin: Springer-Verlag.

Gottesman, I. and Shields, J. (1982) *Schizophrenia: the epigenetic puzzle*. Cambridge: Cambridge University Press.

Gould, L.N. (1949) 'Auditory hallucinations and sub-vocal speech', *Journal of Nervous and Mental Diseases* 109: 418–27.

Gunnell, D.J., Peters, T.J., Kammerling, R.M. and Brooks, J. (1995) 'Relation between parasuicide, suicide, psychiatric admissions and socioeconomic deprivation', *British Medical Journal* 311: 226–30.

Haddock, G., Bentall, R.P. and Slade, P.D. (1993) 'Psychological treatment of chronic auditory hallucinations: two case studies', *Behavioural and Cognitive Psychotherapy* 21: 335–46.

Hare, E. (1988) 'Temporal factors and trends, including birth seasonality and the viral hypothesis', in H.A. Nasrallah (ed.) *Handbook of Schizophreni* vol. 3. Amsterdam: Elsevier, pp. 345–77.

Harrison, G. and Mason, P. (1993) 'Schizophrenia – falling incidence and better outcome?', *British Journal of Psychiatry* 163: 535–41.

Harvey, I., Persaud, R., Ron, M. *et al.* (1994) 'Volumetric MRI measurement in bipolars compared with schizophrenics and healthy controls', *Psychological Medicine* 24: 689–99.

Harvey, I., Ron, M., Du Boulay, G. *et al.* (1993) 'Diffuse reduction of cortical volume in schizophrenia on magnetic resonance imaging', *Psychological Medicine* 23: 591–604.

Hays, P. (1984) 'The nosological status of schizophrenia', *Lancet*, June 16: 1342–5.

Healy, D. (1990a) 'The psychopharmacological era: notes toward a history', *Journal of Psychopharmacology* 4: 152–67.

Healy, D. (1990b) *The Suspended Revolution*. London: Faber and Faber.

Healy, D. (1991) 'D_1 and D_2 and D_3' *British Journal of Psychiatry* 159: 319–24.

Healy, D., Thomas, P., Savage, M. and McMonagle, T. (1997) *Abusive Prescribing*. Forthcoming.

Helmholtz, H. (1866) *Handbuch der Physiologischen Optik*. Leipzig: Voss.

Hermanzohn, P.C. and Siris, S.G. (1992) 'Akinesia: a syndrome common to Parkinsonism, retarded depression and negative symptoms of schizophrenia', *Comprehensive Psychiatry* 33: 221–32.

Herrera, J.N., Sramek, J.J., Costa, J.F. *et al.* (1988) 'High potency neuroleptics and violence in schizophrenia', *Journal of Nervous and Mental Diseases* 176: 558–61.

Heston, L.L. (1966) 'Psychiatric disorders in foster home reared children of schizophrenic mothers', *British Journal of Psychiatry* 112: 819–35.

Hirsch, S., Cramer, P. and Bowen, J. (1992) 'The triggering hypothesis of the role of life events in schizophrenia', *British Journal of Psychiatry* 161 (supplement 18): 84–7.

Hirsch, S., Gaind, R., Rohde, P., Stevens, B. and Wing, J.K. (1972) 'Outpatient maintenance treatment of chronic schizophrenics with fluphenazine decanoate injections: a double blind placebo trial', *British Medical Journal* 1: 633–7.

Hodgkin, P. (1996) 'Medicine, postmodernism and the end of certainty', *British Medical Journal* 313: 1568–9.

Hoenig, J. (1983) 'The concept of schizophrenia: Kraepelin-Bleuler-Schneider', *British Journal of Psychiatry* 142: 547–56.

Hoffman, R.E. (1987) 'Verbal Hallucinations and language production processes in schizophrenia', *Behavioural and Brain Sciences* 9: 503–48.

Hoffman, R.E. and McGlashan, T.H. (1993a) 'Neurodynamics and schizophrenia research: editors' introduction', *Schizophrenia Bulletin* 19: 15–19.

Hoffman, R.E. and McGlashan, T.H. (1993b) 'Parallel distributed processing and the emergence of schizophrenic symptoms', *Schizophrenia Bulletin* 19: 119–40.

Hogarty, J., Anderson, C.M., Reiss, D.J., Kornblith, S.J., Greebwald, D.P., Javana, C.D. and Madonia, M.J. (1986) 'Family psycho-education, social skills training and maintenance chemotherapy in the after-care treatment of schizophrenia: 1. One year effects of a controlled study on relapse and expressed emotion', *Archives of General Psychiatry* 43: 633–42.

Holmes, J. (1996) 'Can poetry help us become better psychiatrists?', *Psychiatric Bulletin* 20: 722–5.

Horowitz, H.W. (1996) 'Poetry on rounds: a model for the integration of humanities into residency training', *Lancet* 347: 447–9.

HRH The Prince of Wales (1991) Lecture given as Patron, to the Royal College of Psychiatrists, Brighton, 5 July 1991. *British Journal of Psychiatry* 159: 763–8.

Huber, G., Gross, G. and Schuttler, R. (1979) *Schizophrenie. Eine verlaufs und sozial-psychiatrische langzeituntersuchungen an den 1945–1959 in Bonn hospitalisierten schizophrenen kranken.* Berlin, Heidelberg, New York: Springer.

Huckle, P. and McGuffin, P. (1991) 'Familial factors in going to medical school', *Medical Education* 25: 13–15.

Ineichen, B., Harrison, G. and Morgan, H.G. (1984) 'Psychiatric hospital admissions in Bristol I: geographical and ethnic factors', *British Journal of Psychiatry* 145: 600–11.

Jablensky, A. (1988) 'Epidemiology of Schizophrenia', in P. Bebbington and P. McGuffin (eds), *Schizophrenia: The Major Issues.* London: Heinemann.

Jackson, J.H. (1889) 'On post-epileptic states: A contribution to the comparative study of the insanities', *Journal of Mental Science* 34: 490–500.

Jakob, H. and Beckman, H. (1986) 'Prenatal development disturbances in the limbic allocortex in schizophrenics', *Journal of Neural Transmission* 65: 303–26.

Jaspers, K. (1963) *General Psychopathology* (trans. J. Hoenig and M.W. Hamilton). Manchester: Manchester University Press.

Javitt, D.C. and Zukin, S.R. (1991) 'Recent advances in the phencyclidine model of schizophrenia', *American Journal of Psychiatry* 148: 1301–8.

Jaynes. J. (1976) *The Origins of Consciousness in the Breakdown of the Bicameral Mind.* Boston: Houghton Mifflin.

Johnson, D.A.W. (1979) 'Further observations on the duration of neuroleptic maintenance therapy in schizophrenia', *British Journal of Psychiatry* 135: 524–30.

Johnson, D.A.W., Pasterski, G., Ludlow, J.M., Street, K. and Taylor, R.D.W. (1983) 'The discontinuance of maintenance neuroleptic therapy in chronic schizophrenic patients: drug and social consequences', *Acta Psychiatrica Scandinavica* 67: 339–52.

Johnson, F.H. (1978) *The Anatomy of Hallucinations.* Chicago: Nelson Hall.

Johnson, P.B., Ramirez, P.M., Opler, L.A. and Malgady, R. (1994) 'Relationship between neuroleptic dose and positive and negative symptoms', *Psychological Reports* 74: 481–2.

Johnstone, E.C., Crow, T.C., Frith, C.D. *et al.* (1976) 'Cerebral ventricular size and cognitive impairment in chronic schizophrenia', *Lancet* ii: 924–6.

Johnstone, E.C., Crow, T.J., Johnson, A.L. and Macmillan, J.F. (1986) 'The Northwick Park study of first episodes of schizophrenia: I. presentation of the illness and problems relating to admission' *British Journal of Psychiatry* 148: 115–20.

Jones, P. and Murray, R.M. (1994) 'The genetics of schizophrenia is the genetics of neurodevelopment', *British Journal of Psychiatry* 158: 615–23.

Jones, P., Murray, R.M. and Rodgers, B. (1994) 'Child development preceding adult schizophrenia', *Schizophrenia Research* 11: 97.

Jones, S.C., Forster, D.P. and Hassanyeh, F. (1991) 'The role of unemployment in parasuicide', *Psychological Medicine* 21: 169–76.

Joseph Rowntree Foundation (1995) *Inquiry into Income and Wealth.* York: Joseph Rowntree Foundation.

Kammerling, R.M. and O'Connor, S. (1993) 'Unemployment rate as predictor of rate of psychiatric admission', *British Medical Journal* 307: 1536–9.

Kane, J.M. and Freeman, H.L. (1994) 'Towards more effective antipsychotic treatment', *British Journal of Psychiatry* 165 (supplement 25): 22–31.

Kane, J.M., Honigfeld, G., Singer, J. *et al.* (1988) 'Clozapine for the treatment resistant schizophrenic', *Archives of General Psychiatry* 45: 789–96.

Kane, J.M. and Smith, J.M. (1982) 'Tardive dyskinesia – prevalence and risk factors, 1959 to 1979', *Archives of General Psychiatry* 39: 473–81.

Karlsson, H. and Kamppinen, M. (1995) 'Biological psychiatry and reductionism: Empirical findings and philosophy', *British Journal of Psychiatry* 167: 434–8.

Kavanagh, D.J. (1992) 'Recent developments in expressed emotion and schizophrenia', *British Journal of Psychiatry* 160: 601–20.

Kendell, R.E. (1975) 'The concept of disease and its implications for psychiatry', *British Journal of Psychiatry* 127: 305–15.

Kennedy, I. (1981) *The Unmasking of Medicine.* London: George Allen and Unwin.

Kennedy, J.L., Guiffra, L., Moises, H. *et al.* (1988) 'Evidence against linkage relationship between chromosome 5 in a northern Swedish pedigree', *Nature* 336: 167–70.

Kety, S. (1974) 'From rationalisation to reason', *The American Journal of Psychiatry* 131: 957–63.

Kingdon, D.G. and Turkington, D. (1991) 'A role for cognitive-behavioural strategies in schizophrenia?' *Social Psychiatry and Psychiatric Epidemiology* 26: 101–3.

Klawans, H.L. (1973) 'The pharmacology of tardive dyskinesia', *American Journal of Psychiatry* 130: 82–6.

Klein, M. (1930) 'The importance of symbol formation in the development of the ego', *International Journal of Psychoanalysis* 11: 24–39.

Klerman, G. (1977) 'Mental illness, the medical model and psychiatry', *Journal of Medicine and Philosophy* 2: 220–43.

Kolers, P.A. and von Grünau, M. (1976) 'Shape and color in apparent motion', *Vision Research* 16: 329–35.

Kraepelin, E. (1913) *Psychiatrie, ein Lehrbuch fur Studierende und Artzt* [Psychiatry, a textbook for students and practitioners] (8th edn), vol. 3. Leipzig: Barth.

Kraupl Taylor, F. (1976) 'The medical model of the disease concept', *British Journal of Psychiatry* 128: 588–94.

Kristeva, J. (1991) *Strangers to Ourselves* (trans. L.S. Roudiez). New York: Columbia University Press.

Lam, D. (1991) 'Psychosocial family intervention in schizophrenia: a review of empirical studies', *Psychological Medicine* 21: 423–41.

Lamb, H.R. (1992) 'Is it time for a moratorium on deinstitutionalisation?', *Hospital and Community Psychiatry* 43: 669.

Lane, E.A. and Albee, G.W. (1965) 'Childhood intellectual differences between schizophrenic adults and their siblings', *American Journal of Orthopsychiatry* 35: 747–53.

Langenbach, M. (1995) 'Phenomenology, intentionality, and mental experience: Edmund Husserl's *Logische Untersuchungen* and the first edition of Karl Jaspers' *Allgemein Psychopathologie*', *History of Psychiatry* 6: 209–24.

Langenbach, M. (1996) 'Time for a linguistic turn in psychiatric theory', *Journal of Theoretical Medicine*, forthcoming.

Leff, J.P., Kuipers, L., Berkowitz, R., Eberlein-Fries, R. and Sturgeon, R. (1982) 'A controlled trial of social intervention in the families of schizophrenic patients', *British Journal of Psychiatry* 141: 121–34.

Leff, J.P. and Wing, J.K. (1971) 'Trial of maintenance therapy in schizophrenia', *British Medical Journal* 3: 599–604.

Leonhard, K. (1980) 'Contradictory issues in the origin of schizophrenia', *British Journal of Psychiatry* 136: 437–44.

Leudar, I. and Thomas, P. (1994) *Guide-lines for Establishing Pragmatic Aspects of Voices – Voice Hearer Talk*. Manchester: Department of Psychology, University of Manchester.

Leudar, I., Thomas, P., and Johnston, M. (1992) 'Self-repair in dialogues of schizophrenics: effects of hallucinations and negative symptoms', *Brain and Language* 43: 487–511.

Leudar, I., Thomas, P. and Johnston, M. (1994) 'Self-monitoring in speech production: effects of verbal hallucination and negative symptoms', *Psychological Medicine* 24: 749–61.

Leudar, I., Thomas, P., McNally, D. and Glinski, A. (1997) 'What can voices do with words? Pragmatics of verbal hallucinations', *Psychological Medicine*, forthcoming.

Lewander, T. (1994) 'Neuroleptics and the neuroleptic induced deficit syndrome', *Acta Psychiatrica Scandinavica* 89 (supplement 380): 8–13.

Lewis, A. (1936) 'Melancholia: Prognostic study and case material', *Journal of Mental Science* 82: 488–588.

Lewis, S. (1993) 'A controlled quantitative study of computed X-ray tomography in functional psychoses', MD thesis, University of London.

Lewis, S. and Murray, R. (1987) 'Obstetric complications, neurodevelopmental deviance, and risk of schizophrenia', *Journal of Psychiatric Research* 21: 413–21.

Lewis, S., Owen, M.J. and Murray, R.M. (1989) 'Obstetric complications and schizophrenia: methodology and mechanisms', in S.C. Schulz and C.A. Tamminga (eds), *Schizophrenia: A Scientific Focus*. New York: Oxford University Press.

Lowry, S. and Macpherson, G. (1988) 'A blot on the profession', *British Medical Journal* 296: 657–8.

Ludwig, A.M. and Othmer, E. (1977) 'The medical basis of psychiatry', *American Journal of Psychiatry* 134: 1087–92.

McGue, M., Gottesman, I.I. and Rao, D.C. (1985) 'Resolving genetic models for the transmission of schizophrenia', *Genetic Epidemiology* 2: 99–110.

McGuffin, P. (1984) 'Genetic influences on personality, neurosis and psychosis', in P. McGuffin (ed.), *Scientific Principles of Psychopathology*. London: Grune and Stratton.

McGuire, P., Silbersweig, D.A., Wright, I., Murray, R.M., David, A.S., Frackowiak, R.S.J. and Frith, C.D. (1995) 'Abnormal monitoring of inner speech: a physiological basis for auditory hallucinations', *Lancet* 346: 596–600.

McKeigue, P.M., Richards, J.D.M. and Richards, P. (1990) 'Effects of discrimination by sex and race on the early careers of British medical graduates during 1981–7', *British Medical Journal* 301: 961–4.

McKellar, P. (1957) *Imagination and Thinking*. New York: Basic Books.

McKenzie, K. (1995) 'Racial discrimination in medicine', *British Medical Journal* 310: 478–9.

McManus, I.C. (1982) 'The social class of medical students', *Medical Education* 16: 72–5.

McManus, I.C. (1995) 'Humanity and the medical humanities', *Lancet* 346: 1143–5.

McManus, I.C. and Richards, P. (1984) 'Audit of admission to medical school: I – acceptances and rejects', *British Medical Journal* 289: 1201–4.

McManus, I.C., Richards, P. and Maitlis, S.L. (1989) 'Prospective study of the disadvantage of people from ethnic minority groups applying to medical school in the United Kingdom', *British Medical Journal* 298: 723–6.

McMillan, J.F., Gold, A., Crow, T.J., Johnson, A.L. and Johnstone, E.C. (1986) 'The Northwick Park study of first episodes of schizophrenia: IV. Expressed emotion and relapse', *British Journal of Psychiatry* 148: 133–43.

Magliozzin, J.R., Mungas, S., Laubly, J.N. and Blunden, D. (1989) 'Effect of haloperidol on a symbol digit substitution task in normal adult males', *Neuropsychopharmacology* 2: 29–37.

Markowe, M., Steinert, J. and Heyworth-Davis, F. (1967) 'Insulin and chlorpromazine in schizophrenia: a ten year comparative study', *British Journal of Psychiatry* 113: 1101–6.

Marmot, M.G., Smith, G.D., Stansfield, S., Patel, C., North, F., Head, J., White, I., Brunner, E. and Feeney, A. (1991) 'Health inequalities among British civil servants', *Lancet* 337: 1387–93.

Mead, G.H. (1934). *Mind, Self and Society: From the standpoint of a social behaviorist*. Chicago: Chicago University Press, 1962.

Mechanic, D. (1972) 'Social psychological factors affecting the presentation of bodily complaints', *New England Journal of Medicine* 286: 105–15.

Mednick, S.A., Huttunen, M. and Machon, R. (1994) 'Prenatal influenza infections and adult schizophrenia', *Schizophrenia Bulletin* 20: 263–7.

Mednick, S.A., Machon, R., Huttunen, M. and Bonett, D. (1988) 'Adult schizophrenia following prenatal exposure to an influenza epidemic', *Archives of General Psychiatry* 45: 189–92.

Mehtonen, O.-P., Aranko, K., Malkonen, L. *et al.* (1991) 'A study of sudden death associated with the use of antipsychotic or antidepressant drugs', *Acta Psychiatrica Scandinavica* 84: 58–64.

Menninger, K. (1963) *The Vital Balance*. New York: Viking Press.

Mettler, F.A. and Crandell, A. (1959) 'Neurological disorders in psychiatric institutions', *Journal of Nervous and Mental Diseases* 128: 148–59.

Mohr, J. (1976) 'Broca's area and Broca's aphasia', *Studies in Neurolinguistics* 1: 201.

Mukherjee, S., Rosen, A.M., Cardenas, C., Varia, V. and Orlarte, S. (1982) 'Tardive Dyskinesia in psychiatric outpatients: a study of prevalence and association with demographic clinical and drug history variables', *Archives of General Psychiatry* 39: 466–9.

Murray, R.M. (1994) 'Neurodevelopmental schizophrenia: the rediscovery of dementia praecox', *British Journal of Psychiatry* 165 (supplement 25): 6–12.

Norman, R.M.G. and Malla, A.K. (1993) 'Stressful life events and schizophrenia 1: a review of the research', *British Journal of Psychiatry* 162: 161–6.

O'Callaghan, E., Sham, P., Takei, N. *et al.* (1991) 'Schizophrenia after prenatal exposure to 1957 A2 influenza epidemic', *Lancet* 337: 1248–50.

Owen, F., Crow, T.J., Poulter, M., Cross, A.J., Longden, A. and Riley, G.J. (1978) 'Increased dopamine-receptor sensitivity in schizophrenia', *Lancet* ii: 223–5.

Pakkenberg, B. (1987) 'Post-mortem study of chronic schizophrenic brains', *British Journal of Psychiatry* 151: 744–52.

Pallis, D.J. and Stoffelmeyer, B.E. (1973) 'Social attitudes and treatment of orientation among psychiatrists', *British Journal of Medical Psychology* 46: 75–81.

Pardo, J.V., Pardo, P.J. and Raichle, M.E. (1993) 'Neural correlates of self-induced dysphoria', *American Journal of Psychiatry* 150: 713–19.

Pasamanick, B., Scarpitti, F.R., Lefton, M., Dimitz, S., Wernent, J.J. and McPheeters, H. (1964) 'Home versus hospital care for schizophrenics', *Journal of the American Medical Association* 187: 177–81.

Pembroke, L. (1993) 'Surviving Psychiatry', *Nursing Times* 87(49): 29–32.

Pincus, H.A., Henderson, B., Blackwood, D. and Dial, T. (1993) 'Trends in research in two psychiatric journals in 1969–1990: Research on research', *American Journal of Psychiatry* 150: 135–42.

Posey, T.B. and Losch, M.E. (1983) 'Auditory hallucinations of hearing voices in 375 normal subjects', *Imagination, Cognition and Personality* 3(2): 99–113.

Rees, W.D. (1971) 'The hallucinations of widowhood', *British Medical Journal* 4: 37–41.

Renton, C.A., Affleck, J.W., Carstairs, M. and Forrest, A.D. (1963) 'A follow up of schizophrenic patients in Edinburgh', *Acta Psychiatrica Scandinavica* 39: 548–600.

Reveley, A.M., Reveley, M.A., Clifford, C.A. *et al.* (1982) 'Cerebral ventricular size in twins discordant for schizophrenia', *Lancet* 1: 540–1.

Reynolds, G.P. (1994) 'Antipsychotic drug mechanisms and neurotransmitter systems in schizophrenia', *Acta Psychiatrica Scandinavica* 89 (supplement 380): 36–40.

Reynolds, G.P., Riederer, P., Jellinger, K. *et al.* (1981) 'Dopamine receptors and schizophrenia: the neuroleptic drug problem', *Neuropharmacology* 20: 1319–20.

Rogers, A., Pilgrim, D. and Lacey, R. (1993) *Experiencing Psychiatry: User's views of services.* London: MIND/Macmillan.

Romme, M.A.J. and Escher, A.D.M.A.C. (1989) 'Hearing Voices', *Schizophrenia Bulletin* 15(2): 209–16.

Romme, M.A.J. and Escher, A.D.M.A.C. (1993) 'The new approach: a Dutch experiment' in M.A.J. Romme and A.D.M.A.C. Escher (eds), *Accepting Voices.* London: MIND.

Romme, M.A.J., Honig, A., Noorthoorn, E.O. and Escher, A.D.M.A.C. (1992) 'Coping with hearing voices: an emancipatory approach', *British Journal of Psychiatry* 161: 99–103.

Rosenthal, D., Wender, P., Kety, S.S. *et al.* (1971) 'The adopted-away offspring of schizophrenics', *American Journal of Psychiatry* 128: 307–11.

Royal College of Psychiatrists (1995) The Twenty-second Annual Report. London: Royal College of Psychiatrists.

Russell, B. (1961) *A History of Western Philosophy.* London: Allen and Unwin.

St Clair, D., Blackwood, D., Muir, W. *et al.* (1989) 'No linkage of chromosome 5q11-q13 markers to schizophrenia in Scottish families', *Nature* 339: 305–9.

Sabshin, M. (1990) 'Turning points in twentieth-century American psychiatry', *American Journal of Psychiatry* 147: 1267–74.

Sartorius, N. (1993) 'WHO's work on the epidemiology of mental disorders', *Social Psychiatry and Psychiatric Epidemiology* 28: 147–55.

Sass, L. (1992) *Madness and Modernism: Insanity in the light of modern art, literature and thought.* New York: Basic Books.

Schneider, K. (1957) 'Primäre und Sekundäre symptomen bei schizophrenie' [Primary and secondary symptoms in schizophrenia] *Fortschritte der Neurologie Psychiatrie* 25: 487.

Schooler, N. (1991) 'Maintenance medication for schizophrenia: strategies for dose reduction', *Schizophrenia Bulletin* 17: 311–24.

Schooler, N.R. (1994) 'Deficit symptoms in schizophrenia: negative symptoms versus neuroleptic-induced deficits', *Acta Psychiatrica Scandinavica* (supplement) 380: 21–6.

Scott, J. (1993) 'Homelessness and Mental Illness', *British Journal of Psychiatry* 162: 314–24.

Seeman, P., Lee, T., Chau-Wong, M. and Wong, K. (1976) 'Anti-psychotic drug doses and neuroleptic/dopamine receptors', *Nature* 261: /17–19.

Segal, H. (1975) 'Psycho-analytic approach to the treatment of schizophrenia', in M.H. Lader (ed.), *Studies of Schizophrenia.* London: Royal College of Psychiatrists, pp. 94–7.

Sherrington, R., Brynjolfsson, J., Petursson, H. *et al.* (1988) 'Localisation of a susceptibility locus on chromosome 5', *Nature* 336: 164–7.

Sidgewick, H., Johnson, A., Myers, F.W.H. *et al.* (1894) 'Report on the census of hallucinations', *Proceedings of the Society for Psychical Research* 34: 25–394.

Sims, A.C.P. (1988) *Symptoms in the Mind.* London: Bailliere Tindall.

Sims, A.C.P. (1994) '"Psyche" – spirit as well as mind?', *British Journal of Psychiatry* 165: 441–6.

Simpson, G.M., Davis, J., Jefferson, J.W. *et al.* (1987) 'Sudden deaths in psychiatric patients: the role of neuroleptic drugs', in *American Psychiatric Association task force report, 27.* Washington DC: American Psychiatric Association.

Singh, M.M. (1976) 'Dysphoric response to neuroleptic treatment in schizophrenia and its prognostic significance', *Disease of the Nervous System* 37: 191–5.

Slade, P. and Bentall, R. (1988) *Sensory Deception: Towards a scientific analysis of hallucinations.* London: Croom Helm.

Slater, E. and Roth, M. (1977) *Clinical Psychiatry.* London: Bailliere Tindall and Cassell.

Smith, R.C., Strizich, M. and Klass, D. (1978) 'Drug history and tardive dyskinesia', *American Journal of Psychiatry* 135: 1402–3.

Smythies, J.R. (1992) 'Neurophilosophy', *Psychological Medicine* 22: 547–9.

Snyder, S.H. (1976) 'The Dopamine Hypothesis of Schizophrenia; focus on the role of the dopamine receptor', *American Journal of Psychiatry* 133: 197–202.

Somers, A.A. (1985) '"Negative symptoms": conceptual and methodological problems', *Schizophrenia Bulletin* 11: 364–79.

Special Hospital Service Authority (1993) *Big, Black and Dangerous?* London: Special Hospital Service Authority.

Spitzer, M. and Uehlein, F.A. (1993) 'Phenomenology and Psychiatry', in M. Spitzer, F. Uehlin, M. Schwartz and C. Mundt (eds), *Phenomenology, Language and Schizophrenia*. New York: Springer-Verlag.

Steinberg, H.R. and Durell, J. (1968) 'A stressful social situation as a precipitant of schizophrenic symptoms: an epidemiological study', *British Journal of Psychiatry* 114: 1097–105.

Suddath, R.L., Christison, G., Torrey, E.F. et al. (1989) 'Quantitative magnetic resonance imaging in twin pairs discordant for schizophrenia', *Schizophrenia Research* 2: 129.

Suddath, R.L., Christison, G., Torrey, E.F. et al. (1990) 'Anatomical abnormalities in the brains of monozygotic twins discordant for schizophrenia', *New England Journal of Medicine* 322: 789–94.

Tarrier, N., Barrowclough, C., Vaughn, C., Bamrah, J.S., Porceddu, K., Watts, S. and Freeman, H. (1988) 'The community management of schizophrenia: a controlled trial of a behavioural intervention with the families of schizophrenic patients', *British Journal of Psychiatry* 153: 532–42.

Thomas, P. (1995) 'Thought disorder or communication disorder: linguistic science provides a new approach', *British Journal of Psychiatry* 166: 287–90.

Thomas, P., Kearney, G., Napier, E., Ellis, E., Leudar, I. and Johnston, M. (1996) 'Speech and Language in First Onset Psychosis: Differences Between Schizophrenics, Manics and Controls', *British Journal of Psychiatry* 168: 337–43.

Thomas, P., King, K. and Fraser, W.I. (1987) 'Positive and Negative Symptoms of Schizophrenia and Linguistic Performance', *Acta Psychiatrica Scandinavica* 76: 144–51.

Thomas, P., Leudar, I., Kearney, G. et al. (1996) 'Syntactic Complexity and Negative Symptoms', *Cognitive Neuropsychiatry* 3: 191–200.

Thomas, P. and McGuire, R. (1986) 'Orofacial Dyskinesia, Cognitive Function and Medication', *British Journal of Psychiatry* 149: 216–20.

Thompson, C. (1994) 'The use of high-dose antipsychotic medication', *British Journal of Psychiatry* 164: 448–58.

Thornicroft, G., Margolius, O. and Jones, D. (1992) 'The TAPS project. 6: new long-stay psychiatric patients and social deprivation', *British Journal of Psychiatry* 161: 621–4.

Tien, A.Y. (1991) 'Distributions of hallucinations in the population', *Social Psychiatry and Psychiatric Epidemiology* 26: 287–92.

Tienari, P. (1992) 'Implications of adoption studies on schizophrenia', *British Journal of Psychiatry*. 161 (supplement 18): 52–8.

Tienari, P., Lahti, I. and Sorri, A. (1987) 'The Finnish adoptive family study of schizophrenia', *Journal of Psychiatric Research* 21: 437–45.

Toone, B.K., Murray, R.M., Clare, A., Creed, F. and Smith, A. (1979) 'Psychiatrists' models of mental illness and their personal backgrounds', *Psychological Medicine* 9: 165–78.

Trimble, M.R. (1988) *Biological Psychiatry*. Chichester: John Wiley.

Van Putten, T. (1974) 'Why do schizophrenic patients refuse to take their drugs?', *Archives of General Psychiatry* 31: 239–55.

Vaughn, C.E., Snyder, K.S., Jones, S., Freeman, W.B. and Falloon, I.R.H. (1984) 'Family factors in schizophrenic relapse: replication in California of British research on expressed emotion', *Archives of General Psychiatry* 41: 1169–77.

Vygotsky, L.S. (1978) *Mind in Society: the development of higher psychological processes*. London: Harvard University Press.

Wallis, G.G. (1965) 'An epidemiological and follow-up study of schizophrenia in the Royal Navy', MD thesis, University of London.

Warner, R. (1985) *Recovery from Schizophrenia: Psychiatry and Political Economy*. London: Routledge and Kegan Paul.

Weinberger, D.R., Cannon-Spoor, E., Potkin, S.G. *et al.* (1980) 'Poor premorbid adjustment and CT scan abnormalities in chronic schizophrenia', *American Journal of Psychiatry* 137: 1410–13.

Wertsch, J.V. (1991) *Voices of the Mind: a sociocultural approach to mediated action*. London: Harvester Wheatsheaf.

Willis, J.H. and Bannister, D. (1965) 'The diagnosis and treatment of schizophrenia: A questionnaire study of psychiatric opinion', *British Journal of Psychiatry* 111: 1165–71.

Windelband, W. (1904) *Geschichte und Naturwissenschaft* (3rd edn). Cited in Allport, G.W. (1938) *Personality: A psychological interpretation*. London: Constable.

Windgassen, K. (1991) *Schizophreniebehandlung aus der sicht des patienten. Untersuchungen des behandlungsverlaufes und der neuroleptischen therapie unter pathischem aspekt*. Berlin: Springer-Verlag.

Wittgenstein, L. (1953) *Philosophical Investigations*. Oxford: Blackwell, 1967.

Wong, D.R., Wagner, H.N., Tune, L.E. *et al.* (1986) 'Positron emission tomography reveals elevated D_2 dopamine receptors in drug-naive schizophrenics', *Science* 234: 1558–63.

Wyatt. R.J. (1986) 'The dopamine hypothesis: variations on a theme (II)', *Psychopharmacology Bulletin* 22: 923–7.

Wyatt, R.J. (1991) 'Neuroleptics and the natural course of schizophrenia', *Schizophrenia Bulletin* 17(2): 325–51.

Yiangou, C., Wood, M., Wright, P., Choi, S., Lam, T.H., Morris, O., Mortimore, I. and Poole, S. (1988) 'Inner city deprivation and medical education: a survey of medical students by medical students', *Medical Education* 22: 2–7.

Zubin, J., Magaziner, J. and Steinhauer, S.R. (1983) 'The metamorphosis of schizophrenia: from chronicity to vulnerability', *Psychological Medicine* 13: 551–71.

Name Index

Subject Index